Eustache Deschamps

Routledge Medieval Texts

Routledge Medieval Texts makes the literary masterworks of the Middle Ages available in volumes translated by leading scholars. Suiting the needs of both general and advanced readers, each book contains an edition of the original with facing English translation. Based on the best available manuscripts, originals are presented in accurate, conservative versions, with minimal editorial or linguistic apparatus. Faithful, line-by-line translations in modern, colloquial English serve all audiences, from readers with no knowledge of the original language to those who need help with difficult constructions or unfamiliar vocabulary. Each volume features an introduction with a full discussion of important literary and critical questions, including the life of the author and the place of the work within either the authorial oeuvre or genre; the work's literary value and importance; the source materials drawn upon; the influence exerted on other writers; the manuscript tradition and printed history; and a select bibliography listing previous editions and major critical and historical studies. While the series includes texts from all medieval languages and literary traditions, important works from French, German, Italian, Occitan, Latin, and Hispanic literatures are its principal focus. Routledge Medieval Texts is overseen by an editorial board of eminent medievalists.

Series Titles

Walther von der Vogelweide
The Single-Stanza Lyrics
Edited and translated by Frederick Goldin

Eustache Deschamps
Selected Poems
Edited by Ian S. Laurie and Deborah M. Sinnreich-Levi
Translated by David Curzon and Jeffrey Fiskin

Eustache Deschamps
Selected Poems

Edited by

Ian S. Laurie
and
Deborah M. Sinnreich-Levi

Translated by

David Curzon
and
Jeffrey Fiskin

LONDON AND NEW YORK

First published 2003 by Routledge

Published 2016 by Routledge
711 Third Avenue,
New York, NY 10017, USA

Published in Great Britain by
Routledge
2 Park Square, Milton Park,
Abingdon, Oxon OX14 4RN

Routledge is an imprint of the Taylor & Francis Group, an informa business

First issued in paperback 2015

Library of Congress Cataloging-in-Publication Data
Deschamps, Eustache, 1346?–1406.
[Poems. English. Selections]
Eustache Deschamps: selected poems / edited by Ian S. Laurie and Deborah M. Sinnreich-Levi ; translated by David Curzon and Jeffrey Fiskin.
p. cm.
ISBN 978-0-415-94243-0 (hbk)
ISBN 978-1-138-99362-4 (pbk)
1. Deschamps, Eustache, 1346?–1406—Translations into English. I. Title: Selected poems. II. Laurie, Ian S. III. Sinnreich-Levi, Deborah M. IV. Curzon, David. V. Fiskin, Jeffrey. VI. Title.
PQ1455 .A25 2003
841'.1—dc21

2002012107

Dedicated to the memory of
Katherine Washburn

Contents

Acknowledgments

This collection of editions, translations, and apparatus is the result of five years' collaboration by four very different people, helped along the way to publication by others too numerous to name. We would, nevertheless, like to chronicle this book's genesis and render some thanks.

David Curzon cordially approached Deborah Sinnreich-Levi in January 1997 with an invitation to lunch at the U.N. Delegates Lounge to discuss a topic of mutual interest, the poetry of Eustache Deschamps. She asked if she might bring along an even more knowledgeable colleague, Ian Laurie. At this fateful lunch, David explained that he had published some translations of Eustache Deschamps's poetry and been asked by Katherine Washburn to translate more for a volume in a series she was planning. And as luck would have it, Ian and Deborah were already coincidentally planning such a volume of their own, based on transcripts Ian had already made directly from the manuscript in the Bibliothèque Nationale de France (BNF Fonds français 840). A collaboration was born. David, based in Manhattan, was going to also be working with Jeffrey Fiskin of Hollywood. Deborah had just left Manhattan for the wilds of suburban New Jersey, and Ian shortly thereafter returned to Australia. Thousands of e-mails ensued as the two medievalists, Deborah and Ian, worked with the two gifted poets, David and Jeffrey, to render accurately into graceful English verse the varied voices of our poet.

Sadly, Katherine Washburn did not live to see this volume—or the series she had planned—completed. We dedicate the volume to her memory.

R. Barton Palmer, now general editor of the Routledge Medieval Texts series, introduced our volume to Garland, and shepherded us through the transition as that press became an imprint of Routledge. He has been a most supportive friend and colleague throughout these years.

Emily Vail and Lisa Vecchione at Routledge patiently and conscientiously guided us through the production of this volume.

We owe a debt to Jean-François Kosta-Théfaine, who has recently completed his Ph.D. in Paris. Jean-François generously gave of his time helping us acquire books from France and tirelessly haunted the Bibliothèque Nationale de France, documenting a flaw in the microfilm of our base manuscript and transcribing sections of one poem that had eluded us for five years.

Finally, our circles of friends and family have long been subjected to tales of wayward manuscript folios, false-friend etymologies, scansion, medieval kings, biblical references, mustard, and grimaces. For their patience and humor, much thanks.

Introduction

Life

Eustache Deschamps *dit* Morel (c. 1340–1404) was one of the most innovative French poets of the Middle Ages. Before him, at least in theory, French lyric poetry had been most valued when it had confined itself to the themes of conventional love (or, much less commonly, religion) and also when it was accompanied by music. In the first art of poetry written in French, Deschamps broke formally with this view that the lyric was no more than a love song, claiming first that the intrinsic music of the spoken word was superior to instrumental music and also that lyric poetry might be about any subject, limited only by the inspiration of the author.

This challenge to close on three centuries of French lyric poetry was not limited to mere theorizing: Deschamps's complete works exploded most of its traditions. French poetry was never the same after him: the old order fell as completely as did the conventions of the French opera with the intervention of Rousseau in the eighteenth century.

Deschamps's success in changing the directions of French poetry are partly explained by the fact that he used his skills as a writer to gain a position of great prominence in the French establishment of his day. His posts in the royal administration brought him into regular contact with most of those who determined the course of public events during his lifetime—kings, dukes, military leaders, and administrators—not only in France but also in other parts of Europe. He is not, of course, the only French writer to have had a successful career in the French administration. It is notable in his case, however, that the posts to which he was appointed had no obvious connection with formal academic credentials, for it is likely that he never completed a university degree. His career may not even have had much to do with any influence that may have been exercised by his family: his origins were probably fairly modest. The fact is that he probably owed his success in what in modern times would be called public service mainly to his reputation as a poet.

He was born about 1340,[1] making him a contemporary of Chaucer (b. 1340), whose poetry he alleged to be superior to his own (Balade 285). His birth places him near the beginning of the Hundred Years' War between France and England (1337–1453), during which he served in several military campaigns and in which his country scored few successes before his death in 1404. His birth occurred a few years before the outbreak of the Black Death, which devastated Europe between 1347 and 1351, and which also broke out again in other years during Deschamps's lifetime; there are frequent references to the plague in his poetry.[2] It was given to Deschamps to live in persistently difficult times: the second of the two kings of France he served, Charles VI, went violently mad while continuing to exercise all the powers of a reigning monarch. In spite of such difficult circumstances, or perhaps because of them, Deschamps had an extraordinary feeling for the comic element in life.

The place of his birth was Vertus in Champagne. Nothing is known about his family although, given the insult of "cobbler" (*savetier*) which he claims was leveled at him,[3] it is possible that he was not of noble birth or was at most of very minor nobility. If true, this status may explain why, in all official references to him before 1389, he is never given the name Deschamps nor credited with any title to nobility. He was addressed simply as Eustache Morel from Vertus. Eustache Morel is also the name likely to have been used by his friends for the whole of his life and even by his admirer the poet Christine de Pizan shortly before his death.[4]

In the surviving records at Vertus for the 100 years before Deschamps's birth, there is no mention of anyone named Deschamps.[5] However, there was a Colinet Morel serving in the local administration there around the time of Deschamps's birth.[6] If he was related to the poet, it is conceivable that Deschamps owed his first relatively minor post in the local administration at Vertus as much to family connections as to his poetry.

Even if he was not born with the name Deschamps, it is certainly connected with a property he owned near Vertus at least by 1370. That property, the "maison des champs," is first mentioned in a comic verse epistle that he dated from there in November 1370 (Lettres 1402). He may have begun to use the name Deschamps, perhaps almost as a joke, in Balades 835 and 866, which were written shortly after an attack made on that house by an English raiding party in 1380: in those poems he referred to himself and his house as burned-out cases, more exactly, as "Buslé Deschamps."

Joke or not, he appears to have persuaded the authorities to use the name Deschamps in official documents, the first of which is dated in 1389, in which he first gives himself the grand style of "Eustache Deschamps, *dit* Morel" and also claims to be a nobleman. It is possible that he owed his title to nobility to the purchase of property at this period, for example an estate at Barbonval. Any such conclusion must, however, remain tentative; it has to be admitted that some of the posts he held with his patrons long before 1389, from the mid-1360s, were most often held by men who had some title to nobility.

The earliest statements about Deschamps's career stem from his own verse, an unreliable source of information for the biographer. The earliest of these, made in Balade 456, was that he first entered the service of love and the ladies at the age of fourteen and a half. This assertion is reinforced in Balade 1105, written much later, perhaps in old age, in which he claims to have spent in womanizing the years he passed as a student at the University of Orléans. There is no reason to doubt that he did attend this university, but there is no way of testing his assertions about his activities there. He may well have left Orléans, however, before completing his degree. He is never in French given the title of master and only once in Latin, where it may have been used by the scribe simply as a courtesy (Lay 310). He even regretted that he had little academic learning to recommend him (Balade 878).

Whatever the truth about his life as a student at Orléans, he appears to have returned to the place of his birth, Vertus, at least as early as 1365. This time frame may be deduced from his earliest datable poem, Chartre 1398, dated Vertus, December 9, 1368. In this poem, which is a mock-legal constitution for a local club, the *fumeux*, a claim is made that the author is in his third year of office as president of the society. (See note to Balade 813, p. 220.) On the generous assumption that he was telling the truth, it is likely that he had resumed residence in Vertus at least by December 1365.

What kind of poetry was Deschamps writing before 1368? If we attach autobiographical significance to the assertions made in Balade 456 about his early entry in to the service of love and interpret these to mean that he had begun writing love poetry when he was fourteen and a half, it is possible that he had begun trying to establish his credentials as a poet of courtly gallantries as early as the mid-1350s. By June 1375, he could assert, in Lettres 1411 (82–87), that he had just written the most melancholy virelai he had produced for ten years. Given the fact that the most common subject of his virelais was love, it would not be too much of a stretch to imagine that Deschamps was already active, at least as a love poet, by 1365.

In this context, Chartre 1398 has a special importance. Its sense of the comic, based on mock-legal language, belongs to that category of parody much favored by law students at French universities in the fourteenth and fifteenth centuries. This genre is itself no more than a subset of a much broader and older parodic tradition, not necessarily associated with the law at all. If one goes no further afield than French and Occitan poetry, it can be traced back at least to the end of the eleventh century in the work of troubadour William of Poitu. Such poetry has a continuing history in French literature after Deschamps to the present day—even with the name *fumiste*, which he might have recognized among, for example, groups such as the Hydropathes and the Incohérents (counterculture and avant-garde artists and writers) of the late nineteenth century.

The conclusion to be drawn is that Deschamps began his life as a poet as the heir to two long and very specific literary traditions. The first is that of the courtly lyric, which again goes back at least to the twelfth century in French and Occitan. The second is that of medieval parody. The value to be attached to such poetry of either vein in the establishment of Deschamps's biography is less certain although in the case of some of the parodic epistles, their careful dating by the author establishes his whereabouts at the time.

Are Deschamps's activities as a poet to be attributed simply to native talent or did he have a poetic mentor? The name that comes to mind in this respect is the great French poet and musical composer of the fourteenth century, Guillaume de Machaut. It has often been said that Deschamps may even have been Machaut's nephew. This story, first told by the fifteenth-century author of the *Règles de séconde rhetorique*,[7] may have been based on the text of a poem that can, unfortunately, bear several interpretations (Balade 447).[8] In this poem, Deschamps states that Machaut was the person "Qui m'a nourri et fait maintes doucours." A cautious translation of these words might be "Who looked after me and did me many kindnesses." "Nourri" could, however, also be interpreted as "brought me up" or "raised me." On the assumption that the words mean just this coupled with references to the siege of Rheims in the 1360s in Deschamps's *Le Miroir de mariage* (ll. 11,660–98), in which Deschamps claims to have a personal memory of the events but actually lifts the whole of his account from the author of the *Chroniques des règnes de Jean II et de Charles V* (Delachenal, III:xviii), a whole construction of his youthful education under Machaut at Rheims has sometimes been erected. One might be as skeptical about this theory as about his claim in lines 11,833–51 of *Le Miroir* that he was present at the conference of Chateaudun in 1360, but it would be imprudent to rule both possibilities out. It is not impossible that Deschamps did meet Machaut at a relatively young age, and it is even possible that he was Machaut's nephew although it is surprising that Deschamps never claimed him as his uncle. What is probable is that Machaut did act as his mentor, at least for a period, tutoring him in such things as those lyric forms that Machaut had done so much to fix and to popularize, perhaps even as early as 1355 if the interpretation given above to Balade 456 is correct. Deschamps certainly expressed the hope that he would be recognized as Machaut's natural successor (Balade 127; Lay 306, ll. 296–99).[9] It is also possible that Machaut played some part in introducing Deschamps to his first patrons. That said, however, it has to be added that Machaut may have been in the habit of encouraging more than one young author. The most famous of them, whether real or part fictional, is Peronne, the lady with whom Machaut claims to have carried on an affair as well as a poetic correspondence in his *Voir dit*. In her case, as perhaps in that of Deschamps, the mentoring involved may have generally consisted of little more than distance education. After Machaut's death in 1377, Deschamps even asked Peronne to take him on as her lover to replace Machaut (Balade 447). It is difficult to believe that this eccentric method of attempting to secure Machaut's poetic mantle was to be taken too seriously especially since Deschamps followed this poem with Balade 493, in which he admitted that Peronne had turned him down, driving him to proposition a lady by the name of Gauteronne, to whom he discloses that she was only his second choice.[10]

There is, however, an indication of close personal contact between the two poets in the fact that Machaut entrusted Deschamps with a commission to deliver a copy of a major work, the *Voir dit*, to Count Louis III of Flanders at Bruges. The visit is recorded in Balade 127, in which Machaut is assured that the work was much appreciated at Bruges. It is impossible to date the visit more accurately than to some time between the composition of the *Voir dit* in 1365 and Machaut's death in 1377, but the presentation would have had more point if it occurred not too long after the completion of the work, perhaps in the period 1365–68, when Deschamps was in residence in Vertus. There are laments for the death of Machaut, which occurred in April 1377, in more serious poems (Balades 123 and 124). In a verse epistle Deschamps sent from Vertus to his lady, a nun at Andely in Normandy, on May 28 of the same year, he mentions including these laments (Lettres 1416). So, finally, one can only hypothesize about Deschamps's relation to Machaut. Deschamps may have been Machaut's nephew, and Machaut may have helped financially or otherwise with Deschamps's education, but if so, it is curious that Deschamps says so little about it. One could even entertain the somewhat far-fetched hypothesis that this desire to avoid indiscretion on Deschamps's part might be explained by the possibility that he himself was the result of an even greater indiscretion on Machaut's part, given that cleric's fondness for the ladies.

Moving from the indications about his early career that can be found in his poetry to the more prosaic evidence of surviving archives, the first reference to Eustache Morel dates from 1367, when he is first mentioned as a *juré* (juror) of the count of Vertus. The duties that related specifically to this post are not known but may not have been much more than these of a notary clerk; in any case they are of less importance than the fact that the count at this time was the duke of Milan, John Galeas Visconti. Deschamps probably owed his appointment to the duke's French wife, Isabelle de France, who may have liked his poetry. In Balade 250, Deschamps claims that Isabelle and the count invited him to Lombardy, perhaps at the time of the wedding celebrations there in 1366 and in any event before her death in 1372. It is impossible to know how close his relationships were with John Galeas Visconti himself, although Deschamps did lament the duke's death on September 3, 1403 (Balade 1212).

The fact that Deschamps visited Italy in his mid- to late twenties may well have been important for his development as a poet. Unfortunately, nothing is known about what he did there. Deschamps's best descriptions of his travels in and outside France date from later periods, the 1380s and 1390s, but even then he has nothing very specific to say about Italy. Perhaps the most important fact to register is that he came to believe that all foreign travel, no doubt including travel to Italy, was a remedy for ignorance, stating, "Il ne scet riens qui ne va hors" (Balade 1311).[11] Never much given to understatement, he even claimed that he had been a world traveler, going as far afield as Cairo, Babylon, and Tartary (Balade 169).[12] Since he has nothing specific to say about these places and reserves his punch line in that poem for the assertion that there is nowhere in the world fit to be compared with Paris, it would seem to be prudent to discount such journeys in establishing his biography.

The most important event in Deschamps's life at this period was his entry into the royal service under Charles V in 1368. We do not know what position he held in the royal service at this date. Perhaps he was no more than an *escuyer*, a squire, just as he was in the service of Duke Philip of Orléans by 1375.[13] The first references to his entry to the royal service occur in three enthusiastic poems (Lay 311 and Virelais 755 and 756), which read almost like the beginning of a love affair: for better or worse, he appears to have fallen in love with the royal service. It took him ten, perhaps twenty, years to come terms with the fact that it might not necessarily have fallen in love with him—at which point his poetry became more satirical.

Deschamps's benefactor Charles V is remembered as a great patron of the arts. Together with the fact that Isabelle de France must have known Deschamps's poetry, the appointment to the royal service is the best indication we have that he had already become well known as a poet.

What was it about Deschamps's early work that might have appealed to Charles V? It is perhaps unlikely that the king was much impressed by the comic epistles or virelais on the topic of unhappy love that have been mentioned so far. Charles was a supporter of weighty works, for example translations from Latin into French and also of chronicles of historical events. Perhaps some of Deschamps's many moralizing lyrics on the state of the world were written at this period, but we have no means of dating them. In later years, Deschamps claimed that he had been commissioned by Charles V and Charles VI to produce a chronicle, to which he gave the title *Le Livre de memoire*; he refers to it in Balade 1130, written in 1396. Unfortunately, this work is now lost. We have no independent confirmation that the work ever existed, but Deschamps does claim that it involved attendance at events of public importance to which his post at court gave him privileged access. If it was a chronicle in verse and not prose, it almost gives Deschamps a claim to have had something in common with what was later to be called a poet laureate. No doubt this conjecture exceeds the evidence, but

Deschamps's claims about the importance of his role at court give some support to it, although the poems concerned are very self-interested. An example is his claim that he served the royal children, Charles and Louis, in their infancies.[14] There is no reason to doubt this claim, but the fact that he made a point of reminding the court of it, not only at the time but also much later, is best interpreted as calling in a debt of gratitude on the part of Charles and Louis in the hope of further acts of patronage. Such an interpretation might be placed on Balade 55, for example, in which an account is given of the time and place at which Charles and Louis were born and which is addressed to Charles as reigning monarch (see also page 8).

Deschamps married no later than 1373 but lost his wife in childbirth in 1375 or 1376. The marriage appears to have been happy: Deschamps still remembered his wife fondly in 1393, when he wrote Balade 1151, commending her to his daughter as an example to follow at the time of her marriage in that year. Deschamps's apparent happiness in marriage is worth pointing out since he is often described, somewhat unfairly, as a misogynist. He must have had a reputation at least as a misogamist in so far as he felt an obligation to justify his decision to marry to a friend, Simon Ployart (Balades 829, 830, and 831). Ployart had accused Deschamps of being a moral fraud, claiming that no one would now be able to take the poet's advice against marriage seriously. Deschamps justified himself on the grounds that he was genuinely in love with his wife. This assertion may have been true, but there were likely more practical motives, too: in Balade 875, he claims that the marriage will rescue him from poverty. If this claim is to be taken seriously, it may confirm the view that he did not come from a wealthy family. Deschamps's marriage produced at least three children: a daughter, whose name has escaped historical record,[15] and two sons, Laurent and Gilles, whose careers and fortunes he actively assisted.

By March 1375, Deschamps had obtained his first major post in the administration by becoming the bailiff of Valois, in the service of Duke Philip of Orléans and his wife, Blanche. (A *bailli* was an officer of the king charged with the administration of justice in the district assigned him by royal authority.) At least in his verse, Deschamps was not inclined to take his duties too seriously, and produced a series of comic epistles in verse (Lettres 1401, 1418, and 1419) written from some of the places to which his duties as a judge on the circuit took him: Crépy-en-Valois (the administrative center of the bailiwick), Gournay, Brie Comte Robert, and Vitry. In another one of these epistles (Lettres 1321), probably written before the death of his wife (if lines 60–61 are a reference to her), he mentions that he has also become the master forester of Rest, a further mark of his patron's esteem. Philip died on September 1, 1375, but Deschamps remained in the service of his widow, Blanche, at least until April 25, 1380. Not long after that date, he complained that she had excluded him from her new house in Paris (Balades 818 and 820), and it is likely that this ban meant she had dismissed him from her service.

Not long after the death of Machaut in April 1377, Deschamps either went on a military campaign with the duke of Anjou and the great French general, Bertrand du Guesclin, or, at least, asked in Balade 808 that provision be made for one of the campaigners. The name of the campaigner, Jehan Tastevin, looks rather like one of the convivial names Deschamps was fond of giving to himself.

Shortly after 1375 and probably by 1378, Deschamps was promoted to the highest office he was to attain at the royal court, a sergeant-at-arms (*huissier d'armes*) of Charles V. This post gave Deschamps privileged personal access to the king, described in Balade 1000, and Deschamps remained in this position serving Charles VI for the rest of his life, even after the king's first fit of madness in August 1392. Deschamps himself saw this position as critical to his career as a court poet. At the most modest level, it meant that he wrote new year's greetings in verse (Balade 293) to the king's son, Louis; praised the young prince (Balade 222); put his readers through an account of Louis's and his brother Charles' births (Balade 55);[16] and recalled, in later years, how he had served both princes in their childhood (Balades 1146, 1190, 1379, and 1459). At a somewhat higher level, he versified the itinerary of Charles V when he made a tour of inspection in the Vermandois, which began on March 22, 1379 (Balade 144 and Chanson Royale 393). If Deschamps accompanied the king on this journey, it would have been in his capacity as *huissier d'armes*. These are examples of the official or public verse that probably justified his appointment. There is another more vigorous poem in the same category, Balade 157, written in the same year, in support of the royal disapproval of the behavior of John, duke of Brittany, who had transferred his allegiance to the English. Versified prose of this kind, however, does not much enhance his reputation with modern readers. Those whose admiration for Deschamps is not based on these potboilers will be more interested to know that it was probably in the same year, on October 26, 1379, that he wrote another comic epistle in verse, drawing attention to the risks of his life as bailiff of Valois, where the plague had made it impossible for his friends to attend his sessions (Lettres 1417).

The year 1380 was marked by the deaths of Bertrand du Guesclin, on July 13, and Charles V, on September 16. Among the commemorative laments Deschamps wrote at this time are Balades 206 and 207 (du Guesclin) and Balades 164, 165, and 166 (Charles V). Between these events, Deschamps went off on campaign with the duke of Burgundy. Deschamps may have had the opportunity to make this trip because Blanche of Orléans had terminated his appointment as bailiff of Valois. Balade 165 also laments Pope Urban V, who had left Rome to die at Avignon ten years earlier in 1370. The fact that the poem passes over his successor, Gregory XI, who left Avignon to die in Rome in 1378, is the first indication we have of the poet's views on the great papal schism: Charles V had declared his allegiance to the Avignon pope, Clement VII, in 1378 and Deschamps, by implication, supported the official French line.

In August 1380, while he was away on campaign, his house at Vertus, the "*maison des champs*," was sacked by Thomas of Buckingham. Deschamps describes in vivid terms the effects of this raid not only on his house but also on Vertus itself (Balades 835, 836, 845, and 864). He was left a refugee by the war, he claims, and also 2,000 francs in debt, which justified a versified claim for compensation from his patrons, partly in order to buy a house in Paris. Charles VI and Deschamps's other patrons appear to have agreed to at least some of his requests, for he was in possession of a house in Paris in the rue du Temple by 1384. Charles VI had also given him a place to live in the shape of a castle at Fismes in Champagne early in 1381 (Balade 1190), although he had to defend himself in the courts against a rival claimant, winning the case in September 1382.

Deschamps's career at court was at first not much changed under the new king. He was invited to the coronation of Charles VI at Rheims on November 4, 1380 (Balade 489), declaring his loyalty (Balade 488), praising Rheims (Balade 172) and giving the thirteen-year-old king the benefit of his advice about prosecuting the war against the English (Balade 168). He did, however, have worries that his post of *huissier d'armes* might not be confirmed under the new monarch; typically, he versified his requests for confirmation (Balades 247 and 250). These pleas were successful, perhaps because, as he claims in Balade 1125, the king and his brother, Louis, had asked him to become their official biographer. There is nothing in his surviving work which looks like such a biography; in Balade 1125 he may have been referring to his *Livre de memoire*.[17] He also continued to write public poetry in 1381, for example, laments on the deaths of Jean de Sempy and Guichard d'Angle (Balades 13, 495, and 981; Chanson Royale 365; and Rondeau 661), managing to include glum prophecies on the perturbing future that was believed to lie in wait for the world in the year 1400. These poems present only historical interest for the modern reader.

One turns with pleasure to a less solemn Deschamps in the persona of a war refugee in Paris in 1380–82, waiting for his offices to be confirmed and his monetary problems resolved. A surly innkeeper and the voracious appetites of Deschamps's horses, which did not have as many friends to feed them as he did himself, were his main problems, all presented with a color and a verve that his public poetry lacks (Balades 791, 794, 857, 866, 882, 884, and 891; Rondeaux 666, 669, and 1439). Worse troubles occurred: the revolt of the Maillotins broke out on February 28, 1382, and Deschamps was forced to run away from Paris like a hare (Chanson Royale 379), taking vengeance on the rioters in a poem written in Latin (Latin 1332).

In his description of the events of the period 1380–82, Deschamps managed to identify his personal fortunes with those of his country. Some caution needs to be exercised before we accept all of these poems as strictly autobiographical—not least because he was a gifted caricaturist and often used his own persona as a target—but these poems greatly increase the interest of his life for modern readers.

Examples taken from his acquisition of the castle of Fismes illustrate this point. He presented it as a kind of handyman's special (Balades 103 and 104), which finally resulted in Charles VI's making him a grant for repairs on November 3, 1388. He also presented it as an eerie place, subject to strange, melancholy, nocturnal noises, in which he spent a period of three months as a convalescent (Balade 1202).[18] It may be that his illness was not unrelated to one of the campaigns to Flanders he went on in the 1380s, the first with Charles VI in November 1382. Some of Deschamps's best poetry was produced on the subject of these campaigns, poetry for which there is no parallel in the history of the French lyric before him although there are a small number of similar poems by Froissart written on the same campaigns, and prose writers had long since given expression to the discomforts and horrors of war. There are not only attempts to raise morale (Balades 17, 19, 94, 96, and 201) but eyewitness accounts of the battle of Roosebecke on November 27, 1382 (Chansons Royales 334 and 347), and even condemnation of the incompetence of Count Louis of Flanders, the ruler whom the French campaigners aimed to defend against the riotous citizens of Ghent (Chanson Royale 389 and Balade 158). Also surprising, at least in the context of the French lyric, are his comic descriptions of the discomforts of the campaign (Balade 801), and his discontent at losing his horses and his relief at going home (Balade 876).

Skepticism about the competence of the authorities may perhaps explain Deschamps's pleas for clemency (Balade 193 and Chanson Royale 385) when reprisals against the defeated Maillotins in Paris took place from January 11 to March 1, 1383, although the fact that one of his friends, Desmares, named in Lettres 1417, was one of those executed may also have influenced his judgment.[19] Shortly afterward, on April 18, 1383, Deschamps presented to Charles VI his translation of Innocent III's *De contemptu mundi* (*On Despising the World*), which he renamed the *Double lai de fragilité humain* (*Double lai of human frailty*). It is likely that he had been working on the project for some time, probably intending it to be presented to Charles V, since it is his name that still appears in the manuscript.

In August 1383, Deschamps was again away on campaign in Flanders with Charles VI and saw such events as the capture of Bourbourg on September 14, and he produced more campaign lyrics to mark his participation (Balades 17 and 19 and Chanson Royale 334). Damage to his property again occurred while he was away but this time not at the hands of the English: it involved a house he owned at Givry-lez-Loisy, and involved him in a protracted lawsuit until he won his case, in 1389.[20] The fact that he never mentions this event in his verse has its own interest; he also passes over in silence his success in gaining possession of the local leprosarium at Fismes together with its endowments, even getting the concession extended to his son Gilles after his death (Prieur 1904, 513). Perhaps the possession of these properties would have cast doubt on the image Deschamps preferred to give of himself as a homeless and impoverished but loyal royal servant. So would the fact that he certainly did not lack for powerful patrons: he names several of them in Balade 1047, written between March 1384 and October 1386. They included Philip, duke of Burgundy; his son John, the count of Nevers; Louis of Valois; Philip of Bar; Charles (perhaps Charles of Bar); Peter of Navarre; and also Marie de France, duchess of Bar, and her family (Balades 88 and 89). The only free time Deschamps had from them, he claimed, was from July until October, when he saw to the harvest on his own estates.

Charles VI was also prepared to entrust his favorite poet with missions of some responsibility, for example, to inspect the fortresses and defenses in Picardy in August and September 1384.[21] Deschamps may well have delivered a report in prose about this visit, but the reports from him that have survived are in verse (Pastourelles 337, 344, and 359). The genre in which these poems are composed suggests idyllic scenes of shepherdesses flirting on the grass with wandering knights, but the country people in Deschamps's poems have nothing in common with such traditional figures. They are well informed about politics and the course of the war against the English, and are not backward when it comes to giving their advice about the necessity of restoring Calais to France. The first pastourelle of this kind was not written by Deschamps but by Froissart in 1382, and it may well be that Deschamps borrowed the idea from the great historian.[22] Calais was a city that Deschamps actually visited, probably at this time, under safe conduct with the poet Oton de Grandson, who could not resist playing a practical joke on him by pretending to give him up as prisoner to the English (Balade 893 and Rondeau 596[23]). It may also have been at this period, when negotiations for peace were going on at Boulogne (May–August 1384), that Deschamps wrote Chanson Royale 765 on Philippa of Lancaster, when it was suggested that she marry Charles VI. More important, it may also have been then, during a time of truce with the English, that he wrote his famous balade to Chaucer, sending samples of his own work while modestly admitting that he deserved to be no more than a nettle in Chaucer's own garden (Balade 285).[24] This poem may also have been written later, about 1390, when Deschamps was in contact with the English knight Clifford, to whom Deschamps may have entrusted this poem as well as other selections from his own work.[25]

By October 1384, Deschamps was back in Paris, this time in possession of his new house in the rue du Temple, where he entertained Charles VI, who promised to give him 200 francs to mark the occasion. Four years later, Deschamps was still waiting for payment of this gift (Balade 788), in spite of the fact that he must have had many opportunities when he was in the king's company to remind him; for example, at a tournament at Saint Pol on February 16, 1385 (Balade 501); at Cambrai on April 12 for the wedding of the count of Nevers (Balades 468 and 469 were probably written to praise the bride, Marguerite of Bavaria); at Compiègne from April 22 to 26 (Rondeau 623); at Vincennes; and then at Beauté-sur-Marne, where he presented the king with Lay 307, the *Lai de franchise*, for May Day, 1385, issuing warnings about a collection of vices, sloth, cowardice, extravagance, and covetousness.

Deschamps was also present at the wedding of Charles VI and Isabeau of Bavaria at Amiens (Chanson Royale 1124), perhaps even having been closely enough involved with the events to know that Charles may have first selected his bride with the aid of a portrait (Balade 463). The charming story told by the Monk of St. Denis has it that Isabeau was one of three finalists under consideration to be Charles's wife.[26] No contemporary sources support this story except Deschamps's own lines: "Car qui verroit sa doulce pourtraiture / Plus l'aymeroit que creature née" ("Whoever saw her portrait / Loved her more than any living woman") (Balade 463, ll. 15–16). Although this reference is admittedly not sufficient, it is also true that the close friendship Deschamps enjoyed with the king meant that the poet is unlikely to have accepted a false story, however charming. Deschamps certainly presented himself as the counselor whose advice had been sought by Louis of Valois over a similar matter, when there were negotiations that Louis marry Mary of Hungary (Balade 1001).[27]

Soon after the royal wedding, Deschamps again accompanied the king on campaign to Flanders, and took part in the siege of Damme from July 31 to August 30, 1385. This trip produced more campaign lyrics, most of them comic, on the discomforts of the campaign (Balades 19, 781, and 782; Chansons Royales 331 and 334). Deschamps had not lost his taste for verse epistles and produced one for a friend, Galhaut, in which Deschamps imposed grotesque terms for the loan of his house in Paris (Lettres 1403).

Preparations began in August 1386 for the invasion of England from Sluys, a plan Deschamps did not greet with much enthusiasm for what he calculated to be his fourth Flanders campaign (Balades 17 and 854 and Virelai 548). The queen gave birth to a son, Charles, on September 25, 1386, an event Deschamps duly commemorated in Balades 521 and 1142, and there is also a poem written probably for her by Deschamps in which a lady laments the imminent departure of a king who is about to invade England (Balade 1040). This latter poem elicited a reply, also written by Deschamps, in which the king discounted the possibility of the invasion—which in fact was in any case abandoned at the end of November. If these two poems are taken at face value, Deschamps was sufficiently trusted by the king and queen of France to write their love letters in verse. There are a number of poems written about the fiasco of the invasion—some encouraging it, some condemning it (Balades 8, 48, 62, 847, 848, 1059, 1060, and 1085). One of his best-known poems, on the difficulty of belling the cat, may well have been written at this time (Balade 58).[28] Some of the criticisms he leveled in these poems at the campaigners may have aroused resentments: it was perhaps on this campaign that he was beaten up and marched around the camp seated backward on his horse (Balades 772, 773, and 803). Certainly, he went home promising never to go on campaign again (Virelai 548[29]), asserting that he had no regrets about its outcome

(Balade 17), and rejecting in advance all future requests that he participate (Balade 855). Composing laments for the death of those still on active service—for example, for the death on August 17, 1387, of Milon de Dormans when he was about to set out on a mission to the duke of Brittany (Balade 46)—were probably more to Deschamps's taste than actual campaigning.

Downsizing in the royal administration on February 9, 1388, could have threatened Deschamps's position at court, but he was one of the lucky eight *huissiers d'armes* to retain his post.[30] On March 10, the king ordered payment to him of various gifts, and then visited him at Vertus on August 26, where the king was shown that the damage done by the raid of 1380 had not been repaired and promptly offered to make a grant to have the work carried out.[31] Did the king's generosity account for the fact that Deschamps forgot his undertaking never to participate in another military campaign? Deschamps embarked on the Guelders campaign immediately after the royal visit to Vertus, taking leave of a lady he does not name (Balade 39). His comments on the campaign were hostile: humiliating the duke of Guelders for him was nothing more than a distraction from the main business of conducting the war against the English (Chanson Royale 327, Pastourelles 336 and 1009, and Balade 919). In spite of his skepticism about the campaign, the defeat of the duke of Guelders is presented as a great triumph for Charles VI (Balades 229 and 1124).

On November 2, 1388, the king proclaimed his majority at Rheims, and appointed his ministry, visiting Deschamps at Fismes on the following day and making him further gifts for repairs.[32] By the time Deschamps returned to Paris, however, he found that he had lost twenty days' pay due him as squire to Louis, who had become duke of Touraine on October 13, 1386 (Balade 797). This poem is the first indication we have that Deschamps held this salaried post. Debt again became one of his preoccupations since the sums promised him by the king were not paid (Balades 788, 902, and 1168).

Perhaps by way of answer to Deschamps's complaints about losses during the war, his patrons had him appointed to the highest post he was to occupy in the administration: bailiff of Senlis. He took the oath for this position on February 9, 1389.[33] He probably viewed it as a more appropriate form of service than campaigning; certainly Guelders was his last campaign, and he advised men over fifty to give up fighting and stay at home (Balade 191).

There was every inducement to do give up campaigning, given the rise in his personal status from his new post. He now had jurisdiction from Pontoise to Compiègne, three houses, servants (Balade 1375 and Supplication 1425), and a better salary (one franc per day). His first receipt for this salary, dated May 23, confirms this improvement in his status, since it is the first occasion on which he repackages himself as a nobleman, lord of Barbonval (a small fief near Fismes), and calls himself Eustache Deschamps, *dit* Morel, much more impressive than his earlier, simple style of Eustache Morel de Vertus.

Professional pomposity was, however, a vein that he preferred to confine to his salary receipts and, perhaps, to his conduct in his own law courts, where, in his poetry, he presents himself as a clay idol ("idoyle de terre," Balade 1036[34]). In his verse, the emphasis is rather on the fact that his duties in his bailiwick kept him from the company of women in Paris and obliged him to live in uncomfortable accommodation (Balades 918 and 1036). One would not suspect from such poems that Senlis was one of the resorts most favored by his friend Charles VI. One might also note that Deschamps's duties at Senlis did not do too much to discourage his attendance at court. For example, he was present at spectaculars such as the tournament in Paris in May 1389 to commemorate the death of du Guesclin (Balade 444). The poet also found time for a little horse trading with Louis of Touraine on May 11, 1389; he also wrote Balade 249 for Marguerite, duchess of Burgundy, about the same time; and received the king as a visitor at Senlis on June 17 of the same year, when he was promised a royal gift of 600 gold francs to set himself up in suitable residences there and in Compiègne. At the time of this royal visit, Deschamps was resolving a dispute between the bishop and the mayor of Beauvais on the construction of roads, perhaps an example of what he presented as the tedious nature of his duties (Balades 1022 and 1205; Chansons Royales 913 and 1285).[35] It is not possible to date most of his satirical poems on the life of the country bailiff; they are not limited to presentations of the criminals brought before him (Balades 804 and 908; Chansons Royales 909, 910, 912,[36] 1217, and 1477), but also lampoon his colleagues (Balade 1492).

If one assumes that most of Deschamps's poetry survives, it has to be noted that satirical poetry of the kind just mentioned tends to displace purely ceremonial, public poetry from about the time he took up his post in Senlis. There are even what would appear to be curious oversights in his verse (again, if one assumes that poems have not been lost). By way of example, it is curious that there are no poems that celebrate the elevation of Louis first to the dukedom of Touraine in 1386, and then to that of Orléans in 1392. Together with Charles VI, Louis was Deschamps's principal patron, and at an earlier period he may even have sought a comment from Deschamps about a prospective bride.[37] However, on August 17, 1389, when the duke married Valentina Visconti, Deschamps does not seem to have written a poem to celebrate the event. It may be, as Deschamps claims, that his duties at Senlis had reduced his appearances at ducal as well as royal courts. Some of his biographers have supposed that Louis had never liked the poet and had begun to discourage Deschamps from attending his court. But this scenario is unlikely. The duke and duchess granted Deschamps thirty gold francs on October 2, 1389, about the same period when he wrote a comic poem on how he waited in Paris for the king and the duke to return from a journey to Languedoc (Balade 920).

Comic and satirical poetry appeared to interest Deschamps more and more. Remembering his resolution not to participate in any more campaigns, he limited himself to writing a farewell to those still on active service—Bourbon, Bar, Eu, Harecourt, Coucy, and Bresch—when they set off for the Barbary Crusade in 1390 (Balade 769). Just what one is to make of his promise to look after their women while they are away is not clear. Neal has argued that the poem answers fears on the subject of fidelity expressed in a poem by Jean de Garencières (33–34). It may well have been the fidelity in love of the crusaders as much as that of their ladies which was in doubt; that at any rate is the message conveyed in Rondeau 686, in which a woman doubts the fidelity of her husband, who is off on crusade in Prussia (November 1390–April 1391). "Stay faithful" ("loyauté tenir") was the motto of the Ordre de la Couronne, founded by Coucy in 1390 and praised by Deschamps (Rondeaux 655 and 656 and Balade 212). Such poetry suggests that Deschamps did keep up with at least some fashions at court: Balade 536, written about the same time, asks Eu, Bresch, Harecourt, and Louis of Touraine to give their judgment in a love dispute involving the English knight Clifford. Given the fact that it was also to Clifford that Deschamps entrusted copies of some of his poems when writing his balade to Chaucer,[38] it is conceivable that this well-known poem was written at this later period, about 1390, rather than in 1384. The king's esteem of Deschamps remained high, and he records another royal visit in Senlis in Lettres 1413, dated December 20, 1390.

Nevertheless, the duties of Deschamps's post at Senlis did begin to provide an excuse for the administration to reduce his entitlements in Paris. In 1391, the king's minister Jean de Montaigu perhaps used these duties as justification for forcing Deschamps to sell his prized house in Paris for what the poet claimed was a below-market price (Balades 784 and 799). At the same time, Deschamps's patrons Louis of Touraine and Philip of Burgundy took him off with them to Italy from February 5 to March 23, 1391, to visit John Galeas Visconti in Pavia. Balades 1037 and 1117 take a positive view of the visit, but Balade 1471, on the rare pleasure of getting a bed to oneself in Lombardy, may be more typical as is the description of the horrors of the return journey through the mountains. He expresses the somewhat contradictory hope that he will be left at peace in Senlis in future—a surprising sentiment, given his numerous poems on the superiority of life in Paris (e.g., Balade 1036[39]).

Deschamps was invited to a tournament on July 23, 1391, to celebrate the birth to the duchess of a son, Louis, but uses the poem not so much to praise the ducal couple as to make a call to arms against the English (Chanson Royale 357). The public poetry is addressed rather to Charles VI on the occasion of the birth of a son on February 6, 1392 (Balades 68, 81, 273 and Virelai 759). Unfortunately for Deschamps, such poetry became irrelevant when the king suffered his first fit of madness on August 5, 1392. Deschamps was, however, involved in more important work for other patrons, although we are left to guess at the identity of the patron for whom he wrote the first art of poetry in French, *L'Art de dictier* of November 25 of the same year.[40]

Louis, who had become duke of Orléans on June 4, 1392, continued to have confidence in Deschamps's administrative skills and promptly asked him to take possession in his name of his inheritance on the day after the death of the duchess Blanche on February 7, 1393. Armed with titles not used by him before this date, ducal *conseiller* and *maistre d'hostel*, as well as with a hundred gold francs, a clerk, a squire, a cook, a servant, a page, and six horses, Deschamps traveled around Champagne, Brie, and Normandy, doing such practical things as making Jean Dumont captain of Oulchy on March 5, and Jean de Viney of Neuilly-Saint-Front on March 9.[41]

Deschamps's schedule must have been tight, for by March 18, 1393, he was back at his post in Senlis involved in matters that varied from litigation with the count of Vertus to the administration of a bankrupt abbey.[42] He was still able to find time to visit the duke of Burgundy at Leulingham (where peace negotiations were going on) in order to present him with a solemn work, the *Complainte de l'eglise*, dated April 13, 1393 (Complainte 1397). Deschamps was also occupied with arrangements for his daughter's marriage to Renaud de Pacy, lord of Plessis-Pomponne, a chamberlain of the duke of Orléans and also a poet. The bridegroom was in debt from which Deschamps rescued him on the wedding day by making him a loan of 500 francs; the duke himself was moved to make Deschamps a handsome gift of 500 francs for the dowry although a wait of three years was required to extract even a first installment from the treasurer.[43] Balades 1149, 1150, and 1234 make satirical comments on these expenses, but there is also a more elevated poem, Balade 1151, addressed to his daughter on his sadness at parting with her. The duke made Deschamps other gifts in the same year, money and a horse[44] and in addition made him his *maistre des fores* (master forester) in Champagne and Brie by the beginning of October.[45] Charles VI is not mentioned except in Balade 1029, which offers reasons for an order given by the king's physicians that he be left to eat his meals in peace; the king had had his first relapse into madness in June 1393.

It was clear by this period, perhaps since Deschamps's troubles in 1380, that no subject was safe from his quill. Balade 1277 illustrates this exuberance; it is a counterblast to the communal assembly at Senlis, which, at its session on July 19, 1394, had decided to offer wine to the bailiff only on the first day of his assizes.[46] The duke of Orléans again used him as an envoy in November of the same year, asking him to go from Paris to Chalons to meet Saint Dizier.[47] Again in the same year, on November 18, while Charles VI was staying with the duke at Asnières-sur-Oise, Deschamps was commissioned to distribute one hundred crowns to the king's officers.[48]

On May 28, 1395, Deschamps appears to have been at his post in Senlis, transacting business,[49] and it may have been later in the same year that he wrote Balade 1375, probably his first poem to Charles VI since the king's illness; the subject is not unlike Balade 1277's, since it is concerned solely with Deschamps's pay and conditions.

It had, however, become obvious that without Charles VI to protect him, Deschamps's cavalier attitude toward his duties in his bailiwick and frequent appearances at court would have consequences. In 1396, the royal treasurers refused to pay him two terms of his salary as bailiff citing this reason. His response in Supplicacion 1425 was somewhat rash since he put himself on record as preferring to lose the post if the sums due were not paid. Royal ordinances of October 18, 1394, and March 28, 1396, attempted to impose residence requirements on royal officers by the withdrawal of salary.[50] Deschamps defended his position (Balades 952, 1110, and 1111; Rondeaux 648 and 649), but it was his position at court as *huissier d'armes* that most obviously contravened the legislation. Threats to deprive him of this court office are attacked in Supplicacions 1190 and 1206, and it is possible that his defense was successful, since Balade 1306, written about four years later, speaks of thirty-two years in court service. In any event, Deschamps used the title of *huissier d'armes*, with or without justification, for the rest of his life. Against the view that he kept the post is the fact that he was excluded from the wedding ceremonies of Richard of England and Isabelle, the daughter of Charles VI, on November 4, 1396. Balades 1124, 1125, and 1130 protest at this exclusion, and present his decision to abandon his *Livre de memoire*,[51] his record of events of public importance and state occasions. Given the fact that this work is now lost, it is conceivable that Deschamps destroyed it in a moment of anger. He may have been genuinely taken aback by his exclusion, since he had produced Balade 1181 in support of the marriage soon after the contract was signed on March 9, 1396, and also promised to immortalize both kings as peacemakers in the same *Livre de memoire* (Balade 1148). The duke of Orléans had even invited him to a meeting with Richard and Isabelle in October,[52] and he was with the duke at Saint Omer at this time (a meeting Deschamps mentions in Balade 452).

At least his position with the duke of Orléans as steward and master forester seemed secure[53] although Deschamps took risks when he defended the duke's wife, Valentina, against charges of sorcery in Balade 771;[54] it was the duke himself who had exiled her to Asnières in March 1396. Again, even if he had indeed lost his position at the royal court, he did not fail to comment on public events, forecasting victory against the Turks in Balade 67 but lamenting the defeat at Nicopolis (September 25, 1396) when the news arrived in Paris in December (Balades 1313, 1316, and 1427).[55] There is also a lament in Balade 1366 for the death of his patron, Enguerrand de Coucy.[56]

The confidence in Deschamps displayed by the duke of Orléans makes a contrast with the hostility of the royal administration. The fact that Deschamps kept his post as bailiff of Senlis until the year of his death can best be explained by the duke's own intervention. An instance of this confidence is that the duke entrusted Deschamps on January 18, 1397, with a difficult and important mission to Bohemia and Moravia.[57] One purpose of the mission was to persuade King

Wenceslas to intervene in Italy,[58] another to convince the marquis of Moravia that he should consent to arbitration in a dispute with the king.[59] Deschamps abstained from versifying these delicate matters but instead wrote some of his most colorful poetry about the events of the journey, the risk of attacks by highwaymen, the glories of Prague, and the extraordinary scenes in foreign inns (Balades 1302, 1305, 1317, and 1318; Versus 1304; Chanson Royale 1325; Rondeaux 1303, 1323, 1326,[60] and 1330). There can be no doubt about his personal courage in undertaking this mission; indeed, it might be argued that age (he was approaching sixty) had done little to curb his inclination toward rash speech and behavior. How else does one explain Rondeau 1321, which celebrates an injury to his eye suffered while jousting in a tournament in Prague?

Back in Paris on July 18, 1397, Deschamps received 200 francs from the duke to compensate him for the loss of his horses on the journey. Then, in January 1398, he received another gift, a fur coat.[61] In September 1398, Deschamps was also commissioned to purchase books for the duke's library.[62] All these activities suggest that his relationship with the duke was fairly close. It is therefore somewhat surprising that Deschamps's political poetry written on the subject of the withdrawal of French recognition of the Avignon pope, Benedict XIII, which took place on July 27, 1398, condemned that pope (Balades 938, 948, and 951 and Dictiés 1260 and 1261), who was supported by the duke of Orléans but opposed by the dukes of Berry and Burgundy. Deschamps's views, so different from the duke's own, did not discourage the duke of Orléans from having the poet accompany him on a diplomatic mission to explore the attitudes of the Breton nobility after the death of Duke John IV and the deposing of King Richard II of England on September 29, 1399. Deschamps lodged at the *ostel de la plederie* in Pontorson in his capacity as the duke's *maistre d'ostel* on November 18, although this is the last occasion on which he is recorded in that position.[63]

Apart from these special services for the duke of Orléans, Deschamps continued to be active elsewhere in the years 1398–99, acting on forestry business on July 8, 1398,[64] defending the rights of the officers of the bailiff of Vitry in Lettres 1406, dated from Fismes on December 24, 1398; lamenting the death of Marguerite de Saint Dizier, a nun at Soissons, on May 8, 1399, in Complainte 1357; and also acquiring another property in the area, the Rouge Bois at Grauves in Champagne in 1399 (SATF 11:87).

The year 1400 had long since been presented as a year of doom in Deschamps's verse (e.g., Prophecies 1041 and 1446), but Deschamps also celebrated it as the jubilee of Boniface IX, the pope in Rome (Balades 1488 and 1490). There are suitably gloomy thoughts on the murder of Richard II on February 14, 1400, in Balade 1200 and Prophecie 1046, and similar poems on the deposition of Wenceslas as emperor by the Rhenish electors on August 20, 1400, in Balade 1204. The betrothal of Jeanne de Navarre, duchess of Brittany and widow of Duke John, to Henry of Lancaster is viewed as a positive step toward peace in

Balade 1488. The themes of this poetry contrast with fashions at court in the same year, notably with the establishment of a court of love in Paris on February 14, 1400 (SATF 11:87). The court named Deschamps as a member, but far from acknowledging or accepting the honor, he announced his intention of retiring from the court and living in the country, probably in the same year (Balades 1265 and 1306). At about the time of the first meetings of the court, Deschamps was involved in more serious activities in Senlis, calling a meeting of citizens on February 28 to discuss a tax to pay for repairs to the fortifications in his jurisdiction.[65] There were also inquiries from the queen as to whether Senlis had been affected by plague.[66] It may be that some of his poems on how the body of a sixty-year-old man begins to let him down (e.g., Balade 1266) were also written at this period.[67] None of these poems on aging, however, diminished his sense of the comic, and later that same year, he was convoking a mock parliament at Epernay and Lens, dating his invitation from Fismes on October 16–17, 1400 (Dit 1404 and Balade 1405). It is likely that he had become rather more active in his bailiwick after his retirement from the court, passing judgment himself on a thief, Jeanne de Beauvais, in 1400 and 1401,[68] although Deschamps appears to have reduced his commitments as master forester of the duke of Orleans; Deschamps is last mentioned in that post in August 1401.[69]

Retirement from court service did not reduce Deschamps's verse output, which continued to defy easy categorization. Balade 1282 is a comic poem on the marriage of Antoine de Bourgogne at Arras on April 25, 1402; Balade 86 in October of the same year supports the duke of Orléans in his plans to crush a rebellion in Metz; Balades 1186 and 1187 lament the death of Louis of Champagne (died February 6, 1403); Balade 1198 is inspired by the rotten fish in Lent 1403; and Lettres 1407 and Balade 1346 satirize the marriage of a cleric. Lettres 1407 is also interesting insofar as Deschamps includes a description of his life in retirement, happy among his books in his house at Compiègne and visited by close friends. He had not lost his talent for abrasive political poetry, however. Balade 1208 is a satire on the reversal of French policy on the competing popes: on July 30, 1403, the duke of Orléans had persuaded Charles VI to transfer French allegiance back to the pope at Avignon, again coming into conflict with the duke of Burgundy on this issue. Deschamps comes close to declaring a plague on both factions, Burgundian and Orleanist. One cannot know whether he intended such poetry only for those of his friends who called on him in his library. If he really intended it for a wider audience, he was living somewhat dangerously. Balade 1212 is another political poem, with allusions to the spread of heresy in Bohemia, the death of John Galeas Visconti on September 3, 1403, and, perhaps, to an expedition to Italy planned by the duke of Orléans.[70]

Deschamps was pleased and flattered by an epistle addressed to him on February 10, 1404, by the poet Christine de Pizan,[71] and wrote her an appropriate reply in Balade 1242.[72] There were, perhaps, doubts about his state of health at this time: the duke of Orléans's wife, Valentina Visconti, and her friends began praying for him when they heard rumors that he had died. He thanked them for their prayers and reassured them in Balades 1344 and 1345. Unluckily for Deschamps, this or a subsequent rumor was given credence by the duke, who promptly had the office of bailiff of Senlis given to his *maistre d'ostel* Pierre de Précy in spite of Deschamps's protests in Balade 1255. Deschamps's last receipts for his salary as bailiff are dated March 24 and May 14, 1404;[73] he was forced to give up the post five days later on May 19.[74] The duke and Charles VI felt the need to make amends, however, and undertook to have Deschamps appointed royal treasurer instead on June 14.[75] This appointment in turn was canceled at the end of a week, on June 21, according to Balade 1248. In Balade 1252, Deschamps points out that all he gained from the promise was the obligation to pay seal duty on the new office and yet another promise from the king that he would appoint Deschamps financial general instead. This promise rated no mention in the archives, however.

Balades 1248 and 1252 are Deschamps's last datable poems. His son Gilles was already involved in a dispute about his father's estate on March 26, 1405. Given the fact that Deschamps, very atypically, raised no protest about the failure to honor the promise to appoint him financial general, it is likely that he died not long after of the "sudden and fatal illness" mentioned by the copyists of BNF Fonds français 840.[76]

Artistic Achievement

Deschamps, as Walter Besant remarked, "wrote no fewer than 90,000 verses, an amount which represents four times the work of Virgil and twice that of Homer" (82).[77] If he had a career as a writer of about fifty years, from the mid-1350s until his death in 1404, that figure translates as about ten lines of verse for every day of his adult life. The very counting of the 1,501 works of poetry and prose that appear in the eleven-volume Société des Anciens Textes Français (SATF) edition[78] of his works has been an occasion of division among scholars, mainly because a few works appear two or three times, and also because some defy easy categorizing. With this caveat, our count produces 1,014 balades, 138 chansons royales, 173 rondeaux, 84 virelais, 14 lays, 34 nonstrophic dits, 10 non-fixed-form lyrics, and 11 pieces in Latin. In addition, there are also four prose works, one in Latin, and, most significant, *L'Art de dictier*. Deschamps's works occupy the entire length of one of the most voluminous manuscripts in medieval French literature, BNF Fonds français 840.

To say that Deschamps was a prolific writer is an understatement. He was also a compulsive writer, turning out verse while presiding in his own law courts to rescue himself from the tedium of his office as judge of those brought before him. He also admits to writing poetry in church. Given the angry reactions to his verse while he was on active military campaign, there is every reason to suppose that he wrote there too as perhaps he did in the inns of Bohemia or while watching diners at court.[79] The epistolary character of much of his verse almost suggests that he preferred poetry to prose as his everyday means of communication, including as his correspondents the Deity and certain elevated allegorical or mythological personages, kings, princes, aristocrats, courtiers, the middle classes, peasants, enemies, criminals, foreigners, friends, his children, and, most of all, himself. The list might be extended to include animals, inanimate objects such as the castle of Fismes, and also certain parts of the body, which are made to deliver speeches or take part in conversations.[80]

Deschamps wrote as unhesitatingly about the state of nations as he did about toothache.[81] He was as forceful in condemning the morals of the nobility as he was about the behavior of waiters who insisted on serving the food before pouring the wine.[82] Even what he believed to be the misconduct of the war against the English and the callous oppression of the French peasantry by their own countrymen were presented no more hallucinatingly than the horrors of foreign hotels.[83] As is the case with most French lyric poets before him, he was capable of turning out pretty verses in praise of women, but he was even more eloquent about the advantages of getting a bed to himself.[84] He shared the conventional medieval view of the wisdom of the ancients as compared with the folly of his own times but was also inclined to believe that the true gift of omniscience was more likely to belong to contemporary domesticated dogs prowling the streets of Paris.[85]

Deschamps enjoyed many foreign cities, and praised their good qualities lavishly,[86] but never relinquished his regional chauvinism: Paris and its environs were the uncontested center of the universe.[87] His poems are peopled with historical and archetypal characters culled from the law court, the royal court, and the peasants' courtyard. Some of the poems are raucous and scurrilous by modern standards;[88] yet others, staid and moralizing, prophesying doom for the ungodly.[89] The latter have contributed to his unduly somber reputation in recent times, but they were among the first poems recognized in the eighteenth century, whose critics praised the poems' morality while condemning contemporary decadence. But the range of Deschamps's voice, expressed best in the short verse forms as well as the range of his topics, is on the whole comic and benign rather than condemnatory or preachy. True, he mocked hypochondriacs, women of fashion, impotent men, crones, peasants, and their social betters; he catalogued kinds of laughter, excesses of courtly manners, the horrors of senescence and disease; he peered into kitchens and dining rooms, battlefields and bedrooms. But he found himself the most amusing character of all, reveling in his own self-contradictions and eccentricities; he made poetry out of his own authorial pretensions as well as his own real or imagined personal predicaments with the same zest as he spoofed knights, nobles, thieves, and judges. What is remarkable is that this public servant, who survived in his offices until his death, not only expressed his personal discontent, but also rebuked his patrons, including the king of France and his brothers, for their poor judgment, contradictions, and misdeeds. The liberties Deschamps allowed himself bear witness to the authority given him by his writing as well as to his courage.

Confronted by the daunting problem of imposing some order on the apparently random collection of his complete works and perhaps following the author's own wishes, the copyists of BNF Fonds français 840 (see note 111, p. 45) attempted to place at least some of Deschamps's lyric works in two general categories according to subject matter: love poetry and moral poetry, "poesies amoureuses and poesies morales." We know that the distinction must have been important to Deschamps because of the sheer number of poems on love topics versus other topics, so we do him the courtesy of taking account of it in categorizing his works. At a rough count, 68 percent of his virelais, 43 percent of his rondeaux, 18 percent of his balades, and 5 percent of his chansons royales can be described as love lyrics. Since there are fewer than 400 virelais, rondeaux, and chansons royales but over 1,000 balades, one needs to add together all these lyric forms to get perspective: just over 23 percent of the total number of virelais, rondeaux, balades, and chansons royales are love lyrics. It is not possible to continue this exercise with the longer poems, and Deschamps's copyists made no attempt to bring them into their categorization system. In any case, most of them cannot be described as love poems of any sort and the others treat multiple subjects including love.

The conclusion that may be drawn is that Deschamps wrote more on what he himself calls "other subjects" than he did on love.[90] Deschamps's choice of topics no longer seems remarkable to us, but it was almost revolutionary in the context of medieval French lyric poetry before him, where the preferred subject, indeed for many poets the only suitable subject, was love. It becomes easier to understand why Deschamps, followed by his copyists, was at such pains to distinguish love poetry from "other" poetry. The fact that he wrote more on "other subjects" was his artistic signature: it is what distinguished him from other lyric poets in the eyes of his contemporaries. Philippe de Mezières, writing during Deschamps's lifetime, praised him as the author of solid, weighty, and edifying poetry ("dictez vertueulx")[91] and even includes him in the same company as Saint Augustine on a list of recommended reading for the young Charles VI. Philippe contrasted Deschamps's works with those of frivolous writers of mere chansons and virelais, the implication being that Deschamps was exceptional simply because he was not a courtly poet whose inspiration was confined to gallantry. Christine de Pizan also praised him in similar terms in the year of his death.[92]

Among Deschamps's greatest claims to fame is *L'Art de dictier* (Prose 1396), written in 1392, the first *ars poetica* in French.[93] Machaut had maintained the traditional indivisibility of the poem and its musical setting, as had earlier lyric poets in both the south and north of France, at least in theory. Deschamps specifically states that music might intrude on the private enjoyment of poetry, for according to him, poetry has its own "natural music," superior to the "artificial," that is, instrumental, variety. This classification was an inversion of the usual medieval definitions, and a view shared by most French poets ever since. Deschamps also affirmed music's recreational and hygienic qualities.

L'Art de dictier is composed of two main parts: a treatise on the seven liberal arts and a prescriptive poetics. The former treats all of the arts except music very briefly. Grammar is the eldest art, and facilitates the study of all the other arts. The focus on the remaining arts is on their practical applications: the use of logic yields subtle arguments, discernment of the truth, and men skilled beyond their peers. Rhetoric produces correct speech. Geometry is used in many practical applications, from architecture to ship building; arithmetic is useful to all manner of professions, most notably coinage and money-changing, as well as to those who are concerned with calculating the passage of time. Astronomy is suited to medical and agricultural applications.

The section on music is the longest section of the liberal arts treatise by far. It focuses on the restorative, hygienic aspects of music, which rehabilitates those exhausted by the pursuit of the other arts or by hard work. There are two kinds of music, natural and artificial. The latter is produced either by instruments or the human voice, but the former is lyric poetry. They go well together, but natural music is vastly superior: it can be learned only by the talented, and it can be performed where instrumental music cannot be, for example, in the private chambers of the nobility. Music refreshes the exhausted: "[T]he hearts and minds of those who [are] fatigued, burdened and bored in practicing the [liberal] arts through thought, imagination, and work of their hands, are healed, renewed and rendered more able thereafter to study and work on the other six arts. (Musique . . . tant que par sa melodie delectable les cuers et esperis de ceuls qui aux diz ars, par pensee, ymaginacion et labours de bras estoient traveilliez, pesans et ennuiez, sont medicinez et recreez, et plus habiles apres a estudie[r] et laboure[r] aux autres vj ars dessus nommez) (*L'Art de dictier* 61, 60). And music, that is, recited poetry, is therapeutic: it can be performed for the sick in the privacy of their rooms (*L'Art de dictier*, 65, 67).[94] There is no indication that Deschamps ever wrote any music himself, but musical settings for Balades 123 and 124, laments for the death of Machaut in 1377, were written by F. Andrieu at the time, and it is possible that Deschamps approved of them, given the fact that Machaut was the greatest French musical composer of his time.[95] This introductory section of *L'Art de dictier* also includes a cursory discussion of linguistics and euphonics.

The balance of *L'Art de dictier* is taken up with a prescriptive poetics. The various forms of the balade, the sirventes, the virelai, the rondeau, and the lay are presented, and the chanson royale and the pastourelle are mentioned.

L'Art de dictier was intended for an audience of people who were at least conversant with poetic theory, even if they themselves were not poets. The treatise is incomplete, and gives signs of haste or impatience[96]—perhaps because it was composed at the behest of a powerful patron. However flawed, it is the product of a prolific and respected poet, and so affords a view into fourteenth-century poetic theory and practice.

Deschamps's longest and best-known work, *Le Miroir de mariage* (Poem 1498), is incomplete in spite of its 12,103 lines.[97] The *Miroir* examines whether the allegorical main character, Franc Vouloir, should marry. It is a scholarly, if basically misogynistic, treatise in which both the pros and cons of domestic life are presented. It is even-handed insofar as marriage is presented as being difficult for women as well as men. Its language and imagery are colorful and often comic until Franc Vouloir's hopes of finding a young, obedient, wealthy wife are dashed by his only true friend Répertoire de Science in a misogamist, misogynist tract based on classical arguments.[98] The discussion breaks off abruptly, and the reader never finds out Franc Vouloir's decision.

Influence

What influence did Deschamps have on other poets? He was certainly in contact with other French writers, for example Oton de Grandson, with whom he shares the innovation of adding an envoy (a short final summarizing stanza) to the balade; Christine de Pizan; and possibly Jean Froissart, with whose pastourelles his own have something in common and whose rival he may have been in the genre.[99] Christine called Deschamps her "dear master and friend" in a verse epistle that praised the moral dimensions of his work.[100] It is also possible that the great fifteenth-century poet Charles d'Orléans knew Deschamps's work, for Deschamps had been closely affiliated with both Philippe d'Orléans and Louis d'Orléans from 1375 to 1404 and had also been a close friend of Louis's wife, Valentina. Some of François Villon's urban poetry is also reminiscent of Deschamps's, but nothing can be said about influence in either his case or that of Charles d'Orléans. The same point can be made about fifteenth-century farces: there are moments in which they may remind one of Deschamps, but the truth is rather that they have sprung from similar plots of ground. Of particular note in this regard is the *Pathelin*, which presents some distant analogies with Deschamps's *Trubert et Antroignart*, a farce on the alleged theft of an almond from a rural confidence man who is outwitted by the greater pretense of the lawyer hired to prosecute the case (Rime plate 1359).

One of the more interesting questions concerns Deschamps's influence on foreign writers, especially Chaucer, with whose work Deschamps's has something in common.[101] Much has been written on this question, the consensus appearing to be that some of Chaucer's shorter poems may have been influenced by Deschamps's lyrics, and the *Prologue to the Legend of Good Women*, by Deschamps's *Lay de franchise*.[102] None of this influence is impossible, but it is doubtful that, as is often claimed, Deschamps's *Miroir de mariage* influenced Chaucer's *Merchant's Tale* and the Prologue to the *Wife of Bath's Tale* if only because Deschamps may still have been working on the *Miroir* in 1404, four years after Chaucer's death, as a manuscript note at the end of the work suggests.[103] Chaucer may have seen early sections of the work, but there is no evidence that Deschamps circulated incomplete works although it remains in the realm of possibility. Deschamps may have sent Chaucer copies of some of his works, perhaps in the 1380s, writing Balade 285 to accompany them. There is no evidence about which works these might have been. The idea that sections of an incomplete work such as the *Miroir* might have been included in this or other packages seems strained. Moreover, there is the difficulty that Deschamps, in his balade to Chaucer (Balade 285), does not assume the role of the greatest living poet: rather, with disarming authorial modesty and an irrepressible comic sense, Deschamps actually tells Chaucer that he feels he is worthy to be no more than a weed in Chaucer's garden. Toward no one else, except his own master, Machaut, does Deschamps adopt the role of awed disciple.[104] His attitude is remarkable given that Deschamps was no older than Chaucer, and that England and France were at war. Could Deschamps have understood enough English to read Chaucer for himself? If so, any influence could have been two-way. Whatever the truth of this matter, Deschamps's astonishing and novel thematic variety and his exceptional capacity to construct character lyrics, which altered French poetry permanently, may have had at least some English roots. It is also possible that Deschamps's work may have had some Italian ones, but the question of whether Deschamps, who visited Italy several times, learned anything from Italian poets or even influenced them has never yet been the subject of systematic inquiry.[105]

By the sixteenth century, Deschamps's work was forgotten. In the seventeenth century, even his descendants who were using his title to nobility as a means to avoid taxation left no indication that they knew his poetry.[106] In the eighteenth century, the lexicographer La Curne de Sainte-Palaye made a fair copy of the unique complete manuscript, largely for the linguistic and historical interest it provided: his dictionary includes many references to Deschamps's poetry. When nineteenth-century editors and critics tended to praise Deschamps's work, it was because they thought it expressed and thus defended traditional values against the ideas of the Enlightenment. Twentieth-century critics, notably Johan Huizinga in his *The Autumn of the Middle Ages*, have quoted selectively from Deschamps's 1,500 poems in order to sustain very different cultural or political agendas: Deschamps served as a scapegoat for everything Huizinga disapproved of in the later Middle Ages. Such treatment may explain why the poet did not perhaps win the reputation he deserved through the publication of his complete works by the Société des Anciens Textes Français between 1878 and 1903.[107] There would be great advantages in a new complete edition, and the present editors hope that the selection offered will contribute to that end as well as to the resurgence of Deschamps studies.[108]

Selection Principles

The main criteria used to select the poems in this collection were their enduring literary quality and their modern appeal. An additional, equally important principle was the possibility for graceful translation into English verse. Also, these poems are a sampling of Deschamps's work in shorter verse forms—the balade, the rondeau, the chanson royale, among others—because such short works can stand on their own and because Deschamps was at his best in these forms. Selecting snippets of his longer works does not do them justice. And having just said that, it seemed nevertheless impossible to completely omit *Le Miroir de mariage*, so a short, often-quoted passage of that work is also included here, since it has been used as hard evidence that Deschamps influenced Chaucer.[109] Among the poems are many that present concrete universals: characters from the court or the countryside, from military campaigns or Deschamps's bailiwick of Senlis, from Paris or those countries where he traveled on royal commissions, as well as the assorted characters whose personas Deschamps donned himself. Some of the poems are minidramas that attempt to compress an incident or a many-sided dispute into a short lyric. Many of the poems have some element of the comic in them, for Deschamps wrote more successfully of laughter than he did of tears. The concrete universals enter into any attempt to define that long Renaissance of which Deschamps was a part: more Chaucerian than Petrarchan, closer to Sancho Panza than to the Don. Apart from their literary merits, many of these poems have a sociocultural interest: an argument can be made that Deschamps was an embryonic sociologist.

Editorial Policy for the Texts and Translations

The French texts in this edition were prepared directly from Bibliothèque Nationale Français (BNF) Fonds français 840, the only manuscript that contains the whole of Deschamps's work. In most cases, these are the first edited texts since the Société des Anciens Textes Français edition appeared. The text of the manuscript is reproduced faithfully, and departed from only where a line would be incomprehensible without emendation. All emendations are explained in the textual notes. Modern conventions on capitalization have been adopted. Only such modern punctuation as is strictly necessary to facilitate the comprehension of a passage has been used, for we have no idea how Deschamps would have liked his poems to be read.[110] Modern French accents are not used except for the acute on the final sounded *e* of past participles or adjectives to ensure that readers not lose count of the syllables.

Most of the poems selected exist only in BNF Fonds français 840. Given the fact that the copyists of this manuscript refer to Deschamps as having died recently, it can be presumed that it must have been completed soon after 1404. It may have been planned before then, in part in fulfillment of Deschamps's own wishes.[111] Deschamps's text has not been emended where there appears to be a defect in metrics, given the possibility that the error may have been Deschamps's own, for we have every reason to believe that he often wrote in haste. We have, however, noted such lapses and, wherever possible, suggested how the line might be scanned in pronunciation to regularize it. Where a line appears to be missing, we have suggested this lack by using the time-honored convention of a line of ellipsis points, always on the understanding, again, that the apparent error may have been Deschamps's own. No attempt has been made to regularize Deschamps's spelling except to avoid confusion where different spellings are used for a word repeated in a refrain from one strophe to the next. These exceptions are noted in the textual notes. As is to be expected from the conventions of medieval handwriting, Deschamps's copyists frequently made no distinction between certain consonants, for example between *t* and *c*, between *v*, *u*, and *n*, and between *i* and *j*. These instances are resolved in line with modern conventions. The later medieval fad for Latinized spelling is honored where there is no doubt about the consonant, provided that it could have been justified at that time by the relationship—often spurious, it is true—between that word and a Latin word similar in meaning, for example, *dictier* instead of the earlier and phonetically more correct versions without a *c*. If these spellings are indeed Deschamps's own and not merely those of his copyists, they may reveal a little of Deschamps's fondness for droll legalistic or learned language in comically inappropriate contexts.

This sense of the comic is part of what drew Ian Laurie to selecting and editing approximately 120 poems from Deschamps's oeuvre that he thought would be most likely to appeal to the modern reader. When Laurie and Deborah Sinnreich-Levi first collaborated in the 1990s, it was on the volume *Eustache Deschamps, French Courtier-Poet: His Work and His World*. And it was serendipitous that the very summer Laurie and Sinnreich-Levi were beginning to assemble a volume of translations and editions, David Curzon and Jeffrey Fiskin approached them with a plan for a similar volume. On the basis of a meticulous review of Ian Laurie's editions, he and Deborah Sinnreich-Levi produced free translations into English, keeping strictly to the literal sense of the lines. David Curzon and Jeffrey Fiskin then rendered these exact but inelegant translations into English verse. Their poetic translations were then compared again with the French and emended where necessary. The collaboration between two French medievalists and two modern poets has produced, we hope, accurate translations that are also colloquial English poems.

Deschamps's Metrical Forms

The poems selected (except for the selection from *Le Miroir de mariage*) are written in the fixed forms: rondeau, the virelai, the balade, and the chanson royale.[112]

In analyzing them, we adopt the convention that rhymes in the refrain are identified by capital letters, and rhymes in the strophe, lower-case letters. A feminine rhyme (i.e., one which ends in a mute *e* and that includes whole verb endings where the termination ceased to be pronounced in the thirteenth century such as *ils aiment* or *ils aimaient*) is signified by adding an asterisk after the letter which denotes the rhyme; that is, "A*" denotes one line of the refrain that is also a feminine rhyme, whereas "a" denotes a line of the strophe that is a masculine rhyme.

The metrical forms represented in this anthology,[113] the fixed-form refrain lyrics of the fourteenth century—the rondeau, the virelai, the balade, and the chanson royale—may be traced back in part to the simpler refrain lyrics of the twelfth and thirteenth centuries, where they appear under various names, for example the *rondel*, the *verenli,* and the *ballette*. However, at least in the case of the longer forms, the balade and the chanson royale, the origins are also to be sought in the twelfth- and thirteenth-century courtly lyric, notably the chanson, which had no refrain. Our discussion begins with the older forms although we must note that Deschamps himself preferred the balade to all other forms, the preponderance of his oeuvre consisting of balades.

Rondeau

The regular rondeau or rondel has only one strophe. It begins with a refrain of variable length (usually from two to four lines), followed by a line or lines of strophe, and followed by the repetition of a portion of the refrain to match the line or lines of this part of the strophe. This partial repetition of the refrain is followed without interruption by a number of lines of the strophe equal to the number of lines in the complete initial refrain. This refrain is repeated in its entirety at the end of the poem. Two rhymes only are employed. The simplest rondeau form is *ABaAabAB*, called by Deschamps the *rondel sangle* to distinguish it from the *rondel double* with a refrain of four lines: *ABABabABababABAB*. BNF Fonds français 840 frequently abbreviates these refrains with an "*etc*." Systematic abbreviation of the repeated refrains in actual performance as well as in manuscripts is usually claimed to have been a fifteenth- rather than a fourteenth-century phenomenon, but there is no way of determining what Deschamps's intentions were in this matter. The whole refrain is noted in our edition, but the point at which the scribe cuts off a repeated refrain with *etc*. is noted in the textual notes. In the case of the rondeau with a four- (and on one occasion even five-) line refrain, sense and syntax occasionally require the repetition of the second line of the refrain at the end of the poem but never of the third and fourth line. In the case of the rondeau with a two-line refrain, the complete first line of the refrain is followed by an "etc." at the end of a poem often enough in the manuscript to compel us to think that Deschamps did indeed want to have the refrain repeated in its entirety. Abbreviation in performance of the rondeau with a three-line refrain, the form preferred by Deschamps, may also have occurred. There is a shorter variety of rondeau with a three-line refrain, not identified by the SATF editors (11:125) and incorrectly printed by them: 625, 641, 644, 658, and 1330. Here, indeed only one line of strophe should be repeated medially because only one line of strophe precedes it. There are two or three poems given the title "rondeau" or "virelai" in the manuscript that fall outside the genres: the most famous of these is the poem *Sui je belle*, which defies categorization.

Virelai

The virelai, unlike the rondeau, can have more than one strophe. Like the rondeau, but unlike the balade, it begins with a refrain, which Deschamps varies from four to seven lines (with the exception of three irregular pieces). That refrain is repeated in its entirety at the end of each strophe and again before the beginning of the next one. As is the case with the balade and the chanson royale, the strophe itself (excluding the refrain) has a tripartite structure—tripartition being a form almost as old as the French lyric itself. The three parts are called by Deschamps the *ouvert*, the *clos*, and the *tierce*. The *ouvert* and the *clos* are symmetrical; the *tierce* is symmetrical only with the full refrain. More than two rhymes can be used. A favorite strophe in Deschamps's virelai is: *AABBA* (refrain) *bba* (*ouvert*) *bba* (*clos*) *aabba* (*tierce*) *AABBA* (refrain). Deschamps states in *L'Art de dictier* that the virelai ought to have three strophes:[114] twenty-one of his virelais have three strophes, eleven have only one, one has thirteen, and fifty have two strophes. Nothing more than the first line of the repeated refrain appears in the manuscript; again, we have no way of knowing whether this form was abbreviated also in performance.

Balade

The balade is unlike the rondeau and the virelai because it begins with the strophe and not with the refrain.[115] That refrain occurs only at the end of each strophe and also at the end of the envoy, when there is one. By contrast with the rondeau and the virelai, the refrain exercises no obvious influence on the metrical structure of the strophe. It does, of course, have to use one of the rhymes of the strophe and also the same number of syllables as in each line of the strophe (where the balade is isometric). The content of the refrain, by contrast, exercises great influence on the poem, usually determining its whole thrust. The fact that the refrain does have a diminished importance in the balade compared with its importance in the rondeau and the virelai is significant because it distances the genre from earlier refrain songs, in which all fourteenth-century short lyric fixed forms have their origin. The balade was well placed to become a purely literary form, unaccompanied by music, and in the process, to use longer lines and strophes than the virelai or rondeau. The balade is comparable to the virelai, however, insofar as it has the same principle of tripartition in the strophe. The *tierce* in the balade, however, is not symmetrical with the refrain: it is largely independent of it. There are normally three strophes. The envoy remained optional for the poet, not a necessary part of the genre. The envoy is usually composed of two symmetrical parts, the first concluding with the rhyme of the refrain: and the second, with the refrain itself. In the balade, the refrain can almost be considered a part of the strophe. Deschamps may well have been the first French poet to add an envoy to the balade. At the very least, he did more to popularize this practice than any other fourteenth-century poet although it didn't become compulsory until the sixteenth century. Did he use it himself at all at the earliest stage of his career, or perhaps very little or not at all during the reign of Charles V, that is, before 1380? In *L'Art de dictier* (1392; SATF 7:278), he points out that the envoy did not appear in earlier poetry except in the chanson royale.[116] The envoy does not appear in Machaut, Froissart, or Wenceslas de Bohème but is found in ten poems by Deschamps's contemporary and friend, Oton de Grandson. None of these poems by Grandson can be dated with any certainty before those by Deschamps. Unfortunately, most of Deschamps's balades, with or without envoys, cannot be dated with any precision either. However, it can be noted that the exceptions, those poems without envoys, which can certainly or probably be assigned to the period before 1380,[117] outnumber those that do have envoys and that may have been written during the same period but could also have been written much later.[118]

Chanson Royale

The chanson royale in Deschamps is simply an extended balade with five strophes instead of three. The envoy tends to be compulsory; indeed, the envoy of the balade was probably borrowed from the chanson royale, and can be traced back to the French and Occitan verse of the twelfth century.

Rhyme

In his *L'Art de dictier*, Deschamps makes a fairly simple classification of rhymes according to whether they cover a full syllable, *rymes leonines,* or only half a syllable, *rymes consonans* or *rymes sonans* (74, 76). We would probably prefer to say the classification is made according to whether the rhyming vowel is supported by the same preceding consonant. As examples of the former, he cites *monde/onde* and *homme/romme*. As examples of the latter, he cites *clamer/oster* and *presentement/innocent*. For practical purposes, one might refer to these more simply as "rich" and "poor" rhymes, respectively, at least for the purposes of the present selection, although the terminology would not be adequate to describe rhyme in other authors, not least those in later periods of French literary history, since standards for a sufficient rhyme changed along with the terminology. Even for Deschamps himself, the terminology is inadequate to describe his own practice: for example, a rhyme covering two full syllables such as *maintenir/tenir* (76) is also called *leonine* by Deschamps.

Deschamps composed poems of technical virtuosity that were excluded from this selection because they seemed to the editors much less interesting than his poems of personal commentary and social insight. That he was capable of producing such technical tours de force bears mention in the light of criticism that disparaged Deschamps as a mere second-rate versifier. One strophe may serve as an example. The following is the opening strophe of a balade in which the last syllable of one line is picked up (with a different meaning) in the first syllable of the next line.[119]

Lasse, lasse, maleureuse et dolente!
Lente me voy, fors de souspirs et plains.
Plains sont mes jours d'ennuy et de tourmente;
Mente qui veult, car mes cuers est certains,
Tains jusqu'a mort et pour celli que j'ains;
Ains mais ne fut dame si fort atainte;
Tainte me voy quant il m'ayme le mains.
Mains, entendez ma piteuse complainte.[120]

Alas, alas, unhappy and mournful!
Full weary I see myself, burdened by sighs and complaints,
plaints of my days full of torment and ennui.
We may lie, but my heart is sure,
surely pale, unto death, for the one whom I long for,
for never in the past was a lady so wounded.
Dead am I, less than any, if his love decline.
Decline not, Day, to hear my piteous complaint.

Deschamps describes such a strophe as "*equivoque, retrograde et leonime*" (*Art* 74 and 76), that is to say that the rhyme is "*leonine*" because it extends to a full syllable, "*retrograde*" because the first syllable in each line takes up the same syllable as occurred at the rhyme at the end of the line immediately preceding, and "*equivoque*," or a punning rhyme, because the same syllable is used in a different sense from one occurrence to the next. Deschamps describes such virtuosity as surpassing all others in difficulty, but it is fortunate, from the point of view of most modern readers, that he made use of such refinements of rhyme very rarely. We suspect that John Fox may have been correct when he claimed that a full count of Deschamps's rhymes might reveal that the most modest rhyme of all, the *rime sonnant*, probably accounts for more than half of his rhymes (133).

An important element in the French rhyming system is the distinction between masculine and feminine rhymes. Where a French word ends in an *e* that is no longer pronounced in ordinary speech and only in certain defined circumstances in verse or song, for example at the rhyme at the end of the line, that rhyme is called a feminine rhyme. Examples of feminine rhyme from the balade above are "*dolente/tourmente*" and "*atainte/complainte*." The final unpronounced *e* in these examples is generally referred to as a mute *e*. By contrast, a rhyme ending in a vowel that is pronounced, again in the above balade, "*plains/certains/ j'ains/mains*" is referred to as a masculine rhyme. Verb endings such as the third person plural of the present indicative and the imperfect ending in such terminations as "*-ent*" and "*-aient*" and also nouns in the plural ("*complaintes*") are also reckoned as feminine rhymes.

Deschamps does not use the terminology masculine and feminine rhymes but does discuss the problem again in *L'Art de dictier*. Here he takes the view that any poem is improved by a mixture of what we would now call masculine and feminine rhymes. Curiously, he counts what we would call the mute *e* in these rhymes as not mute at all but as a full syllable and argues that a poem is improved by having a mixture of lines of different lengths. Assonance is very rare in Deschamps, but we have included one example in the present selection, Rondeau 554.[121]

Deschamps's Language

Anyone able to read a translation of Deschamps's works into Modern French will probably also be capable of reading them in the original fourteenth-century French, at least as the poems are presented in this edition, with a facing English verse translation and notes to resolve difficulties. Beyond these notes, a few observations about language still need to be made.[122]

The French used from the end of the thirteenth century until some time in the sixteenth century (the dates are somewhat fluid) is sometimes called Middle French, to distinguish it from Old French and Modern French. Some linguists prefer to call it Early Modern French. It may be more accurate to refer to it as Later Medieval French. French at this period has been the subject of excellent studies, some of which are listed in the bibliography. For the purposes of the present edition, it is sufficient to be aware only of some major differences between Later Medieval French and Modern French, including the following: the personal pronoun is often omitted before conjugated forms of the verb; word order is sometimes a little different; and attitudes toward agreement are more relaxed than is the case in Modern French. None of these differences, however, is likely to impede comprehension.

Matters become a little more complicated when one considers the relationship between spelling and pronunciation. Everyone who studies modern French is aware that *s* as the sign of the plural is not pronounced except in liaison with a following vowel, so that the reader will not be inclined to mispronounce, for example, the name Deschamps, which is based simply on the plural "des champs," in which the *s* in both words is not pronounced. Other appearances of a nonpronounced *s* are less obvious. Preconsonantal *s* largely disappeared from pronunciation in the thirteenth century. It has been removed in Modern French and is sometimes replaced by an accent, circumflex or acute, as a guide to pronunciation. In the words *vestus*, *ostel*, *chascun*, and *estoilles*, for example, the *s* before the *t* or *c* is not pronounced and does not appear in Modern French. Less confusion about an unpronounced consonant is likely to be given by final, unsupported *t*, as, for example in many verb endings, since it continues to appear in spelling in Modern French, too, for example in the imperfect and also in the third person plural, and, is of course, not pronounced. The letter *l*, which had been vocalized to the vowel *u* before a consonant in the thirteenth century, frequently still appears in fourteenth-century spelling, or worse, appears along with the *u* to which it had become vocalized. For example, the *l* was not pronounced in the word *moult* or the name *Machault*. Of further note is Deschamps's rhyming of words such as *mer* or *cler* with infinitives that end in *-er*, resulting in an open *e* plus a trilled *r*.[123]

Perhaps the most unfortunate feature of fourteenth-century French is the addition of superfluous letters to the spelling of words that did not formerly possess them. Such additions are explained by the fact that the century was a great one for the translation into French of Latin works. Medieval scholars could not fail to observe how often a French word matched one in Latin. Many found it irresistible to supply letters that seemed to them to be missing from the French but that were a normal part of the Latin spelling. To them, it gave greater dignity to French as a language. In many cases, the analogies that they saw were misleading; for example, they added a *c* (never to be pronounced) to the verb *scavoir* in the mistaken belief that it was a version of the Latin verb *scire*.

Deschamps's *L'Art de dictier* would not have had a *c* in *dictier* in the thirteenth century and that *c* was never pronounced when it was added in the fourteenth. The hope was that the word might appear weightier if it bore a closer resemblance to the Latin *dictum* or *dicere*. While it is fortunate for modern French that some of these strange spellings have disappeared, it makes the reading of Later Medieval French more complicated phonetically than it should be. All that need concern the modern reader of Deschamps is that such letters were for the eye only, to make the French seem more learned and weighty. The surest guide for modern readers, at least for those without a specialist's knowledge of historical French linguistics, is to ignore these spellings and pronounce these words exactly as they are pronounced in Modern French. That, indeed, is probably the best general advice to be given for the reading of all the poems that appear in this edition: in cases of doubt, simply pronounce the word as in Modern French.

There are no more than a few instances in which this method would be unfortunate. The pronunciation of *oi*, for example, as in such words as *oiseau* or *roi* (also written *roy*), or *savoir* is like the English "way" without the second part of this diphthong, not "wa" as in Modern French. Also different from Modern French pronunciation are infinitives in *-er*, which were not pronounced with a closed *e* but rather with an open *e* plus a trilled *r*. Uvular *r* did not exist, and instead that consonant was probably lightly trilled as in Scottish English. Certain consonants, notably final *s* and *t* and also the so-called mute *e*, which were normally not pronounced, might have been heard at a pause in the line, especially at the rhyme. We shall return to this phenomenon in the section on performance.

Apart from these points, the most important fact to be kept in mind with respect to Deschamps's language is that the texts of his work are not those of the author but of the early-fifteenth-century manuscripts in which they are preserved.[124] None of these was completed during Deschamps's lifetime. It is possible, therefore, that judgments about his language may sometimes be more relevant to the linguistic habits of his copyists than to his own. That said, in the case of the manuscript on which this edition is based, BNF Fonds français 840, the copyists do claim to have worked, at least in part, from materials found among Deschamps's belongings after his death, so that the distance between the texts as they might have been offered by the author himself and the version we have may not be very great.

Performance

What has been said so far about the differences between Later Medieval French and Modern French relates mainly to the spelling and pronunciation of words in isolation. This clarification does not go far in addressing the problem of how Deschamps might have intended that his poetry be performed in public or, more simply, be read aloud on more private occasions. That such performance was a matter of some importance to him is beyond doubt. In *L'Art de dictier*, he expresses his conviction that the music of the voice in reading poetry is greatly superior to that of instrumental music.[125] Natural music—for Deschamps, lyric poetry—"is pleasing to hear by itself" but "the lyrics of songs can often be recited in places where they are most willingly heard—even where artificial music would not always be performed, as among lords and ladies in private and secret." Lyrics can be read aloud by a single individual or read "before a sick person" (65, 67).[126] Further support for Deschamps's preference for what he called natural music can be found elsewhere: for example, when condemning those who played the bagpipes at court (Balade 923), Deschamps expressed such dislike of instrumentalists that one suspects he thought of them principally as his great rivals. Difficult as it is to answer it, the question of how his poetry should be read aloud cannot be avoided.

Some assistance, albeit of a purely exclusionary character, may be drawn from the presentation of Deschamps's prose as it appears in BNF Fonds français 840. While not observing in any detail the precepts of medieval manuals of punctuation, the copyists of BNF Fonds français 840 at least generally include the medieval equivalent of a period at the end of a sentence in prose and begin the next one with a capital letter. There can be no doubt that they do so as a means of assisting the reader in identifying sense groups. This division occurs, for example, in the prose passages of *L'Art de dictier*.

The situation is markedly different when the same copyist turns from the prose passages in *L'Art de dictier* to the examples in verse that illustrate the points made in prose. The verse, as is the case with all the verse in the whole manuscript, has so little punctuation that it offers no guide at all as to how it should be read. Certainly a new line beginning with a capital letter is given to each line of verse, but other punctuation marks scarcely appear at all. Where a period or other mark appears, it generally serves to separate a title or rubric, such as "Autre balade" or "Envoi" or perhaps a short summary of the content of the poem in prose, from the actual text of the poem. In the much rarer instances in which a period does appear in the text of a poem, it occurs at the end of the last strophe or envoy, as a means of separating one poem from the next. There are practically no examples of punctuation within the actual texts of the poems themselves, either to identify sense groups or for any other reason. Those marks that do appear are intriguing rather than illuminating. In poems included in the present edition, for example, in Balade 1452, lines 6 and 7 offer a list of place names and persons. In the manuscript, a period follows the word "Troye." The next word, "cartaige," lacks a capital letter. In the next line, "Athenes" is again followed by a period, and this time, the following word, "Alixandre," has a capital. It is, however, not followed by a period but by a mark that is the medieval equivalent of a comma with another capital letter for "Remus." We are dealing with the whim of a copyist and not with the systematic use of punctuation as it appears in the prose passages of BNF Fonds français 840 to identify sense groups. Chanson Royale 912 provides two exceptions to this rule in the first line of the envoy. Here the corrupt judge calls on his officers with one word: "Sergens." They reply, again in one word: "Maistre." In the manuscript, both of these words are followed by a period, which does indeed serve to separate the speakers. It is impossible, however, to attach any importance to these exceptions, since there would have been equal scope for punctuation on these grounds elsewhere in the same poem.

These differences between verse and prose in punctuation and capitalization in BNF Fonds français 840 suggest that poetry did not require punctuation, since the rules for its delivery were known to everyone. If it had been intended that the verse be delivered with appropriate pauses to mark the end of a sense group, that is to say, if it had been intended that the verse be read as if it were prose, one might have expected that the verse be punctuated in the same way as the prose as a guide to the reader. But it is not.

It is clear that a different system of delivery for verse was intended. That system depends on a division of the poem into lines, each of a predetermined number of syllables. The end of each line is marked by a rhyme, and the end of each strophe, by a refrain. The poem may be ended by an envoy, which is itself ended by the refrain. Deschamps describes all of these characteristics in the prescriptive poetics section of *L'Art de dictier*. He also makes reference to what he calls two pauses in the line, the caesura and the rhyme, which divide a line into two parts. They could also be described as stresses.

The longest line used in the present selection is of ten syllables. In most cases, these decasyllabic lines are fairly clearly end-stopped: a pause at the end of them at the rhyme, as suggested by Deschamps's definition, does no violence to the sense and may even make it clearer. There are a few exceptions to this rule, most commonly in the envoy, where a change in the expected rhythm of the poem may signal that it is about to end. The envoy of Balade 923 provides an example. A pause at the end of lines 25 and 26 does nothing for the sense and risks confusing the reader. Again, in Balade 285, a pause at the end of line 7 offends against every rule of French syntax. This offense in itself does not prove that pauses were not required by the meter; more evidence is required before any conclusions can be drawn.

Deschamps's decasyllabic lines usually have a caesura on the fourth syllable of each line. If Deschamps's description of the caesura as a pause is taken seriously, what happens to these lines? The very first poem in our selection provides excellent examples (Balade 24). In twenty-eight of the poem's thirty-four lines, a pause at the caesura is possible even if that pause does not correspond always to what we would now think of as the normal rhythm of the sense group. In the remaining six lines, 3, 15, 16, and 21, such a pause does violence to the sense. Lines 18 and 31 are even more striking since they actually split a word at the caesura just as is the case with Balade 813, line 2 (also included in this collection). There are only three explanations for these occurrences: perhaps Deschamps or his copyists made a mistake; perhaps the caesura falls somewhere else in these lines, for example on the fifth syllable; or perhaps the rhythm of the verse takes no account of the meaning of the words.

Lines shorter than the decasyllable are represented by lines of six, seven, and eight syllables in the present selection. End-stopping is also characteristic of these shorter lines, for example in Balades 58 and 341, Rondeau 554, and Virelai 752. There are also occasional lines where this end-stopping does not occur, for example in Balade 404, lines 14 and 27; Balade 776, line 26; Chanson Royale 912, lines 12, 17, 22, 37, 41, and 51; Balade 1230, lines 1, 25, and 28–30. It is not likely that these shorter lines have a caesura.

How did Deschamps intend that this poetry be read aloud? If we follow his injunction to view both caesura and rhyme as pauses, we must accept that they often take precedence over sense and logic, which would have suggested pauses at quite different points in the lines.

An analogy may be drawn from the instrumental music of the period. Georges Lote examines in some detail the relationship of caesura and rhyme to sense and syntax in French poetry (1:167–290). He concludes that, at least until the sixteenth century and perhaps even until the seventeenth, French composers and poets had no hesitation in sacrificing sense and logic to the metrical demands of caesura and rhyme. It is possible to examine this contention since the same lines of music are repeated unchanged from one strophe to the next. In music, the caesura and rhyme are often marked with longer notes; the note at the caesura may also be higher in pitch than the note at the rhyme, which tends to be a little lower. Deschamps's master, Machaut, is typical: the natural rhythm of French speech, the very sense of the utterance, is sometimes obscured by caesura and rhyme (Lote 1:240–243). This phenomenon would be even more the case if fourteenth-century French speech observed conventions similar to those of Modern French. Here, as any student of the modern language knows, a failure in communication is risked not so much by the mispronunciation of individual words but by the failure to observe grammatical stress. Most vowels in a sentence have approximately equal value: only the last sounded vowel at any pause in the sentence is slightly longer and also slightly higher in pitch. The last sounded vowel at the end of the sentence is also longer, and there the voice tends to fall although there are exceptions to this rule. Such lengthening of vowels and rises and falls in pitch identify sense groups and are essential in communication. If fourteenth-century speech rhythms were similar, the lengthening of notes at the caesura and rhyme in song together with a systematic rise and fall in pitch to mark them out must have made it difficult to follow the words. A system that in speech served to identify sense groups was redirected in song to identify caesura and rhyme. The distance between the delivery of verse and prose must have been great.

The problem for us with Deschamps is whether his view of poetry as "natural music" meant that he followed Machaut in imposing the rhythm of caesura and rhyme on his lines irrespective of their meaning, or whether his own break with instrumental music meant that he also had begun to abandon some of these conventions. In his criticisms of instrumental music, he makes no reference to any need to abandon such conventions: his criticisms are largely based on the complications of bringing instrumentalists into places where they intrude on private life. The strongest evidence that he did not break with Machaut in this respect is his definition of caesura and rhyme as pauses in the line.

Were the caesura and rhyme differentiated from the rest of the line in other respects? It is possible that, following the example of French music and possibly even of normal speech rhythms of the period, Deschamps intended that the voice rise at the caesura and fall at the rhyme. The treatment of so-called mute *e* is also a marker, at least at the rhyme. As we pointed out above (p. 34), ordinarily a nonaccented *e* at the end of a word is not pronounced if it occurs before a following vowel. Before a following consonant, it has the value of a full syllable; this convention survived even in modern times. It has already been pointed out that Deschamps actually reckoned the mute *e* at the rhyme as a full syllable, so turning what we would now think of as isometric poems into heterometric in ways that we would probably find disconcerting in performance.

We can also note that at the two most significant points in the line, the caesura and the rhyme, Deschamps often uses alliteration to reinforce these "strong points." Indeed, this reinforcement also occurs at the other "strong point" in the line, the first word. For example, the first poem in this collection, Balade 24, alliterates in *p* at all these strong points, stressing both the poem's meaning and its rhythm.

We have no reason to believe that Deschamps did not perform his own poetry with full observation of the above conventions, even where they had the effect of distorting normal speech patterns. Poetry readings in ages before our own may have been stranger than we think: one has only to listen to the wax cylinder in the BBC archives of Tennyson chanting a fragment of *Maud* to see how our own conventions have changed over a single century. In Deschamps's case, however, one needs to go beyond conventions and leave room for his own eccentricities and for his reputation for taking people by surprise. It would be tempting to imagine him presenting a character lyric such as Chanson Royale 912, for example, by acting all the parts himself, changing the rhythm of his speech, his voice, and his gesture appropriately. That may not have left much space for the niceties of pause only at the rhyme. We cannot, of course, be sure that he ever did anything of the kind wherever he performed his poetry, at court or on military campaign, but the possibility should not be entirely excluded.

In view of what has been said, the reader may well be surprised that the editors have not hesitated to include modern punctuation in Deschamps's verse. We have done so only to make the meaning clear. That punctuation offers no guide at all as to how the poetry should be performed.

The Presentation of the Poems

The French text and English translation are presented on facing pages. The French text includes the relevant folio numbers. Textual notes are provided mainly only to draw attention to some defect in the text. The number of the poem as taken from BNF Fonds français 840, and the volume and page of each poem as it appears in the Société des Anciens Textes Français's edition are also noted for the interested reader. Literary, linguistic, historical, and biographical notes are also supplied as well as notes concerning translation cruces.

Ian S. Laurie
Melbourne, Victoria, Australia

Deborah M. Sinnreich-Levi
Glen Rock, New Jersey

September 2002

Notes

1. Critics have advanced possible dates ranging from Auguste Molinier's 1338 (4:3346) to Gaston Raynaud and Le Marquis de Queux de Sainte-Hilaire's 1346 (SATF 11:9–10). All references to Deschamps's or his editors' work will be to the Société des Anciens Textes Français (SATF) edition or apparatus unless otherwise noted. Other suggestions for Deschamps's birth date have been made by Hoepffner, between 1340 and 1346 (21–22); Sarradin, between 1338 and 1340 (52–54); and Dupont-Ferrier, 1346 (1942–65, 5:20775). For a more detailed discussion of this or any other aspect of Deschamps's biography, the reader is referred to Ian Laurie's comprehensive biography of the poet.
2. See, for example, Balade 819, which counsels appropriate diet during an outbreak of the plague. See also Rondeau 647, Balades 1162, 1291, and 1452, and Virelai 708. For a discussion of medicine in Deschamps, see Becker, "Eustache Deschamps' Medical Poetry" (in Sinnreich-Levi 1998, 209–23). All references to Deschamps's poems will be to the numbering system in the SATF edition, which follows MS BNF Fonds français 840, the unique complete manuscript of Deschamps's poems. For a discussion of BNF Fonds français 840, see also note 111.
3. Balades 803 and 1199. See also note 79.
4. Christine calls him friend and master in a verse epistle in 1404. See also note 92.
5. There was a Deschamps in Vertus in 1242 (Prieur 1901, 2:518).
6. The reference is for 1340–41 (Longnon 2:318).
7. "Aprez vint Eustache Morel, nepveux de maistre Guillaume de Machault, lequel fut bailli de Senliz et fut tressouffisant de diz et balades et autres choses" (cited in SATF 11:12).
8. Included in this collection.
9. For a discussion of Balade 127 in historical and performance contexts, see Coleman.
10. Both of these poems appear in this anthology.
11. Included in this collection.
12. Included in this collection.
13. Whatever positions in the royal service Deschamps did hold in 1368, they did not have the status of *huissier d'armes* to which he eventually rose. He did, however, serve as a bailiff to Duke Philip (Laurie, 7 and 42, n.30). There is no evidence that Deschamps was ever a royal messenger or royal horseman (Laurie, 38, n.19).
14. See Balades 1146, 1190, 1379, and 1459.
15. Her husband was Renaud de Pacy, only known because Deschamps had to lend him money to get him out of debt on his wedding day. See also page 16.
16. See also above on page 7.
17. See also page 6 for a discussion of *Le Livre de memoire*.
18. Included in this collection.
19. See above page 8.

20. Deschamps's house was laid waste during an ongoing feud in which he was not a participant (Balade 1347). Deschamps sued the leader of the offending party, Huguenin de Charmes, in 1384 (Prieur 1901, 531; SATF 11:40, n.5; 11:42) Raynaud also mentions Balades 2, 5, and 105 in addition to Balade 1347, but these poems contain only vague complaints against lawlessness.
21. BNF Pièces Originales vol. 666, doss. 15570, no. 2, records a royal gift made to Deschamps on March 10, 1388, in recognition of this inspection tour. In this document, which has been misread by previous critics, Charles VI, referring to his *huissier d'armes* Eustace Morel, also the *escuier* of Louis of Touraine, acknowledges services the poet rendered in visiting the Picard frontier and its fortresses. For a fuller discussion, see Laurie 49, n.71.
22. For an excellent discussion of the war poetry of Deschamps and Froissart, see Devaux.
23. Rondeau 596 is included in this collection.
24. Included in this collection.
25. See the notes for Balade 285.
26. See, among others, Marcel Thibault, 45–47; and Verdon, 24–26. As for the use of portraits in matchmaking, Deschamps also refers to this procedure in Virelai 713.
27. Raynaud erroneously associates Balade 463 with this proposed match, and this association has served to obliterate the more likely connection the poem has with the marriage of Charles VI and Isabeau of Bavaria. It should be added that Raynaud also believed that Balades 417, 468, and 469 refer to Mary of Hungary (SATF 11:44–45), but Deschamps says that her name is "Marguerite" (Balade 469, 1.9) and that she is named after a flower (Balade 417, 1. 27).
28. Included in this collection.
29. Included in this collection.
30. There was an ordinance restricting the number of *huissier d'armes* to eight, but it does not name Deschamps specifically (*Receuil des Ordonnances* 7:174–77; SATF 11:52). Deschamps makes further reference to being one of the lucky eight remaining *huissiers d'armes* in Supplicacion 1190: "L'un des VIII restrains suis pour voir / Des huissier d'ordonnances escrys." Raynaud and Hoepffner both misconstrue the implications of the events of this time, leading them to assert that Deschamps was falling from royal favor. In fact, he probably enjoyed the best situation of his career in that regard. For a fuller discussion, see Laurie 55, n.98.
31. For the gift of 400 gold francs on August 26, 1388, for the repair of Deschamps's house, see BNF Pièces originales vol. 666, doss. 15570, no. 3, and SATF, 11:54–55.
32. See BNF Pièces originales vol. 666, doss. 15570, no. 4 and SATF 11:56.
33. See Raynaud (SATF 11:57–58) who also identifies Deschamps's predecessor at Senlis as Jean de Venderesse, who held office from 1374 to 1388 (Dupont-Ferrier, 1942–65, 5:385, no. 20774).
34. Included in this collection.
35. There is a reference to this dispute in BNF Dossiers bleus vol. 167, doss. 4393, fol. 8. (cf. SATF 11:72). For a more complete account, see BNF Cabinet

d'Hozier 85, doss. 2221, no. 8. The complete text of this reference is cited by Laurie 58, n.110.

36. Included in this collection.
37. See note 27, above.
38. See page 11, and note 25, above.
39. Included in this collection.
40. For a fuller discussion of *L'Art de dictier*, see page 22.
41. See Brit. Mus. Add. 11540, fol. 244, no. 633; and fol. 245, no. 641. Cf. SATF 11:72, n.7.
42. For the archival references see Arch. Nat. X 1A 1475, fol. 60 V°, and 1476, fol. 69 V°; cf. SATF 11:72, n.7; Archives Nationales X 1A 1477, fol. 77 V°, and SATF 11:72 n.4. See also Archives de l'Oise, Série H.2, 358, Inventaire (1897), 2:284; and Archives de L'Aisne, Série G. 253, Inventaire (1885) 3:52. These last two references were not mentioned by earlier biographers, but were cited by Laurie with more detailed discussion (61, nn. 122–24).
43. The gift was made on April 18, 1393, but Deschamps only received the initial payment of 100 gold francs on August 9, 1396. For the initial gift, see BNF Latin 17058, no. 78, published by the Bibliothèque de L'Ecole des Chartes 5:69. The gift was confirmed on April 2, 1395 (BNF fr. 10431, 180, no. 1001; see also Brit. Mus. Add. Ms. 11540, fol. 311, no. 1434, and fol. 4186, no. 1001). For complete archival references on the history of this transaction, see Laurie 61, n. 125.
44. The duke of Orléans granted Deschamps 100 gold francs on April 28, 1393, and a horse valued at 80 francs before July 24, 1393. For archival sources, see Brit. Mus. Add. MS. 11540, fol. 294b, no. 1246, and also fol. 276, no. 1027; cf. SATF 11:373.
45. The nomination came after an expedition to Normandy in February, and Deschamps was acting in this capacity by October. His salary was 50 livres parisis a year. See BNF P.O., vol. 666, doss. 15570, no. 13; cf. SATF 11:73. For complete archival sources and further discussion, see Laurie 62, n.130.
46. See Archives Municipales de Senlis, Archives Antérieurs à 1790, B.B. no. 1, Inventaire (1863), Cartulaire des délibérations municipals, 1383–1403, fol. 122. Cf. SATF 11:74, n.3.
47. Deschamps was paid 20 francs for expenses. BNF nouv. acq. fr. 3655, 14, nos. 1897/1989. Cf. SATF 11:75.
48. Deschamps was commissioned on November 18, 1394, to distribute 100 crowns to the king's officers on the following day (BNF P.O., vol. 2153, doss. 48873, no. 207; cf. Raynaud, who incorrectly gives the date as November 14, SATF 11:75).
49. On May 28, 1395, Deschamps delivered to the priests of Senlis the legacy of Jean Lasne (Notre-Dame de Senlis, Bibliothèque de Chartres, *Afforty* 12:114). Other evidence of his and his lieutenants' activities documented in BNF fr. 10431, 49, no. 301, and cf. SATF, 11:75. In Balade 1375, probably written around this time, Deschamps accounts for his expenses in his first poem addressed to Charles VI since the king's collapse, and asks for 500 crowns and the rights to other revenues. Deschamps alleges in this balade that it has been six

years since the king last made him any gift (ll. 46–48). Further evidence of Deschamps's activities at Senlis at this time may be found in Laurie 63, n. 135.

50. Deschamps deplored these ordinances in Rondeaux 648 and 649 and Balades 952, 1110, and 1111. We know that he was, however, bound by them by his presence in Senlis on April 14, 1396, when he handed down a favorable judgment to the chapter of Senlis against laymen living within its precincts (Notre-Dame de Senlis, Bibliothèque de Chartres, *Afforty* 12:114; Archives de l'Oise, G. 2028; and cf. SATF 11:76.)
51. See also page 6.
52. Numerous archival records document Deschamps's journey, for which he was compensated with 80 livres tournois (BNF fr. 10431, Vol. 169, no. 942; Vol. 190, no. 1064, and cf. SATF 11:76). Further evidence for the gift is found in Brit. Mus. Add. Ms. 11540, fol. 412b, no. 942; BNF nouv. acq. fr. 3105, no. 100; BNF fr. 10431, Vol. 207, no. 1164; and cf. SATF, 11:78).
53. BNF fr. 10431, no. 1785; Raynaud 11:78.
54. Raynaud correctly associates Balade 771 with Valentina through her motto "A bon droit" (SATF 11:76–77).
55. It is possible that Balade 67 was written either in 1395 when the crusade against the Turks was first proposed, or in 1396, before the news of the disastrous defeat in Nicopolis reached Paris (cf. SATF 11:77, 78–80).
56. Deschamps mentions Enguerrand de Coucy in Balades 347, 393, 735, and 769, and Rondel 655, among others. Cf. SATF 11:180.
57. Evidence that Deschamps was compensated for this journey is found in the duke's order of January 18, 1397, ordering payment to the poet of 400 francs (BNF fr. 10431, 256, nos. 1440–42). Further discussion of the documentation for this journey and the payments Deschamps received for it may be found in Laurie 64, n.142.
58. See, too, Boüard 231, n.2. In contrast, Raynaud held that the trip's purpose was preparation for the marriage of Wenceslas's niece Isabella to Charles of Orléans (SATF 11:80).
59. See SATF 11:80, and Hoepffner 108.
60. Balade 1326 is included in this collection.
61. Documentation for the reimbursement may be found in BNF fr. 10431, 451, nos. 2581–83. Cf. SATF 11:82, but Raynaud mistakes the date of the payment order for this disbursement as well as that for the fur coat. Further documentation for the furs for the coat may be found in BNF fr. 10431, 430, no. 2445. See, too, Laurie 64, n.144, and 65, n.148.
62. The books were Guillaume de Deguilleville's *Pelerinage de vie humaine*, *Pelerinage de l'ame*, and *Pelerinage de Jesus Christ*. See BNF fr. 10432, Vol. 159, nos. 777 and 827; cf. SATF, 11:85, and Hoepffner 109.
63. See BNF fr. 26030, no. 2998, and SATF 11:87.
64. See BNF fr. 10432, 26, no. 74, and cf. SATF 11:83. For more detailed discussion of Deschamps's and his lieutenants' activities during this period, see Laurie 65, n.152.
65. The other biographers have not mentioned this meeting. See Creil, Archives de Senlis B.B. I f. 138 V°, cited in Flammermont, 579.

66. This information is again not cited by previous biographers. See Arch. Nat. KK 45, fol. 64 V^{O}, April 28, 1400. See also Laurie 66, n.157.
67. For a thorough study of Deschamps and aging, see Magnan.
68. This and other judgments are not mentioned by previous biographers but are documented in the Archives de l'Oise, Série G, 1301, Inventaire (1897) 2:193. For a fuller discussion of Deschamps's and his lieutenants' activities at this time as well as for a summary of Raynaud's perspective on these events, see Laurie 66, n.158.
69. See the Act of Jean de Beaurouvre on February 20, 1400 (BNF fr. 10432, 288, no. 1348; cf. SATF 11:88). For a fuller discussion of documentation for Deschamps's final activities and a comparison with Raynaud's perspective on the same, see Laurie 66, n.159.
70. For Raynaud's argument in favor of associating Balade 1212 with this expedition, see SATF XI:91. The journey was planned in April and began in October, 1403. Cf. Coville, 71.
71. Cf. note 92, below.
72. Included in this collection. Lines 25–28 indicate that Deschamps and Christine clearly were correspondents beyond these epistolary poems.
73. The receipts for Deschamps are documented in BNF P.O. 666, doss. 15570, no. 46, and *Sceaux Clairambault* vol. 28, no. 84. Deschamps was able to give his son authority to collect taxes at Beauvais on February 16, 1403 (BNF Cabinet d'Hozier 85, doss. 2221, No. 8). There is a much more detailed discussion of documentation for these final official records regarding Deschamps in Laurie 67, n.163.
74. See Arch. Nat. 21, F2, fol. 127 verso–128, published by Dupont-Ferrier 1935, article 21. See also Laurie 68, n.164.
75. On the appointment as treasurer, see Dupont-Ferrier 1935, article 21. For a refutation of Raynaud's view that the duke was glad to get rid of a courtier he had long disliked, see also Laurie 68, n.165.
76. "De la matiere de ce livre ne traicta l'auteur plus avant pour maladie qui lui survint de laquelle il mourut" (*Le Miroir de mariage* 9:388); and "Cy mourut l'acteur, et pour ce demoura la fiction cy dessus imparfaicte" (*La Fiction du lion* 8:338).
77. The editors of this volume have not found any source that has counted the number of lines in Deschamps's corpus, but a database currently being assembled on Deschamps's poems will yield numbers that can be used to confirm Besant's assertion.
78. Nine volumes contain the poetry, and two are devoted to ancillary material.
79. See, for example, Balade 803, in which he rebukes the youngish, aggrieved noblemen who said to him, "de savetier fy" (l. 10), and Balade 1199, ". . . savetier, chien, / Suy appelez . . ." (ll. 15–16). Note, too, that Balade 803 includes among those rebuked for their churlish behavior Savoisy and Poitier, who are chastised for their dining habits in Rondel 579, one of the poems presented in this volume.
80. See, for example, Balade 264, spoken by the castle of Fismes; Balade 1056, spoken by the head; Balade 1024, spoken by Jean de Saint Simon's posterior. Balade 1024 is presented in this volume.

81. Balade 834, included in this volume.
82. Balade 1385, presented in this volume.
83. See, for example, Balade 341 and Rondeau 1325, included in this volume.
84. Balade 1028, included in this volume.
85. Balade 1432, presented in this volume.
86. For example, see Rondeau 1330, on Prague.
87. See Balade 924 about Senlis. Balade 169, in the present volume, lauds Paris.
88. See, for example, Balade 892 and Rondeau 670, on the sexual complaints of a *mal mariée*; and Sote Balade 1363, on the foul mouth of a certain M. Regnault.
89. See, for example, Balade 357 on the benefits of Lenten sacrifice; and Balade 969, presented in this volume.
90. In *L'Art de dictier*, in the discussion of music, Deschamps says that natural music derives from love poetry and other subjects—"en autres manieres" (62, 63).
91. Cited in SATF 9:333. Also see Jacqueline Cerquiglini-Toulet, 149, and Collette, 154.
92. See the *Epistre a eustace mourel*, dated February 10, 1404. See also note 4. For an extended discussion of this epistle and Christine's connection to Deschamps, see Earl Jeffrey Richards's chapter "The Lady Wants to Talk: Christine de Pizan's *Epistre a Eustace Mourel*" (in Sinnreich-Levi 1998, 109–22).
93. By contrast, the first in English include Gascoyne's *Certain Notes of Instruction* (1575), Lodge's *A Defence of Poetry* (1579), Puttenham's *Arte of English Poesie* (1589), and Sidney's *Defense of Poesy* (c. 1583, printed 1595); Dante's *De Vulgari eloquentia* (*Concerning the Eloquence of the Vulgar Tongue*) (1303) is less an *ars poetica* than a defense of Italian as a vehicle for poetry although it does categorize poetry and style.
94. For a fine discussion of music and literature as hygienic and therapeutic, see Glending Olson's *Literature as Recreation in the Later Middle Ages*.
95. The music for these poems is published by Thibault and Droz.
96. For example, Deschamps tells those who want to compose lays that they needn't bother with his whole prescription. They "need only take up a lai, for they are numerous enough and would be too long a poem to have included in this little book" (97).
97. The other works Deschamps left unfinished at his death are *La Fiction du lion* and *L'Art de dictier*.
98. This section relies heavily on *Le Roman de la rose*.
99. See also p. 11.
100. He replied in Balade 1242. Lines 22–24 suggest that Christine was one of Deschamps's correspondents quite independent of their poetic contact. Cf. also note 92, above.
101. See, among others, Bryan and Dempster, especially 207–8, 215–22, 333–39; and Lowes. See also the notes for Balade 285.
102. Presented to Charles VI in May 1385.
103. See also note 76, above.
104. See Balades 127 and 447 and Lay 306.
105. Indeed, the questions revolving around Deschamps's knowledge of the English language, his possible acquaintance with Chaucer or Chaucer's poetry, the refer-

ences within Balade 285, and that balade's highly rhetorical form have been the topic of considerable debate. See especially Calin, Crépin, Jenkins, Kooijman, Lerch, Lowes, Mieszkowski, Olson, Pearcy, Shoaf, Thundy, Toynbee; and Young.

106. For a discussion of some of the Deschamps genealogy, see Longnon, 3:318. There is another Deschamps family genealogy dated 1690 (BNF Cabinet d'Hozier 85, doss. 2221 no. 8). This last is more complete than others mentioned by other biographers (cf. SATF 11:20). For a more complete discussion of these archival records, see Laurie 32, n.6.

107. The total number of works includes poems that appear two or even three times. Some defy easy categorizing. See page 20, above. Deschamps did some translations from Latin, including Pope Innocent III's *De contemptu mundi* (*On Despising the World*) which he presented to Charles VI in 1383 in the *Double lay de la fragilité humaine* (*Double Lai on Human Frailty*, Lays 309 and 310), and *Geta et Amphitrion*.

108. At the time we write, the only modern editions of any of Deschamps's work are *L'Art de dictier*; the anthology by Boudet, Millet and Becker, *Eustache Dechamps en son temps*; and the unpublished edition of *Le Miroir de mariage*. James Laidlaw and Christine Scollen-Jimack as well as Jacqueline Cerquiglini-Toulet are also currently preparing collections. A Deschamps society (Société Eustache Deschamps) has been founded in France, and an entire conference (Colloque International Eustache Deschamps) was dedicated to him in 1999 and again in 2002 in Vertus.

109. See, for example, Bryan and Dempster.

110. Only for two of Deschamps's poems do musical settings still exist, and he did not write them, so it seems safe to say he did not expect his poems to be sung as Machaut and the poet-musicians would have. See also the discussion on page 23.

111. It is possible that Arnaud de Corbie either commissioned or owned the manuscript now called BNF Fonds français 840. He was a friend of Deschamps's and was chancellor of France from 1388 to 1413. For a full description of the manuscript, see Tesnière, 340–42; *L'Art de dictier* 7; and SATF 11: 101–6. The editors of the SATF include a prefatory essay by Siméon Luce on the scribe who produced BNF Fonds français 840: "Note sur Raoul Tainguy: Copiste des poesies d'Eustache Deschamps" (2:vi–xvi). Luce classes Tainguy as a revisionist, especially with respect to political topics, citing three Froissart manuscripts. Luce also contends that Tainguy was an amateur poet, possibly not above inserting his own poems into BNF Fonds français 840, and probably not beyond making corrections to Deschamps's poems (see also Luce 245–59). The current editors see little evidence of such emendations or additions, at least not in the poems selected for this anthology. Bradley also discusses Tainguy, but doesn't mention BNF fr. 840 (282–84). More recent and relevant mention of Tainguy can be found in Monfrin (253). Tainguy, in our opinion, did his best to see that his scriptorium produced a fine manuscript, as faithful to Deschamps's own copies as possible. That there are mistakes in that manuscript is obvious; that any of them was deliberate or that Tainguy rewrote some of the poems to suit himself seems to us to be very unlikely.

112. For a lengthier discussion of Deschamps's metrical forms, see SATF Vol. 11, and Poirion.
113. Every selection except the excerpt from *Le Miroir de mariage*.
114. *L'Art de dictier* 84–85.
115. This form should not be confused with the ballad, the English narrative verse form.
116. Deschamps also favored the alternation or at least the mixture of lines of masculine and feminine lines, in other words, lines of odd and even numbers of syllables. This innovation became standard in French prosody, but is unjustly credited to sixteenth-century writers such as Ronsard.
117. Balades 123–124, 127, 157, 164–66, 172, 202, 222, 250, 263, 421, 447, 489, 493 (included in this collection), 808, 821–22, 829–31, 835–36, 864, and 866.
118. Balades 293, 790, and 1184.
119. In *L'Art de dictier*, from which this exemplary strophe is taken, Deschamps says, "Et sont les plus fors balades qui se puissent faire" ("These are the hardest balades that can be written") (74–77). This balade, Balade 477, can be found in its entirety in SATF 3:297. Of similar construction is Balade 461 (SATF 4:277).
120. This strophe is from Balade 477 (3:297). The additional two strophes that complete the balade continue the concatenation as well as duplicate its rhyme scheme. BNF Nouvelles acquisitions françaises 6221 adds two more strophes to the balade.
121. On assonance, see also the section on performance, page 34, above.
122. The editors have made no attempt to present a complete overview of fourteenth-century French, but will elucidate those points pertinent to Deschamps's versification. Interested readers may see such texts as Fournier, Kibler, and Elsabe.
123. See Balades 84 and 235 for examples.
124. BNF fond français 840 is the only complete collection. BNF Nouvelles acquisitions françaises 6221 includes *L'Art de dictier* and 155 other pieces, not all by Deschamps. There are several less important manuscripts of which the most significant are BNF Nouvelles acquisitions françaises 6235 and 20029 and BNF Fonds français 850. For a fuller discussion of the manuscripts, see Tesnière and Raynaud in SATF 11:101–11.
125. For a discussion of Deschamps's views on artificial and natural music see the introduction to *L'Art de dictier*.
126. "plaisant a ouir par soy . . . les diz des chancons se puent souventefoiz recorder en pluseurs lieux ou ilz sont moult voulentiers ois, ou le chant de la musique artificiele n'aroit pas tousiours lieu, comme entre seigneurs et dames estans a leur prive et secretement, ou la musique naturele se puet dire et recorder par un homme seul, de bouche, ou lire aucun livre de ces choses plaisans devant un malade, et autres cas semblables . . ." (64,66). See also page 23.

Poets' Introduction

The range of experience captured in Deschamps's poetry is so wide that *Larousse* calls this oeuvre "la gazette d'une époque" (the newsletter of an epoch). Modern readers remark the great variety of subject matter, personas, stances, and tones of voice, and the penetration and accuracy of the poet's psychological, political, and social observations. In many of the poems, the persona is presented as if it were Deschamps himself, talking to us as a charming and loquacious companion, and telling us of his experiences and what he has made of them.

Because we were so taken with the content of Deschamps's poems, we tried to be strict with ourselves on basic accuracy of meaning, word choice, level of diction, and syntax. In the choice of individual words, while our scholarly collaborators kept us aware of meaning and *faux amis*, we tended to prefer the obvious English word when the meaning was close. But our primary unit of translation was the phrase; we were after line by line or phrase by phrase equivalents in contemporary English. And very often there were relatively straightforward equivalents to the medieval French, as in the opening of Balade 969,

> Charongne a vers, povre fragilité,
> Qui puez estre comparee a la rose
> Qui est boutons et naist ou temps d'esté . . .

which became

> Carrion for worms, a poor fragility
> which may be likened to a rose,
> a bud born in the summer . . .

Where Deschamps was using idioms or epithets, we tried to come up with corresponding idiomatic phrases and epithets drawn from the same domain, but selected for rhyme or rhythm in English, just as he had done in French. In Chanson Royale 912, for example, an officer of the court is told to make an arrest, and an exchange ensues with the miscreant:

"Voluntiers; venez en prinson
Puis que la chose est commandée."
"Je n'ay meffait a ame née;
Que je parle au prevost a part."
"Adieu! Il est huimais trop tard."

The original is almost conversational, and we have tried to retain this level of diction in the translation:

"Glad
to do it. Custody for you, my lad.
Orders are to put you in the hole."
"But I haven't harmed a living soul.
Let me talk in private to the judge."
"By God, it's now too late to budge."

We felt free to take a poetic catalogue and move the sequence of items around in order to get an English rhyme and rhythm, since Deschamps had obviously done the same to get the original French rhyme. For example, the sequence of place names in Balade 169 is:

Et visité en chascune partie,
Jherusalem, Egipte et Galilée,
Alixandre, Damas et la Surie,
Babiloine, le Caire et Tartarie

which in translation became:

and visited all places, every one,
seen Egypt and Jerusalem and Galilee,
Damascus, Alexandria and Babylon,
Cairo and Syria and Tartary.

We have occasionally added phrases not in the original, but usually have restricted them to exclamations in the voice of the protagonist of the poem, not new content. We have also occasionally transposed lines or moved conceptions around in a sentence, in order to translate all thoughts, and get a rhyme. When the wife in Balade 853 complains,

> Je n'ose aler en bois, ville ne plaine,
> Danser, chanter, manger, boire de vin,
> Que le villain, a guise d'un mastin,
> Ne m'abbaie, crians: "Que fais tu la?"

these lines are translated, shifting the concept of daring from the beginning to the middle of the sentence,

> If I go to the woods, the town, the fields, or dare
> to dance, or sing or eat or drink some wine,
> the villain, like a dog, barks his one line
> and shouts at me, "What are you doing there?"

The two scholars have added footnotes pointing out what they thought were our most serious departures from the French. By and large, however, the two poets believe they got as close as the languages permit to the form and meaning of Deschamps's poems, and that all departures are in the spirit of the author.

As to versification, we decided that Deschamps, who wrote in a highly formal manner, and was brilliant at it, had to be translated into formal verse in English.

Most of the poems translated are balades, where the main formal interest is not in the rhymes or rhythms but in Deschamps's extraordinary formulation and use of refrains. Consequently, we started with as accurate, idiomatic, and powerful a translation of the refrain as we could get. We presume, as anyone who has ever written a poem would, that Deschamps often started with the refrain and worked up a poem to bring out its meaning. In any case, a strict concern with rhyme and rhyme schemes would have necessitated departing too far from exact meanings, which we took to be the primary interest of the balades we selected. All balades were translated into an iambic meter, usually a pentameter, and for quite a few this was as much formality as we felt was needed, and we rested content with blank verse. In a few cases, usually those where the mood was somber, we added the requirement of an unstressed ending to each line.

But for most balades we required of ourselves a translation into iambic meter and full rhyme. We chose rhymes of opportunity, and did not attempt consistent rhyme schemes in balades. Full rhymes of opportunity seemed preferable to half rhymes in a consistent pattern. Deschamps was a court poet, and the satisfaction, the click, of full rhyme was part of his display of virtuosity and wit. A courtly audience would not have considered half rhymes witty. At our most lax, which was rare, we allowed full rhymes separated by three intervening lines. We also sometimes allowed ourselves a five- or even six-stress line where the equivalent length would have been shorter. The extra syllables gave us room to get a natural syntax and rhyme word.

For other technical matters we did what we could, attempting, for example, to match enjambment when it seemed of poetic importance in the original and possible in the translation. And sometimes this was indeed possible, as in Chanson Royale 912, where the thief is giving a bribe:

> "Prevost, pour Dieu, aiez regart
> A cent frans que vez ci; tenez;
> Je suis prodoms."

which we translated as:

> "Judge! have a look, for heaven's sake,
> at the hundred francs I've brought for you to take:
> I am an honest man."

For poems in the form of rondeaux or virelais, we tried to follow the line lengths and rhyme schemes of the original, since these features are a dominant part of the effect of such highly stylized poems. And for one of the best of Deschamps's poems, which defies categorization in any of the fixed forms, *Sui je belle* (Virelai 554), the fifteen-year-old protagonist looks in the mirror and says *inter alia* (in lines so short they leave little wiggle room for a translator, and with a charming and consistent diction):

> J'ay dur sain et hault assi,
> Long bras gresles, doys aussi,
> Et par le faulz sui greslette:
> Dictes moy se je sui belle.
> J'ay bonnes rains, ce m'est vis,
> Bon dos, bon cul de Paris,
> Cuisses et gambes bien faites:
> Suis je, suis je, sui je belle?

After many drafts, we had her saying:

> My breasts are firm, and they are high;
> Slim arms and fingers, by the by,

and my small waist is very fine:
tell me if I'm lovely.

My hips are good, it seems to me,
good back, good Paris butt on me,
and my legs and thighs are just divine:
am I, am I, am I lovely?

David Curzon
New York City

Jeffrey Fiskin
Hollywood, California

September 2002

The Poems

Plus ne prestray livre quoy qui aviengne[1]

fol 6d J'ay mes livres en tant de lieux prestez
Et a pluseurs qui les devoient rendre
Dont li termes est failliz et passez
Qu'a faire prest ne doy james entendre
Laiz ne chancons ne faiz d'amours comprandre
Hystorier n'oneur ramentevoir
Quant je me voy sanz cause decevoir
Et retenir mon labeur et ma paine.
Dolens en sui: a Dieu jure et pour voir
Plus ne prestray livre quoy qui aviengne

Il souffist bien que je soie entestez
Que j'aie mis mon labeur et ma paine
Et se j'ay fait en mes chetivetez
Chose qui soit ou biens se doye prandre
Donnez le vueil liement, non pas vendre,
Mais qu'on face de l'escripre devoir
En mon hostel; pour ce a tous faiz scavoir
Que nulz desormais requerir n'emprangne
De mes livres ne mes papiers avoir:
Plus ne prestray livre quoy qui aviengne.

Perdu en ay maint dont je suis troublez
Par emprunter, et ce me fait deffendre
Que jamais nul ne m'en sera ostez
Par tel moien, a quoy nul ne doit tendre.
De ce serment ne me doit nulz reprandre,
Mais qui vouldra de mes choses scavoir,
Tresvoulentiers l'en feray apparoir
Sanz porter hors; veoir vers moi les viengne
Se sires n'est qui ait trop grant povoir:
Plus ne prestray livre quoi qui aviengne.

L'envoy
Prince, Eustaces, qui a la teste tendre,
Supplie a tous que des or leur souviengne
De mes livres non retenir n'emprandre:
fol 7a Plus ne prestray livre quoi qui aviengne.

I'll never lend a book again no matter what

My books are now lent out in many a place
to people I was sure would have the grace
to give them back, but they're long overdue.
I won't consent to one more loan; I'm through
with lending chronicles, or songs, or lays
recording deeds of love, or honor's praise;
I was needlessly deceived, I see,
and all my pain and labor gone from me.
And my unhappiness, God knows, has this upshot:
I'll never lend a book again no matter what.

To stick to this idea I must be tough,
but I've put myself to trouble and toil enough
and if, in my modest way, what I produce
includes some things that prove to be of use,
I'm happy to give them all away for free
provided people are ready to come to me
and copy; I proclaim to all that they can not
assume henceforth that they, by demand or design,
can get a paper or any book of mine:
I'll never lend a book again no matter what.

I've lost a lot, and this distresses me,
through borrowing, and so I must forbid
any and all to take from me as once they did,
which no one should protest as far as I can see.
No one will be excluded from this oath.
If someone wants my stuff I am not loath.
In fact, I'm happy to give access if he
does not take it outside; let him come to me,
unless he is a powerful lord, and see what I've got:
I'll never lend a book again no matter what.

Envoy
Prince! Eustache, whose head is his tender spot,
begs everyone remember from now on to not
keep any books of mine they may have got:
I'll never lend a book again no matter what.

Fors aux commis a departir argent[2]

fol 9c Quant j'ay veu tous les mondains estas
Des lieux royaulx et de chevalerie
Et advisé des plus haulx aux plus bas
Les pratiques et la mahommerie
Tant sur les queux qu'en l'eschanconnerie
Et autre part je voy communement
Qu'il n'est homme en ceste mortele vie
Fors aux commis a departir argent.

Aucuns parlent d'onourer advocas
Et les autres, clers en theologie,
Mais ce sont ceuls qui ont plaiz et debas
Car un chascun ne les honoure mie.
On se retrait souvent de seignourie,
Mais je ne voy grace avoir entre gent
N'oneur donner a nul, quoy que l'en die,
Fors aux commis a departir argent.

Dieux sont mondain qui ont argent en tas
Et aourez tant comme ydolatrie.
On les poursuit humblement pas a pas;
Si grant n'y a qu'a eulx ne s'umilie
En deffublant a genoulx on les prie
En obeissant a leur commandement
Ne secours n'est qu'aucuns ait ne aie
Fors aux commis a departir argent.

Except for those who hand the money out

Now that I've come to know each worldly estate,
from royal palace to the noble's gate,
and contemplated life both high and low,
the servile practices and simpering show
from bearers of the cup down to the scullery,
and others, too, when I look around, I see
there's none in this mortal life men care about
except for those who hand the money out.

I hear some speak of giving honor to
lawyers, which others feel is the cleric's due,
but pleas and arguments are all they get;
no one has given them honor as yet.
Authority quite often loses face,
but among the folk, I've seen no grant of grace,
none getting honor—there simply is no doubt—
except for those who hand the money out.

They're earthly gods, the ones with piles of pelf;
they're worshipped to the point of idolatry.
They're humbly followed, step by step. I never see
a man so great he won't humiliate himself
by doffing his hat, by pleading as he kneels,
by obeying commands from those who make the deals.
No one can help: there's none who've got the clout,
except for those who hand the money out.

"Qui pendra la sonnette au chat?"[3]

fol 14a Je treuve qu'entre les souris
Ot un merveilleux parlement
Contre les chas, leurs ennemis
A veoir maniere comment
Elles vesquissent seurement
Sanz demourer en tel debat.
L'une dist lors en arguant:
"Qui pendra la sonnette au chat?"

Cilz consaulz fut conclus et prins;
Lors se partent communement.
Une souris du plat pais
Les encontre et va demandant
Qu'om a fait; lors vont respondant
Que leur ennemi seront mat
fol 14b Sonnette aront ou coul pendant:
"Qui pendra la sonnette au chat?"

"C'est le plus fort," dist un ras gris.
Elle demande saigement:
"Par qui sera cilz fais fournis?"
Lors s'en va chascune excusant;
Il n'y ot point d'executant;
S'en va leur besogne de plat.
Bien fut dit mais au demourant:
Qui pandra la sonnette au chat?

L'envoy
Prince, on conseille bien souvent
Mais on puet dire, com le rat,
Du conseil qui sa fin ne prant:
Qui pendra la sonnette au chat?

"But who's the one to bell the cat?"

Among the mice, so runs the tale,
a brilliant convocation sat
against their enemy the cat
to see if they could formulate
some means by which they could prevail
without getting lost in endless chat.
One asked, in the course of the debate,
"But who's the one to bell the cat?"

A motion was adopted; then
they were parting from each other when
a lady mouse from the low lands met
them all and asked what did they get
accomplished. They responded they
will conquer their enemies today:
they'll bell their necks; that will be that.
"But who's the one to bell the cat?"

"That's the hardest part," said an old grey rat.
The lady asked, and wisely too,
"Who'll do this deed of derring-do?"
Now each of them proceeds to secede:
there wasn't one who'd do the deed
so in the end the plan fell through.
They were fine words, but only that:
"But who's the one to bell the cat?"

Envoy
Prince, advice is often tossed about
but we can comment, like the rat,
on counsels which won't be carried out:
"But who's the one to bell the cat?"

Qui ainsi fait ce n'est pas sens de beste[4]

fol 19d Je vous souhaide entre vous, gens de mer,
Qui avez chaut dedenz vostre galée,
De ce bon vin frisque, friant et cler
Dont a la cour est ma gueule arrousée,
Poucins, perdriz, connims a la gelée,
Et de ce pain legier de Carpentras,
Lit et coissin, la lavande et blans draps,
Beau cueuvrechief pour couvrir vostre teste,
Eaue douce, gesir hault et non bas;
Qui ainsi fait ce n'est pas sens de beste.

Car vous estes en peril de tumer
Souventefoiz en tempeste formée,
Et lors vous fault en la soulte avaler,
Gesir envers et la gueule baée,
Pour la pueur vonnir mainte goute,
Le cul a bort mettre, crier "Helas!"
Le patron est en poupe souvent las,
Qui doubte fort le vent et la tempeste
En requerant Dieu et saint Nicolas;
Qui ainsi fait ce n'est pas sens de beste.

Le patron fait le timon gouverner;
A pouge, a ourse est leur chancon chantée,
Et proue fait les undes trescouper.
Deux mas y a, mainte antene aprestée,
. . . .
Becuit vireux, poulz, puces et ras,
Le vermical, les vers en l'eaue a tas,
Au mieulx venir, un pou de char mal preste:
A Paris sui en joie et en soulas:
Qui ainsi fait ce n'est pas sens de beste.

L'envoy
fol 20a Enfans, vueillez tost aborder,
Car la puet on mener et joie et feste,
Viande et vin et tout bien recouvrer:
Qui ainsi fait ce n'est pas sens de beste.

Whoever acts this way is not a fool

My wish for all you seafarers
inside your galley, stifled by the heat,
is some of the bright, sparkling, tasty wine
with which my throat is watered here at court,
and chickens, partridges, and rabbit in aspic
accompanied by light bread from Carpentras,
a bed, a pillow, lavender, white sheets,
a handsome nightcap to cover up your heads,
fresh water, and a bed above the floor;
whoever acts this way is not a fool.

You are in danger of encountering,
and not so rarely, storms that are genuine
in which you have to go down to the hold,
and lie facing the floor with gaping mouths
while you're in terror, vomiting,
your butts over the side, and crying out, "Alas!"
The often weary captain's on the bridge
in dread, anticipating wind and storm,
and calling on God and Saint Nicholas;
whoever acts this way is not a fool.

The captain moves the rudder, guides the ship
to port, to starboard, as their song is sung,
and makes the prow cut through the waves.
It's a two-master; many spars are readied,
. . . .
and moldy biscuits, and lice, and fleas, and rats;
and the water cistern crawls with worms;
at best, there's a little badly cooked-up meat.
In Paris, I live in pleasure and happiness:
whoever acts this way is not a fool.

Envoy
My boys, come here to land, and quickly too,
for on the land you can have feasts and joy
and food and wine and all good things:
whoever acts this way is not a fool.

Riens ne se puet comparer a Paris[5]

fol 37a Quant j'ay la terre et mer avironnée
Et visité en chascune partie,
Jherusalem, Egipte et Galilée,
Alixandre, Damas et la Surie,
Babiloine, le Caire et Tartarie
Et touz les pors qui y sont,
Les espices et succres qui s'i font,
Les fins draps d'or et soye du pays
Valent trop mieulx ce que les Francois ont,
fol 37b Riens ne se puet comparer a Paris.

C'est la cité sur toutes couronnée
Fonteine et puis de sens et de clergie
Sur le fleuve de Saine située
Vignes, bois a, terres et praerie.
De touz les biens de ceste mortel vie
A plus qu'autres citez n'ont;
Tuit estrangier l'aiment et ameront,
Car pour deduit et pour estre jolis,
Jamais cité tele ne trouveront:
Riens ne se puet comparer a Paris.

Mais elle est bien mieulx que ville fermée
Et de chasteaulx de grant anceserie,
De gens d'onneur et de marchans peuplée,
De touz ouvriers d'armes, d'orfaverie,
De touz les ars c'est la flour quoy qu'on die;
Touz ouvraiges a droit font;
Subtil engin, entendement parfont
Verrez avoir, aux habitans toudis,
Et loyaulté aux euvres qu'ilz feront:
Riens ne se puet comparer a Paris.

Paris is beyond compare

When I've gone round the earth and sea
and visited all places, every one,
seen Egypt and Jerusalem and Galilee,
Damascus, Alexandria and Babylon,
Cairo and Syria and Tartary,
and entered every port,
and seen the spices and the sweets that they make there,
the fine gold cloth and silks which can be bought,
although they're better than the French have got,
Paris is beyond compare.

She is the city crowned above the rest,
the fount of scholarship and wisdom, and its well,
located on the river Seine, possessed
of woods and vineyards, land and dell.
She has more of the mortal good that we embrace
than any other place;
all strangers love her, will always find her fair,
because such elegance, such happiness,
will not be found in any town but this:
Paris is beyond compare.

For she's much better than any fortress town:
she has chateaux built in the days of old,
she's peopled with merchants, men of renown,
and workers of every kind, in armour, gold;
the flower of all the arts, as you've heard tell;
her workmen all excel;
deep understanding and a subtle skill
was found in her inhabitants, and is found still,
and loyalty to the craft that's in their care:
Paris is beyond compare.

D'avoir a court un pié hors et l'autre ens[6]

fol 44d Tant de perilz sont a suir la court
Qu'a grant paine s'en pourroit nul garder;
Qui grace y a, envie sur lui court,
Qui grans y est, en doubte est de verser.
La convient il trop de maulx endurer
Dont, quant a moy, je tien que c'est grant sens
D'avoir a court un pié hors et l'autre ens.

Es grans cours fault souvent faire le sourt,
Qu'om ne voit rien et qu'on ne scet parler,
Autrui blandir et qu'om saiche du hourt,
Faire plaisir, soufrir, dissimuler,
N'il n'est pas bon d'y toudis demourer;
fol 45a Mais pour le mieulx je conseille et consens
D'avoir a court un pié hors et l'autre enz.

L'un pié dedenz s'aucun meschief lui sourt
Fait bon avoir pour grace demander,
L'autre dehors s'aucun mal y acourt
Afin qu'on puist le peril eschiver,
Vivre du sien et qu'on puist demourer
En paix de cuer, autrement ne m'assens
D'avoir a court un pié hors et l'autre ens.

To have one foot in court, and one foot out

There's so much peril at court you can't ensure,
with even great effort, that you will be secure.
If anyone's in favor, envy's always near;
if anyone is great, he's plunged in fear.
There are so many troubles to endure
that it is sensible, and this I do not doubt,
to have one foot in court, and one foot out.

At the great courts you often must be blind,
play deaf, know how to never speak your mind,
to butter up, to understand intrigue,
dissimulate, be pleasing and endure fatigue,
nor is it wise to simply hang about;
my counsel is it's best to join the league
of those with one foot in court, and one foot out.

The one foot in is just in case you're struck
and mercy has to compensate bad luck;
the other's so, if some intrigue has failed,
you won't be close to one of those who's nailed.
Live on in peace of heart in your redoubt,
or else what you must do is not have too much clout:
to have one foot in court, and one foot out.

Pardonnez moy car je m'en vois en blobes[7]

fol 48b J'oy a xii ans grant ymaginative;
Jusqu'a xxx ans je ne cessay d'aprandre,
Tous les vii ars oy en ma retentive;
Je pratiqué tant que je sceus comprandre
Le ciel et les elemens,
Des estoilles les propres mouvemens;
Lors me donnoit chascun gaiges et robes;
Or diminue par viellesce mes sens;
Pardonnez moy car je m'en vois en blobes.

Ou moien temps oy la prerogative,
Je sceu les loys et les decrez entendre
Et soutilment arguer par logique
Et justement tous vrais jugemens rendre;
J'estoie adonc reverens;
L'en m'asseoit le premier sur les rens,
Mais l'en me fait par derriere les bobes;
Je moquay tel qui m'est ores moquans;
Pardonnez moy car je m'en vois en blobes.

Saiges est donc qui en son temps pratique
Que povreté ne le puisse sousprandre,
Car qui vieulx est chascun lui fait la nique;
Chascun le veult arguer et reprandre;
Il est a chascun chargens;
Or se gart lors qu'il ne soit indigens
Qu'adonc seroit rupieus non pas gobes;
Je suis moqué ainsi sont vielle gens;
fol 48c Pardonnez moy car je m'en vois en blobes.

Forgive me, please, for taking leave in rags

I had a great imagination when I was twelve
and didn't cease my studies until thirty. I
had grasped all seven arts. I even used to delve
as far as I could into the how and why
of the elements, the sky,
and the singular motion of each star.
Back then, I got the best rewards by far,
but now, in old age, every power sags;
forgive me, please, for taking leave in rags.

When I was middle aged I had authority
and could interpret every law and each decree,
and argue with logic and with subtlety;
only sound verdicts were delivered by me.
I was thought a mensch:
back then I had the first seat on the bench
and those who sneered took care I didn't see.
I mocked at many; now I'm the butt of their gags;
forgive me, please, for taking leave in rags.

Arranging things in the prime of life is wise
so poverty won't take you by surprise,
since everybody mocks a man who's old,
and everybody wants to argue, scold;
all feel burdened by him.
Let him beware of being left out in the cold.
The sniveling man isn't one who brags.
I'm mocked: all oldsters are considered dim;
forgive me, please, for taking leave in rags.

Que m’est il mieulx de quanque je vi onques?[8]

fol 50a Chascun me dit: “Tu te doiz bien amer
Qui cerchié as honeur en mainte terre
Deca les mons ou pays d’oultre mer
Et en tous lieus que noble cuer doit querre,
Qui as veu mainte dure et fors guerre
fol 50b Et qui amas bien par amours adonques.”
Lors respons je: “Ce m’a fait po acquerre;
Que m’est il mieulx de quanque je vi onques?

“Il est certain que j’ay veu caroler
Et pour amours maint fait d’armes requerre,
En temps de paix tournoier et jouster,
Faire chancons et maint pais conquerre,
Oiseaulx voler, chiens chacer a grant erre
Et tous deduit; or court uns autres mondes;
Dire puis bien de quoy le cuer me serre,
Que m’est il mieulx de quanque je vi onques?

“J’ay veu les roys aux sacres couronner
Et leurs grans cours dont l’en doit po enquerre,
Les chevaliers sur riches draps broder,
Leurs grans tresors de joiaulx mis soubz serre;
Sui les ay; pour ce pas ne me terre;
Rien n’ay acquis et ne puis durer longues
Fors que renom; c’est le vent de soulerre;
Que m’est il mieulx de quanque je vi onques?

L’envoy
“Prince, le temps ne puet gaires durer;
Il fault chascun a son aage finer,
Jeusnes et vieulz, vielles et blondes,
Fors et hardiz, couars au parler,
C’est tout neant; pour ce vueil demander:
Que m’est il mieulx de quanque je vi onques?”

How am I better off for what I've seen?

I'm always told, "You must feel proud to be
a man who has sought honor across the sea,
in many lands, beyond the mountain peak,
and in every place the noble-hearted seek,
a man who has seen many hard and cruel wars
and suffered much in true love's cause."
Then I respond, "And precious little good it's been.
How am I better off for what I've seen?

"It's true I have known dancing and its charms,
and have, for love, raised many needed arms,
in peaceful times delighted in joust and tourney,
conquered many lands and made songs on my journey,
watched birds in flight, dogs hunt game down,
and enjoyed it all, but now that world is gone.
And so I ask, with a troubled heart, again:
How am I better off for what I've seen?

"I've watched the coronations of great kings
and their grand courts, which must not be
too closely scrutinized; I've seen nobility
on rich embroideries, with their fine rings
and jewels locked away. I've seen it all;
I haven't stayed at home. Save some renown,
I have gained nothing, nothing lasts. It's just a squall.
How am I better off for what I've seen?

Envoy
"Prince, time will end for each and every man;
we each must come to our allotted span:
fair women and the grey, young men, and old and weak,
the strong and brave, those too afraid to speak.
All is for nothing. So I ask, of what has been,
'How am I better off for what I've seen?' "

Grant translateur, noble Geffroy Chaucier[9]

O Socrates plains de philosophie,
Seneque en meurs et Anglux en pratique,
Ovides grans en ta poeterie,
Bries en parler, saiges en rethorique,
Aigles treshaulz, qui par ta theorique
Enlumines le regne d'Eneas,
L'Isle aux Geans, ceuls de Bruth, et qui as
Semé les fleurs et planté le rosier,
Aux ignorans de la langue pandras,
Grant translateur, noble Geffroy Chaucier!

Tu es d'amours mondains Dieux en Albie:
Et de la Rose, en la terre angelique,
Qui d'Angela saxonne et puis flourie
Angleterre, d'elle ce nom s'applique
Le derrenier en l'ethimologique;
En bon anglès le livre translatas;
Et un vergier ou du plant demandas
De ceuls qui font pour eulx auctorisier,
A ja longtemps que tu edifias
Grant translateur, noble Geffroy Chaucier!

A toy pour ce de la fontaine Helye
Requier avoir un buvraige autentique,
Dont la doys est du tout en ta baillie,
Pour rafrener d'elle ma soif ethique,
Qui en Gaule seray paralitique,
Jusques a ce que tu m'abuveras.
Eustaces sui, qui de mon plant aras:
Mais pran en gré les euvres d'escolier
Que par Clifford de moy avoir pourras,
Grant translateur, noble Geoffroy Chaucier!

L'envoy
Poete hault, loenge d'escuiye,
En ton jardin ne seroie qu'ortie:
Considere ce que j'ay dit premier,
Ton noble plant, ta douce melodie,
Mais pour scavoir, de rescipre te prie,
Grant translateur, noble Geffroy Chaucier!

Great translator, noble Geoffrey Chaucer!

You are a Socrates, full of philosophy,
a Seneca of morals, worldly as Gellius,
and in your poetry as great as Ovid,
succinct in speech, and wise in your devices,
a lofty eagle, who, by understanding,
illuminates the kingdom of Aeneas—
the island of the Giants, of Brutus—
who scattered flowers, who planted roses,
a guide for those who do not know the language:
Great translator, noble Geoffrey Chaucer!

Of earthly love, you are the God in Albion,
and of the Rose, in the land of Angles,
which comes from the Saxon Angela, which flowered
into the name of Angleterre, which derivation
is where the etymologies have ended;
and you translated the *Rose* into fine English;
and long ago you began an orchard
for which you asked for plants from those you
understood to have authority.
Great translator, noble Geoffrey Chaucer!

And for this reason, from the fount of Helicon
I seek to have from you authentic beverage
from the source that you are now controlling
with which to quench my thirsty fever
and I'll remain in Gaul and paralysed
until the time you let me drink it.
My name's Eustache; you'll have some of my plantings;
but take them graciously, these schoolish writings,
which I will send you by Sir Lewis Clifford.
Great translator, noble Geoffrey Chaucer!

Envoy
High poet, pride of the English squires,
I would be just a nettle in your garden:
remember what I mentioned at the beginning
about your noble plant, and your sweet melody.
But write me back, so that I really know it:
Great translator, noble Geoffrey Chaucer!

"Sa de l'argent! Sa de l'argent!"[10]

fol 112c

En une grant fourest et lée
N'a gaires que je cheminoie
Ou j'ay mainte beste trouvée;
Mais en un grant parc regardoye,
Ours, lyons et liepars veoye,
Loups et renars qui vont disant
Au povre bestail qui s'effroye:
"Sa de l'argent! Sa de l'argent!"

La brebis s'est agenoillée,
Qui a respondu comme coye:
"J'ay esté quatre fois plumée
C'est an ci, point n'ay de monnoye."
Le buef et la vaiche se ploye;
La se complaingnoit la jument;
Mais on leur respont toutevoye:
"Ca de l'argent! Ca de l'argent!"

Ou fut tel paroule trouvée?
De bestes trop me merveilloie.
La chievre dist lors: "Ceste année
Nous fera moult petit de joye.
La moisson ou je m'attendoye
Se destruit par ne scay quel gent.
Merci, pour Dieu, va ta voye:
Sa de l'argent! Sa de l'argent!"

La truie qui fut desesperée,
Dist: "Il fault que truande soye
Et mes cochons; je n'ay denrée
Pour faire argent." "Ven de ta soye,"
Dist li loups, "car ou que je soye,
Le bestail fault estre indigent.
Jamais pitié de toy n'aroye
Sa de l'argent! Sa de l'argent!"

"Out with your money! Out!"

In a forest that was large and wide,
I scarcely had begun to ride
when I found many an animal who
was in a great park I looked into
where leopards, lions and bears abound,
and wolves and foxes, going round
giving the cattle a fright with the shout:
"Out with your money! Out!"

The poor ewe kneeled down and she
answered very peacefully,
"I have been shorn four times this year;
I don't have more to give, I fear."
The bull and cow both bowed down there,
beside the complaining mare,
but all the response they got was the shout:
"Out with your money! Out!"

How could they form such phrases?
That animals could do so still amazes.
The goat then said, "This year
will give us little joy, my dear:
I looked forward to the harvest so
but it's being destroyed by people I don't know.
Mercy! For the love of God, please go without:
" 'Out with your money! Out!' "

One who despaired was the poor sow
who said, "I'll have to become a beggar now
and my piglets too. I have no goods
to sell." "Sell your share of the woods,"
said the wolf. "The herbivore,
in every place I am, is always poor.
Pity you'll have to do without.
" 'Out with your money! Out!' "

Balade 341 (cont'd)

Quant celle raison fut finée,
Dont forment esbahis estoye,
Vint a moy une blanche fée,
fol 112d Qui au droit chemin me ravoye,
En disant: "Se Dieux me doint joye;
Sers bestes vont a court souvent,
S'ont ce mot retenu sanz joye:
Sa de l'argent! Sa de l'argent!"

L'envoy
Prince, moult est auctorisée
Et court partout comunement
Ceste paroule acoustumée:
"Sa de l'argent! Sa de largent!"

Balade 341 (cont'd)

When this discussion was at an end —
and it astonished me, my friend —
there came, all dressed in white, a fairy who
and said, "May God grant me some joy, I pray;
led me back to the right road and true
these beasts, they go to court each day
since they've learnt to repeat this joyless shout:
'Out with your money! Out!' "

Envoy
Prince, now so much is authorized
and everybody gads about,
so these words come as no surprise:
"Out with your money! Out!"

Que nulz prodoms ne doit taire le voir[11]

fol 115b Aucuns dient que je suis trop hardis
Et que je parle un pou trop largement
En reprouvant les vices par mes dis
Et ceuls qui font les maulx villainement.
Mais leur grace sauve certainement,
Verité faiz en general scavoir
Sanz nul nommer fors que generalment
Que nulz prodoms ne doit taire le voir.

L'en pugnissoit les maufaicteurs jadis
Et rendoit l'en partout vray jugement
Et Veritez qui vint de paradis
Blasmoit chascun qui ouvrait laidement;
Par ce vivoit le monde honnestement.
Mais nul ne fait fors l'autre decevoir,
Mentir, flater dont je dy vrayement
Que nulz prodoms ne doit taire le voir.

Par pechié voy les grans acouardiz
Et les saiges gouverner sotement,
Riches avers, larges atruandiz,
Nobles villains, jeune gouvernement,
fol 115c Avoir aux vieulx et jeunes ensement
D'eulx presumer car trop cuident valoir.
Se j'en parle c'est pour enseignement
Que nulz prodoms ne doit taire le voir.

Les mauves sont blasmez par leurs mesdis
En l'escripture et ou viel testament
Et pour leurs maulx les dampnent touz edis
Que l'en souloit garder estroictement.
Mais aujourd'hui verité taist et ment;
Ce monde cy qui ne quiert que l'avoir.
Coupable en est qui telz maulx ne reprant
Que nulz prodoms ne doit taire le voir.

Because no honest man should quash the truth

Some tell me I'm too bold in what I say,
that I speak out too freely when I speak,
when I write poetry condemning vice
and those who perpetrate their ugly deeds,
but with all due respect to these men,
I tell the truth in very general terms
while never naming individuals
because no honest man should quash the truth.

Evildoers were punished in former times
and honest judgments were rendered everywhere
and Truth, which comes from heaven to us,
was used to condemn all those who did bad deeds.
This was the way the world lived decently;
deceiving others is what all practice now,
and lies, and flattery, and I say this
because no honest man should quash the truth.

I see the mighty brought to cowardice by sin,
wise men who govern foolishly,
and wealth turn miser, the generous turn poor,
nobles turn base, government run by youth,
and old and young become the same
and, arrogant of merit, push themselves.
If I report all this, it's for instruction
because no honest man should quash the truth.

The wicked are condemned by their misdeeds
in both the Scripture and Old Testament,
and edicts damn them for their acts;
men used to strictly follow this in ages past.
But truth today is silent; the lying world
that is here below seeks only wealth.
A man is guilty if he's not opposed to this
because no honest man should quash the truth.

Balade 348 (cont'd)

Les bons n'orent pas les cuers effadis
Dont le renom yert pardurablement
Qui conquirent terres, villes et pais,
Juif, Sarrazin et crestienne gent
Qui aux vertus furent si diligent
Que des vices ne vouldrent nulz avoir.
Blasmons les maulx: fi d'or et fi d'argent!
Que nulz prodoms ne doit taire le voir.

L'envoy
Princes, je traiz en hault legierement
Sanz nul ferir s'entechiez ne se sent
Et que sur lui laist mon carrel cheoir
Dont il se puet garder legierement
Par le fuir et dy en concluent
Que nulz prodoms ne doit taire le voir.

Balade 348 (cont'd)

They didn't have faint hearts, those good folk of the past,
the ones whose reputations will endure,
who conquered cities, countrysides, and lands,
the Jews, the Christians and the Saracens,
all those who paid attention to the virtues,
who didn't want a thing to do with vice.
So let's condemn misdeeds; to hell with silver and gold,
because no honest man should quash the truth.

Envoy
Prince, I shoot small arrows to the heights
but don't hit anyone unless he feels he's hit,
and if he doesn't let my arrow fall on him—
and he can easily protect himself
by fleeing—I will give my conclusions voice
because no honest man should quash the truth.

Leur propre nature deffont[12]

fol 138d
Ovides, qui bien figura
Des bestes la proprieté
Et par fiction parla
Ramenans a moralité
L'orgueil, l'ordure et vanité
Des meurs aux hommes bestiaulx
Qui faint les dieux celestiaulx
Ne fut si saiges que ceuls sont
Qui en bestes et en oiseaulx
Leur propre nature deffont.

Car maint, qui bien garde y prandra,
Sont singe, tant sont escourté
Et tant de taiches sur eulx a
Comme panthere loqueté
Sont et de pluseurs draps brodé.
De leurs manches font chalemiaux
Et se souillent comme pourceaux
Es laides ordures du mont.
Helas! Que ne s'avisent ceaulx?
Leur propre nature deffont.

Adam ne Noé ne chaussa
Ne noz peres d'antiquité
Telz solers comme on trouvera
Qui une aulne ont de bec anté
De denz de balaine enhanté
S'en reculent com creviciaulx;
Leur cul monstrent et leurs museaulx
Cueuvrent qui a descouvrir font
Et par ainsi ces gens nouveaulx
Leur propre nature deffont.

They undo their own nature

Ovid, who was well able
to portray animal nature,
talked to us in fiction,
turning into moral fable
pride, vanity, corruption
(a behavior that is bestial
in those faking the Celestial)
was by no means so clever
as those turned bird or creature:
they undo their own nature.

For many, if we pay attention,
are monkey, curtailed of vesture,
and stained, spread with imperfection,
just like the spotted panther,
it's themselves that they embroider.
Their sleeves are like pipes, or wider;
they soil themselves like a piglet
in the world's filthy ordure.
Alas! why can't they see it?
They undo their own nature.

The shoes of Adam and Noah
and every ancestral father
were not those we now discover
with beaks in front a yard long,
with whalebone as protrusion;
these people back up like a crawfish;
they uncover their arses and cover
their snouts, which they should uncover;
and by such new-fangled posture
they undo their own nature.

Balade 404 (cont'd)

Au chien ou envie s'en va
Puelent bien estre comparé;
Au lion qu'orgueil surmonta
Dont maintes d'iceulx sont surmonté
Apparant estre hault monté
fol 139a Veulent bien cuider estre beaux
Par dehors mais dedenz en eaulx
Bonnes vertus ne s'apparront.
Grans queues portent comme veaulx:
Leur propre nature deffont.

Chascuns dieulx par nuit veillera;
Aux suettes sont comparé
Car par jour l'en les trouvera
En lit jusqu'a midi sonné.
A touz gieux sont habondonné
Et a vivre de gloz morseaulx
Et convoitier l'or a monceaulx
Et moquer ceuls qui bien feront
Mais a faire ainsi leurs reveaulx
Leur propre nature deffont.

L'envoy
Princes, ce que j'ay ci recité
Seroit bien de necessité
De laissier aval et amont
Car ceuls qui font tel niceté
Ont plus bestes que homme esté:
Leur propre nature deffont.

Balade 404 (cont'd)

They best can be compared to
a dog that has gone greedy,
a lion overcome with hubris,
which overcomes so many,
who seem to rise up higher
and think that they are handsome
on the outside, but inside
honest virtues aren't apparent.
They wear great tails like calves do:
they undo their own nature.

At night, each one is wakeful;
they are just like the owl is,
since during the day-time
they're in bed until it's midday.
They're given to amusement,
and to living as gluttons,
and to lusting for gold coins,
and to mocking the decent,
but by taking such pleasure
they undo their own nature.

Envoy
Prince, the things I've talked of
should be, without an option,
root and branch, got rid of,
for those doing such folly
are more animal than human:
they undo their own nature.

Que je soie vostre loyal ami[13]

fol 150c Apres Machaut qui tant vous a amé
Et qui estoit la fleur de toutes flours,
Noble poete et faiseur renommé,
Plus qu'Ovide vray remede d'amours
Qui m'a nourri et fait maintes doucours,
Vueilles, lui mort, pour l'onneur de celui
Que je soie vostre loyal ami.

Tous instruments l'ont complaint et plouré,
Musique a fait son obseque et ses plours
Et Orpheus a le corps enterré,
Qui pour sa mort est emmuys et sours,
Ses tres doulx chans sont muez en doulours,
Autel de moy s'ainsi n'est quant a my
Que je soie vostre loyal ami.

fol 150d Eustace suis par droit nom appellé;
Hé, Peronne, qui estes mes recours,
Qui en tous cas bien faictes a mon gré,
Je vous pry que me faictes secours
En recevant mes piteuses clamours
Me recréez s'il vous plaira ainsi
Que je sole vostre loyal amy.

Let me be your loyal friend and lover

Now that Machaut, who loved you with devotion,
who was a flower above all other flowers,
whose writings gave him fame, a noble poet,
greater than Ovid for love's true consolation,
who brought me up, who did me so much kindness,
is dead, I ask you, in his honor,
let me be your loyal friend and lover.

For him, all instruments were weeping
and music sang his requiem, lamenting,
and Orpheus himself has buried the body,
who at this death himself has suffered deafness;
his sweetest songs have been transformed to grieving,
and I myself will be the same unless you
let me be your loyal friend and lover.

Eustache is what I'm rightly called.
Ah, Péronne—you who are my refuge,
whose every act is one that I admire—
I beg for help since, if you help me,
if you accept my wretched pleading,
you'll give me life again, if only you would
let me be your loyal friend and lover.

Recevez moi: j'ai failli a Peronne[14]

fol 160c A vous m'octroy de vray cuer et de bon,
Doulce chantant plus que nulle seraine,
Plaisant a tous, de gracieux renom,
De toute honneur la dame souveraine;
fol 160d Vo maison est toudis de joye plaine
Si vous supplie treshumble, belle et bonne,
Recevez moy, j'ay failli a Perronne.

Je ne requier d'amy fors que le nom
Et si vous aym plus que Paris Helaine
Et se je l'ay j'aray plus que Jason;
Qui ot Dydo, la noble chastellaine;
Trop suis ferus en l'amoureuse vaine
Par vo doulcour tres doulce Gauteronne;
Recevez moy, j'ay failli a Perronne.

Car sanz amours ne puis faire chanson;
Or suy par vous a la clere fontaine
Ou Narcisus ne trouva garison
Aincoiz mouru et j'encourray tel paine
Se de vous n'ay retenue certaine;
Par vo pité, d'onneur escrips a bonne;
Recevez moy, j'ay failli a Perronne.

Accept me, since I missed out on Peronne

With heart sincere and good, I give myself to you
who sing more sweetly than the sirens do,
are kind to everyone, renowned for grace,
a sovereign lady honored in every place.
From your house joy is never gone.
Fair and virtuous lady! humbly I beg of you,
accept me, since I missed out on Peronne.

The title of lover is all I ask, no more;
Paris loved Helen, but I'll love you more,
and if I win this title I shall then have more
than Jason; or than he who had Dido, who
ruled such a noble hall. I'm overwhelmed by you
and the course of love, and your sweetness, sweet Gauteronne:
accept me, since I missed out on Peronne.

For, without love, I can't compose a thing,
and now, because of you, I'm at that crystal spring
where Narcissus found no respite from his pain
but died, and I shall suffer in like vein.
if I don't have a word in pledge from you.
Have pity; write in honor's name that you
accept me, since I missed out on Peronne.

Puis que j'ay passé le Lis[15]

fol 173a Puis que j'ay passé le Lis
Je seray gais et jolis
En ce doulz pais de France
Et vivray a ma plaisance
Maugré Flandres et le pais

Ou j'ay toudis fait penance,
Porté bassinet et lance,
De cote de fer vestis
Geu aux champs en grant doubtance
Eu faim, froit, pluie et soufrance,
Sanz couvert, sanz avoir lis,
Et encor me faisoit pis
Vuacarme, alarme et les cris
Des Flamens que ma finance
Ne que toute ma despence.
De Dieu soient ilz maudis
Puis que j'ay passé le Lis
Je seray gais et jolis
En ce doulz pais de France
Et vivray a ma plaisance
Maugré Flandres et le pais.

Quant il pleut nulz n'y dance
Les chevaulx jusqu'a oultrance
Sont en boe ensevelis;
Maint sommier es chemins lance
Dont il n'est nulle esperance
Que jamais en soit saillis
Desrobez, tuez, murdris
. . . .
D'une pique a en la pance;
Trop mauvais y fait quant g'y pence,
Chevauchier par leur pais
Puis que j'ay passé le Lis
Je seray gais et jolis
En ce doulz pais de France
Et vivray a ma plaisance
Maugré Flandres et le pais.

When I've crossed over the Lys

When I've crossed over the Lys
I'll be gay and bright again
in France, that sweet domain
where I will live as I fancy
in spite of Flanders and that country

where I've always done penance,
helmeted, bearing a lance,
clothed in a coat of mail
in a field, scared to death, I quail,
in pain and starved, in sleet,
with no bed, not even a sheet,
and much worse, the screaming,
the alarms, the noise of the Fleming,
not to mention the terrible cost,
the expenses, the money I've lost.
May God curse them for me.
When I've crossed over the Lys
I'll be gay and bright again
in France, that sweet domain
where I will live as I fancy
in spite of Flanders and that country

where nobody dances in the rain,
horses in the mud remain
sunk to the shoulder and mane,
packhorses fall on the road
without hope that horse or load
will ever be pulled free again;
robbed and murdered, slain
. . . .
with a pike stuck through the belly,
seems a nasty job to me
riding around their country.
When I've crossed over the Lys
I'll be gay and bright again
in France, that sweet domain
where I will live as I fancy
in spite of Flanders and that country

Virelai 548 (cont'd)

Quatre foiz d'une suiance
C'est une fole ventance
J'ay esté entrepris
En peril et en balance
D'avoir grant male meschance
J'en suis hors, bien m'en est prins.
fol 173b Jamais n'y seray reprins.
Voist il qui veult avoir pris:
Je n'i eus onques plaisance.
Eulz regni et leur puissance
Car je les harray toudis
Puis que j'ay passé le Lis
Je seray gais et jolis
En ce doulz pais de France
Et vivray a ma plaisance
Maugré Flandres et le pais.

Virelai 548 (cont'd)

where four times in succession—
this is a fool's confession—
I've been caught in this mess
in danger and under duress
hostage to great misfortune.
Now I'm out, I'm a lucky man,
I'll never be caught there again.
Go, if you still need a name:
I never had joy from acclaim.
I renounce them and all their power;
I hate them from this very hour.
When I've crossed over the Lys
I'll be gay and bright again
in France, that sweet domain
where I will live as I fancy
in spite of Flanders and that country.

"Sui je, sui je, sui je belle?"[16]

fol 173d "Sui je, sui je, sui je belle?"

Il me semble, a mon avis
Que j'ay beau front et doulz viz
Et la bouche vermeillette:
Dictes moy si je suis belle.

J'ay vers yeulx, petis sourcis,
Le chief blont, le nez traitis,
Ront menton, blanche gorgette:
Sui je, sui je, sui je belle?

J'ay dur sain et hault assis,
Longs bras gresles, doys aussis,
Et par le faulz sui greslette:
Dictes moy se je sui belle.

J'ay bonnes rains, ce m'est vis,
Bon dos, bon cul de Paris,
Cuisses et gambes bien faites:
Sui je, sui je, sui je belle?

J'ay piez rondes et petiz,
Bien chaussans et biaux habis,
Je sui gaye et joliette:
fol 174a Dictes moy se je sui belle.

J'ay mantiaux fourrez de gris,
J'ay chapiaux, j'ay biaux proffis
Et d'argent mainte espinglette:
Sui je, sui je, sui je belle?

J'ay draps de soye et tabis,
J'ay draps d'or et blans et bis,
J'ay mainte bonne chosette:
Dictes moy se je sui belle.

Am I, am I, am I lovely?

Am I, am I, am I lovely?

In my own view, it seems to me,
my brow and face are sweet to see,
and my mouth is red and feminine:
tell me if I'm lovely.

My eyes are lively; I've cute brows,
white neck and shoulders, a straight nose,
and hair that's blond, and a good round chin:
am I, am I, am I lovely?

My breasts are firm, and they are high,
slim arms and fingers, by the by,
and my small waist is very fine:
tell me if I'm lovely.

My hips are good, it seems to me;
good back, good Paris butt on me,
and my legs and thighs are just divine:
am I, am I, am I lovely?

My feet are plump and dainty,
I've clothes and shoes in plenty,
and I am gay and pretty:
tell me if I'm lovely.

My coats are fully lined in fur;
I have good prospects, I aver,
and hats, and many silver pins:
am I, am I, am I lovely?

I've cloth of silk and of samite
I've cloth of gold, and brown and white.
I've got so many little things:
tell me if I'm lovely.

Rondeau 554 (cont'd)

Que XV ans n'ay je vous dis;
Moult est mes tresors jolys
S'en garderay la clavette:
Sui je, sui je, sui je belle?

Bien devra estre hardis,
Cilz qui sera mes amis,
Qui ara tel damoiselle:
Dictes moy se je sui belle,

Et par Dieu je li plevis
Que tresloyal, se je vis,
Li seray, si ne chancelle:
Sui je, sui je, sui je belle?

Se courtois est et gentilz,
Vaillans apres, bien apris,
Il gaignera sa querelle:
Dictes moy se je sui belle.

C'est uns mondains paradiz
Que d'avoir dame toudiz
Ainsi fresche, ainsi nouvelle:
Sui je, sui je, sui je belle?

Entre vous, acouardiz,
Pensez a ce que je diz.
Cy fine ma chansonne:
Sui je, sui je, sui je belle?

Rondeau 554 (cont'd)

And I've now reached my fifteenth year;
with all my lovely treasures here
which I guard with a little key:
am I, am I, am I lovely?

Those who'll be lovers of mine one day
will need their courage, I would say,
to catch a young Miss such as me:
tell me if I'm lovely.

But I'll be loyal, by the Lord,
as I live, I give my word,
I will be loyal, unless I waver:
am I, am I, am I lovely?

If he shows all the courtesies,
is valiant, puts me at my ease,
he'll court me, and will win my favor:
tell me if I'm lovely.

It is an earthly paradise
to have someone so fresh, so nice,
a lady in her bloom, so new:
am I, am I, am I lovely?

Among yourselves, you who are shy,
think about all this, say I.
And now my little song is through:
am I, am I, am I lovely?

Je n'ose aler souper a court[17]

fol 177d Je n'ose aler souper a court
Pour Savoisi et pour Poitiers
Qui lopinent trop volentiers.
Sur ce me font souper trop court,
Mangier n'y puis, n'a quart n'a tiers.
Je n'ose aler souper a court
Pour Savoisi et pour Poitiers.
L'un d'eulx a ma viande court,
Et l'autre au vin; poussins, plouviers,
M'arrache des poins, amy chiers,
Je n'ose aler souper a court
Pour Savoisi et pour Poitiers
Qui lopinent trop volentiers.

At court I don't dare dine on anything

At court I don't dare dine on anything
because of Savoisy and Poitiers: those guys
are greedy, gobble everything.
They've cut my dining down to size—
I don't eat a third or quarter of the food I prize.
At court I don't dare dine on anything
because of Savoisy and Poitiers, those guys!
One makes a run at my food, likewise,
the other at my wine; and as for chicken thighs,
dear friends, both grab the very leg I'm handling.
At court I don't dare dine on anything
because of Savoisy and Poitiers: those guys
are greedy, gobble everything.

Est cilz aise qui ne se puet dormir[18]

fol 179c Est cilz aise qui ne se puet dormir
Et qui ne fait toute nuit que viller,
Puces sentir, oyr enfans crier,
Sur un matras et sur cordes gesir,
Avoir ors draps et sur dur orillier;
Est cilz aise qui ne se puet dormir
Et qui ne fait toute nuit que viller?
Et d'autre part oit la grant mer bruir
Et les chevaulx combatre et deslier;
C'est a Calays, Granson, veilles jugier:
Est cilz aise qui ne se puet dormir
Et qui ne fait toute nuit que viller,
Puces sentir, oyr enfans crier?

Can a man be comfortable all night

Can a man be comfortable all night
who cannot get to sleep, who lies awake
hearing kids cry, feeling fleas bite,
on a mattress on cords, for heaven's sake!
And the pillow's hard, the sheets are a filthy sight.
Can a man be comfortable all night
who cannot get to sleep, who lies awake
and also hears the waves of ocean break
and horses slipping ties, the sounds of a fight?
This is Calais, Oton de Grandson! am I right?
Can a man be comfortable all night
who cannot get to sleep, who lies awake
hearing kids cry, feeling fleas bite?

Je ne vueil plus a vous, dame, muser[19]

fol 182b Je ne veuil plus a vous dame muser;
Vous povez bien querir autre musart.
Tart m'appercoy qu'on m'a fait amuser;
Je ne veuil plus a vous dame muser
Ne plus n'espoir en vous mon temps user
Quant d'esprevier savez faire busart;
Je ne veuil plus a vous dame muser;
Vous povez bien querir autre musart.

Lady, on you I will no longer muse

Lady, on you I will no longer muse;
you need another fool; go look again.
I have been slow to see the tricks you use.
Lady, on you I will no longer muse.
On hope for you, I've no more time to lose
because you can convert a hawk to hen.
Lady, on you I will no longer muse;
you need another fool; go look again.

Cilz qui onques encores ne vous vit[20]

fol 182c Cil qui oncques encore ne vous vit,
Vous aime fort et desire veoir;
Or vous verra car en cest espoir vit
Cil qui oncques encore ne vous vit.
fol 182d Car pour les biens que chacun de vous dit,
Vous veult donner cuer, corps, vie et povoir.
Cil qui oncques encore ne vous vit
Vous aime fort et desire veoir.

He has never yet so much as seen you

Though he has never yet so much as seen you,
it's you he loves, and he desires to see.
For in this hope he lives: that now he'll see you
though he has never yet so much as seen you.
Because of all the good all speak about you,
he wants to give his heart, flesh, life, capacity.
Though he has never yet so much as seen you,
it's you he loves and he desires to see.

Venez a mon jubilé[21]

fol 184b Venez a mon jubilé:
J'ay passé la cinquantaine.
Tout mon bon temps est alé,
Venez a mon jubilé.
Mon corps est tout afolé.
Adieu! De moy vous souviengne.
Venez a mon jubilé:
J'ay passé la cinquantaine.

Come to my jubilee

Come to my jubilee:
I've turned fifty today.
The best has been for me.
Come to my jubilee.
My body's in disarray.
Goodbye! Remember me!
Come to my jubilee:
I've turned fifty today.

Au monde n'a au jour d'ui que ces deux[22]

fol 188d Au monde n'a au jour d'hui que ces deux
Eur et meseur, a tout considerer
Dont l'un fait bien et l'autre desperer;
Aler partout peut cil qui est eureux
On ne lui peut ne nuire ne grever;
Au monde n'a au jour d'huy que ces deux;
Eur et meseur, a tout considerer.
Maiz bien se gard toudiz le maleureux
Car il ne peut fors meschance trouver;
Chascuns li nuit si puis dire et prouver
Au monde n'a au jour d'uy que ces deux
Eur et meseur, a tout considerer
Dont l'un fait bien et l'autre desperer.

In all the world today there's just these two

In all the world today, there's just these two,
luck, and bad luck, that's the gist of the affair;
one makes for good, and the other for despair.
Those who have luck can take in every view,
none can torment them; none can touch a hair.
In all the world today, there's just these two,
luck, and bad luck, that's the gist of the affair.
The unlucky must keep watch their whole lives through,
for they'll find nothing but mischance out there;
as I can say, and prove, they haven't got a prayer.
In all the world today, there's just these two,
luck, and bad luck, that's the gist of the affair;
one makes for good, and the other for despair.

Oez de la nonnette[23]

fol 199c Oez de la nonnette
Comme a le cuer joly
S'ordre ne ly puet plere.

"Mes peres et ma mere
N'ont plus d'enffans que mi.
M'envoient a l'escolle.
Je n'y ay riens apriz
Fors un mot d'amourette
Qui m'a fait si gaiette
Que j'auray bel amy;
Autre rien ne me hette."
Oez de la nonnette
Comme a le cuer joly
S'ordre ne ly puet plere.

"Je sui mal de mon frere
Pour ce que j'en yssy
Maiz par l'ame mon pere
Je veil avoir mary
Si comme a Sebilette.
Ne vous chaille d'abeesse
De prieuse autressy;
Cure n'ay de maitresse."
Oez de la nonnette
Comme a le cuer joly
S'ordre ne ly puet plere.

"Adieu le moinage!
Jamaiz n'y enterray;
Adieu tout le mainage
Et adieu Avenay!
Bien voy l'aumosne est faitte;
Trop tart me suy retraicte.
fol 199d Certes, ce poise my.
Plus ne seray nonnette."
Oez de la nonnette
Comme a le cuer joly
S'ordre ne ly puet plere.

Listen to the little nun

Listen to the little nun
whose heart is full of fun
and wishes convent life were done.

"I was the only child
my father and my mother still had
They sent me off to school
where I just played the fool
and only learned to say
a word of love that made me gay,
and wish for nothing in the end
except a handsome friend."
Listen to the little nun
whose heart is full of fun
and wishes convent life were done.

"I know my brother will grieve
that I have had to leave
but, by my father's soul,
a husband is my only goal,
I want to be like Sebilette,
with no Abbess to make me fret,
and also no Prioress.
No, I don't want a mistress."
Listen to the little nun
whose heart is full of fun
and wishes convent life were done.

"Farewell to the convent's border!
Not for me the order;
farewell, the house I leave today
and farewell to Avenay!
But all good men are gone.
I've left too late, I see.
And, yes, this weighs on me.
And I'll never be a nun."
Listen to the little nun
whose heart is full of fun
and wishes convent life were done.

Sur tous autres doy estre roy des lays[24]

fol 205a Se nulz homs doit estre roy de laidure
Pour plus laideur c'on ne porroit trouver
Estre le doy par raison et droiture
Car j'ay le groing con hure de sanglier
Et aux singes puis asses ressambler;
J'ay grans dens et nez camus,
Les cheveulx noirs, par les joes barbus
Suy et mes yeux resgardant de byays,
Par le front sui et par le corps velus;
Sur tous autres doy estre roy des lays.

J'ay des longtemps trop estrange figure,
Comme un more me puet on figurer;
Pintelez sui et formez sanz mesure,
Cours, rons et gros, ne me puis acoler;
L'en me doit bien comme roy couronner;
Je suis courbes et bossius,
Gresles dessoubz et espes par dessus;
De tel forme n'a nul roy au palays
Et par ces poins determine et conclus
Sur tous autres doy estre roy des lays.

D'or en avant faut toute creature
Que l'en pourra veeir et esprouver,
Laide de fait et de sa propre nature
Par devers moy retenir et donner
Aucun estat si s'en veult courser
Tant sera mes subgiez plus;
Toutes mes gens mettre vous fait sus
Et retenez tous hideux pour jamaiz;
Par moy sera ly regnes soustenus;
Sur tous autres doy estre roy des lays.

L'envoy
Princes, nulx homs a moy ne se figure
fol 205b Je souverains mes retenues faiz
Tous estas doing seculiers et de cure;
Sur tous autres doy estre roy des laiz.

Among all other uglies, I should be the king

If any man should be the king of ugliness
because of the great ugliness in him
then I'll be it by reason and by right
since I've got a head just like a wild boar
and have the features of a monkey, too.
I have huge teeth, I have a flattened nose,
I have black hair, and I've got hairy cheeks.
Look and you'll see that I'm a cross-eyed man.
I'm hairy on the body and the brow:
among all other uglies, I should be the king.

For quite a while my face has been very strange;
you can imagine me as a mulberry,
I'm mottled, and I'm out of all proportion,
short, round and fat; can't reach around myself;
I surely should be crowned the king.
I am bent over, hunchbacked, too,
slender below, voluminous above.
No king in any palace has got such a shape
and for these reasons I conclude and decide:
among all other uglies, I should be the king.

Henceforth, I will declare that every creature
who comes into view should get a simple test
to see if ugliness is natural to them;
they must be brought before me and they must
be given some posting, even if this offends,
since then they'll be my subjects all the more;
all my people will be subject to this summons
and all the uglies held perpetually.
This kingdom will have my complete support:
among all other uglies, I should be the king.

Envoy
Prince, no man can be compared to me,
I'm sovereign, and so can hire my staff
and grant positions, religious and secular:
among all other uglies, I should be king.

C'est un grant donneur de bons jours[25]

fol 205c "Qui est cilz compaings si joliz
Si gracieux et si courtoiz
Qui salue les gens toudiz
Et qui s'offre a eulx tant de foys?"
"Voire, que tu ne le congnoiz?"
"Ce ne fay moy." "Moult scet de tours;
Tost a sailly de deux encroiz:
C'est un grant donneur de bons jours.

Est il gaiz, en parler faitiz,
Biaux et blons, gens, longs et adroys,
Juenes, bien chantans, yeux traitis,
Bien dancans, parez comme un roys;
De cuidier est en son droit moys;
Il voit, il oit, il n'est pas sours;
Il fait a ses polses les droiz:
C'est un grant donneur de bons jours.

Il ne tient conte des chetifs;
Il est entrans, il a ses loys;
Il accorde a chascun ses diz;
Il parle ainsis comme tu l'oiz
. . . .
Et proffite entre les seignours;
Cure n'a de ceulx qui n'ont croix:
Cest un grant donneur de bons jours."

L'envoy
Princes, cilz n'est pas esbahis;
Partout veult faire ses honnours
Savoureux, qui tant a d'amis:
C'est un grant donneur de bons jours.

He's great at giving have-a-good-days

"Who is this ever-cheerful man,
so gracious and so courteous,
who is forever greeting us
and offering to do all that he can?"
"So you don't know him? Is it true?"
"I don't." "He has his little ways.
He's everywhere at once when he encounters you:
he's great at giving have-a-good-days.

He's merry, and he speaks with elegance,
gracious, fair, blond and tall, with looks that please,
he's young, sings well, has arching eyes, and he's
all decked out like a king, and he can dance,
and is at the peak of his self-confidence,
and hears—he is not deaf—and sees,
and as to wealth, he's quick to appraise:
he's great at giving have-a-good-days.

He has no patience for the meek;
he's got his rules, he has entree;
he agrees with every word you speak;
when talking, he expresses it your way;
. . . .
those in authority are his mainstays;
your assets yield the interest he displays:
he's great at giving have-a-good-days."

Envoy
Prince, here's a man who's never at loose ends,
who wants to hand out his bouquets
everywhere, since he has many friends:
he's great at giving have-a-good-days.

Tousjours, sanz demander, moustarde[26]

fol 206b En Haynaut et en Brabant ay
Aprins a sauces ordonner;
Es hostez ou je me logay
Me fist on toudiz apporter
A rost, a mouton, a sangler,
A lievre, a connin, a ostarde,
A poisson d'eaue douce et mer
Tousjours, sanz demander, moustarde.

Harens fres quiz et demanday
Carpe au cabaret pour dyner,
Bequet en l'eaue y ordonnay
Et grosses solles au soupper;
A Brusselles fiz demander
Sauce vert; le clerc me regarde;
Par un varlet me fist donner
Tousjours sans demander moustarde.

Sanz li ne bu ne ne mengay;
Avec l'eaue la font meller
Du poisson et ancor say
fol 206c Que la graisse du rost gester
Font en la moustarde et bouster.
D'en servir nulz d'eux ne retarde;
La arez vous pour vostre user
Tousjours sanz demander moustarde.

L'envoy
Prince, gingembre, c'est tout cler,
Clos, sapfran, graine n'ont d'eulx garde
Maiz a chascun font destramper
Tousjours sanz demander moustarde.

Always, never asking, mustard

In Hainaut and Brabant I made
attempts to order sauce with care,
but in every inn at which I stayed
they always brought me, with my fare,
with every roast and mutton dish,
with boar, with rabbit, and with bustard,
with fresh and with salt-water fish,
always, never asking, mustard.

I took fresh herring, said I'd like
carp at the pub for midday dinner,
and called for simple boiled pike
and some large sole, to be my supper.
In Brussels, I asked them for green sauce;
a cleric stared and looked disgusted
and a varlet brought me in, of course,
as always, never asking, mustard.

I couldn't eat or drink without it.
They add it to the water they
boil the fish in and—don't doubt it—
the drippings from the roast each day
are tossed into a mustard vat
in which they're mixed, and then entrusted
to those who bring—they're quick at that—
always, never asking, mustard.

Envoy
Prince, it's clear that ginger, clove,
saffron, pepper are never trusted.
There's just one thing these people serve:
always, never asking, mustard.

Muser souvent et si ne say pourquoy[27]

fol 213b Je doy estre chancelliers des fumeux
Et en l'office tousjours demourer
fol 213c Car de l'ordre maintenir sui songneux
Si c'on ne puet ma personne trouver
En un estat: ains me voit on muer
Soudainement mon scavoir en folye,
Estre dolens et puis faire chere lye.
Ainsi me fait fumée, par ma foy,
Muser souvent et si ne say pourquoy.

De nature sui merencolieux,
Colerique, noir, me puet l'en trouver,
Si sui enclins a estre merveilleux
Naturelment; donc doy je retourner
A ma nature, sans moy desnaturer
Et estre plains de grant merencolie,
Car resister n'est pas de ma partie;
Ains me defuit; ce me fait, en requoy,
Muser souvent et si ne say pourquoy.

Dont je conclus, s'on me voit pou joyeux,
Que je m'en puis par nature excuser,
Car je ne suis pas si ingenieux
Que je sache contre nature aler;
Fumeux seray, riens n'i vault le parler;
Fumeusement menrray fumeuse vie.
Demourer doy en ma chancellerie
Qu'a tousjours maiz me verrez en ce ploy,
Muser souvent et si ne sai pourquoy.

I often brood, not understanding why

I should be chancellor of shadow-men
and stay forever in that post, for then,
if I maintain the order carefully
so no one can discover me
in one condition, they can see my shift
from wisdom into folly and, as swift,
my slide from sorrow into gaiety.
I am a shadow and, by Heaven that is on high,
I often brood, not understanding why.

By nature I'm a melancholy man
and choleric—that blackness is in me—
and so I tend—it's natural—to be
bewildered, and I therefore—if I can
without denaturing myself—must try
to use this melancholic tendency
because resistance isn't something I
can seem to bring about; so, secretly,
I often brood, not understanding why.

And, therefore, if I find that joy is rare,
I have my nature to excuse this weight of care
since I'm not such a very clever guy
that I know how to go against it. I
will be a shadow-figure—that no one can deny—
and, shadowy, I'll lead a shadow life:
I must stay in my chancellery since I
will be forever in this state of strife:
I often brood, not understanding why.

Jamaiz dame forment ne l'aimera[28]

fol 217a Povre signe est que d'avoir mal es rains,
Plaindre son doux et devenir gouteux,
Mal es costez et avoir chaudes mains
Et de sentir quant le temps est pluieux.
Telz signes ne valent rien,
Car qui devient tel astronomien,
Et de certain scet quant il plourira,
Pert ses amours, toute joye et tout bien.
Jamaiz dame forment ne l'aimera.

Car de doleur procedent tous ses plains:
Se plovoir dont il devient angoisseux,
S'il s'est armé, es lieux ou fu attains,
Des cops se deult, qui le font dolereux.
Lors le fault vivre du sien,
Et visiter par le fisicien,
Qui medicine ou puison lui donrra.
Lors dit Amours: "De li airer te tien."
Jamaiz forment dame ne l'aimera.

Seuffre tes maulx, l'en ne veult que gens sains
Et qui soient puissans et vertueux,
Juenes, jolis, de toute joye plains,
Trippens, saillans comme est uns escuireux;
Et se l'omme est ancien,
Voist conceiller et soit saint Julian,
Et le juene non goutteux poursuira,
Car se sain Mort l'atrappe en son lien,
Jamaiz dame forment ne l'aimera.

No lady will ever fall for him

It's a bad sign to have a pain in your back,
and to complain of it, start getting gout,
have a pain in your side, have clammy hands,
be able to predict when it's going to rain.
Such signs do not have value because
a man who becomes an astronomer,
who knows for sure when it will rain
will lose all joy, his lovers, every good.
No lady will ever fall for him.

His talk is all about his aches;
he's twitchy if it's going to rain;
if he bears arms, then each old wound
that's bumped gives rise to new complaints.
And then he needs his private funds
and receives the visits of physicians
who give him potions or medicine.
Then Cupid will say, "Do not disturb."
No lady will ever fall for him.

So suffer. People only want the healthy near,
those filled with strength, the vigorous,
the cheerful, young, those full of life,
who jump like squirrels, and who dance;
and as for those who've reached old age,
they'll be Saint Julian and give advice.
Let youngsters with no gout go love,
for if Saint Maur gives a man the gout,
no lady will ever fall for him.

Il n'est doleur que fors le mal des dens[29]

fol 217b Aucuns dient: grant peine est de veillier
D'avoir tiercaine ou fievre tout a fait,
Ou mal ou ventre, ou d'estre prisonnier,
D'avoir goutes de quoy l'en crie et brait,
Ou gehinez estre pour son meffait;
Maiz c'est tout riens au regart que je prens:
Il n'est doleur que fors le mal des dens.

Tel meschief n'a femme pour travaillier,
Mal de teste telle doleur ne fait,
Car on ne puet ne boire ne mangier,
Mais fault crier mal gré que en ait;
On ne pourroit pis avoir par souhet;
Qui a tel mal plus est que hors du sens:
Il n'est doleur que fors le mal des dens.

On ne pourroit dormir ne sommeillier;
Qui tel mal a, mainte male nuit trait.
Quant il espoint il convient erragier.
La joe enffle, li viaires deffait,
Et d'en garir ont pluseurs moult de plet,
Qui tout gastent quant il touchent dedens:
Il n'est doleur fors que le mal des dens.

There is no pain like a toothache's pain

It's torment to be sleepless, so some say,
to have an ague or a fever come your way,
or stomach-ache, be held in custody,
have gout that makes you scream or be
put to the torture for iniquity.
But all that's nothing; I maintain
there is no pain like a toothache's pain.

No woman in labor has such agony;
a headache doesn't give such misery;
you cannot eat or drink even if you try;
despite yourself, you have to cry;
you couldn't be worse off if you wished to be.
Those who suffer this are beyond insane.
There is no pain like a toothache's pain.

You cannot get to sleep, or even snooze;
this illness gives the all-night blues.
You go out of your wits when you get hit.
It swells the cheeks, the face distorts with strain,
and pleading for a cure, you throw a fit;
you thrash around in bed with it.
There is no pain like a toothache's pain.

Ja ne deissent sur autrui telle goulée[30]

fol 217d
Qui ne chevauche et qui n'est bien montez,
Qui ne poursuit et qui n'a grant estat,
Bassinet nuef et tout entier armez,
Et qui ne va ou l'en se combat,
Chascun dit qu'il ne vault rien;
C'est un chetifs qui espargne le sien;
Onques ne vit sachier du fuerre espée;
Maiz se pluseurs s'avisassent tresbien,
Ja ne deissent sur autrui telle goulée.

Pluseurs y vont qui en sont endebtes,
Qui de paier font sovent grant debat,
Et en la fin en sont desheritez,
Et se portent leurs besongnes de plat.
De telz gens compte ne tien:
C'est droictement un va-tost-et-revien
Sur povres gens qui composent l'armée.
Maiz s'ils sceussent qu'ont fait li ancien,
Ja ne deissent sur autrui telle goulée.

S'uns homs ne va, est il donc reboutez?
Autrui destruire, grever et faire mat,
Et acquerir mille pechez mortelx
Ou nulle honeur maintesfoys ne s'embat?
Nennil: mieulx li vaurroit bien
Vivre envers Dieu, comme vray crestien
Que faire mal pour avoir renommée.
S'aucuns seussent ce mot, or le retien:
Ja ne deissent sur autrui telle goulée.

They wouldn't talk such rubbish of others

A man not riding, not well saddled up,
not in the chase, without great retinue
with no new helmets, not armed to the teeth,
a man who doesn't go where the fighting is,
is someone everyone agrees is worthless,
a wretch who must be saving every cent,
who never saw a sword out of its scabbard.
But if these people only thought a bit
they wouldn't talk such rubbish of others.

Many in debt go off to war this way
and, over payments, often fight a lot
and in the end they're ruined by it all,
their circumstances having then collapsed.
Do not take any notice of such people:
they're just as quick at coming back as entering
on the backs of the poor, who are the army.
But if these speakers knew what our forebears did
they wouldn't talk such rubbish of others.

If someone doesn't go, why is he then rejected?
Should he destroy, oppress, and conquer others
and so commit a thousand mortal sins
in which some honor isn't often found?
No, not at all: he would be better off
to live, like a true Christian, near to God
than do such evil to gain reputation.
If people only knew and understood,
they wouldn't talk such rubbish of others.

Haro! Haro! Est ce bien gracieuse?[31]

fol 217d Haro, dame! Souffrez que l'en vous voye.
Vous me semblez trop precieuse chose,
Maiz sans vo gré approucher n'oseroye
fol 218a Si doulx saffir ne vermeille rose.
Trop est hardiz qui atouchier vous ose:
Vous n'estes pas de maniere aureuse.
Haro! Haro! Est ce bien gracieuse?

Qui vous verroit aler parmi la rue,
Jhesu semblez dedens vostre habit close;
Vous parlez bas afin qu'on ne vous oye,
La Trinité est dedens vous enclose;
Par Saint Trotin homme regarder n'ose,
Car homme voir est chose perilleuse.
Haro! Haro! Est ce bien gracieuse?

Toudiz plourez: nulz temps ne faictes joye,
Ne vostres cuers fors en Dieu ne repose,
Si fait grant bien qui un po vous resjoye;
Et quant a moy je tesmoingne et suppose
Que qui seroit avec vous longue pose
Que vous seriez un po amoureuse.
Haro! Haro! Est ce bien gracieuse?

Come on! come on! is this true graciousness?

Come on, dear lady! please allow a glimpse.
You seem to be a too exquisite thing;
I wouldn't dare approach without permission
so sweet a sapphire, such a red red rose.
He would be bold indeed who dared to touch.
You certainly don't have a happy look.
Come on! come on! is this true graciousness?

To those who see you walking down the street
it looks like Jesus wrapped up in your clothes;
you speak so softly that you can't be heard;
you must enclose the Trinity itself;
Saint Trotin helps you not to look at men
because there's danger if you see a man.
Come on! come on! is this true graciousness?

You're always weeping, never seem to laugh,
and as for your heart, it only lies with God;
a man would do some good if he cheered you up
and yet I swear that I presume you would,
if someone spent enough long hours with you,
end up becoming just a little amorous.
Come on! come on! is this true graciousness?

"C'est droitement Jhesus sur une pele"[32]

fol 218a Telz fait souvent bien le religieux,
Et telle fait aussi la Magdalaine,
Portans cotes et habis marmiteux,
Qui ont toudiz aussi verde la vayne,
Que de telz gens menent vie mondaine
Combien que aucuns dient de tel et telle:
"C'est droitement Jhesus sur une pele."

Devant les gens font cy le gracieux,
Qu'a paine ist il de leur corps poux n'alayne,
Maiz ce font il comme malicieux:
L'en congnoist mal le mouton a la layne.
Tel malice leur voulenté amayne,
A leur effeit rouges sont dessoubz l'ele:
C'est droitement Jhesus sur une pele.

De telles gens dist nostresire Dieux,
Quant on les voit vestus de pel humaine,
fol 218b Comme brebis faisons le precieux,
Que bonne euvre n'est pas en eulx certaine.
Faictes leurs diz maiz nulz leurs faiz ne praigne,
Car qui les voit a leur couleur mortelle:
C'est droitement Jhesus sur une pele.

"They really are the wafer, Jesus on a plate."

Many a man will act as if he were a monk,
and many a woman acts like Magadalene,
wearing their garments of tattered cloth,
but they still have as much lust in their blood
as those who lead a worldly life,
and so some say about such men and women
"They really are the wafer, Jesus on a plate."

When they're in public they are so refined
that scarce a throb or breath comes from their flesh
but this is the behavior of the cunning,
and you can't know a sheep by woolen clothes.
The malice that directs their will is real;
they hide their scarlet underneath drab wings.
They really are the wafer, Jesus on a plate.

Our Lord has told us all about such people
when they're seen wrapped in human skin
pretending that they're meek as lambs
that they can't be depended on to do good works.
Do what they say but don't do what they do
because whoever looks on them sees the color of death:
They really are the wafer, Jesus on a plate.

Pour un perdu, j'en ay deux retrouvez[33]

fol 218b Dieux que je suis dolente et esbahie
Comme je voy sans cause mon ami
Desloyaument faire nouvelle amie,
Qui des long temps s'estoit donné a mi,
Et il se depart et m'a du tout guerpi
Sens dire adieu, li desloyaulx prouvez.
Mais j'en reprendré bon reconfort aussi:
Pour un perdu, j'en ay deux retrouvez.

Qui loyaulx est en l'amoureuse vie
A poine ara james joye de lui,
Maiz qui y ment et sert de tricherie,
Il est amez comme a esté cellui
Qui en mentant m'a de tous poins failli.
Bien est par moy faulx amens esprouvez;
Courcée en sui, or m'en reconforte ainsi:
Pour un perdu, j'en ay deux retrouvez.

Voist donc a Dieu, par ma faulte n'est ce mie.
Pour ce, dames, a toutes vous supplie
Que vous servez de la nappe ploye
A ces amens qui font sy le joly.
Piz leur ferez mieulx arez, je vous dy,
Et plus servans tousjours les trouverrez
D'amours me plaing, maiz au fort, Dieu merci:
Pour un perdu, j'en ay deux retrouvez.

For every one I've lost, I have found two

My God, how thunderstruck and miserable I am
when I see how my lover, for no reason,
takes on another mistress faithlessly;
he long ago had pledged himself to me
and now he's leaving, and I am abandoned
without goodbye; he's proved himself disloyal.
But I can take such comfort just like him:
for every one I've lost, I have found two.

Those who are loyal in the amorous life
should not expect to get much joy from this
but anyone engaged in treachery
will be loved well, just like this man
who lied, and let me down in every way.
But I put my false lover to the test;
when miserable I comfort myself like this:
for every one I've lost, I have found two.

Go then, by God, this is no fault of mine.
And therefore, ladies, I beg all of you
to play a few ploys of your own
with all those lovely lovers that you know.
The worse you treat them the better off you'll be,
you'll always find them more obliging then.
I do complain of love and yet, thank God,
for every one I've lost, I have found two.

Que se semble le ris d'un cardinal[34]

fol 218d Avoir ne puis trop grant merencolie
Des ris que font au jour d'ui mainte gent.
L'un rit des yeux, et en riant colie,
Et l'autre rit qui ne passe le dent;
Li autres rit si tresorriblement
Qu'il semble folz, tant li siet son ris mal,
Que se semble le ris d'un cardinal.

Aucuns font un riz d'ipocrisie
Combien qu'il n'ont de rire nul talent.
Et l'autre rit, qui ne se mocque mie,
Du bon cuer pour quelque esbatement;
Aucuns y a qui rient faintement,
Et l'autre rit qui a joye du mal.
Des oreilles rit aucuns tellement
Que se semble le ris d'un cardinal.

Senz cause rit aucuns par sa folie,
Qui de rire n'a certain mouvement;
L'autre est joyeux, qui a plaine voix crie,
Et qui le fait sans mauvaiz pensement;
Et l'autre rit maiz traiteusement,
Car son ris vient de parfont et d'aval;
Pour ce en tel cas dit on communement:
Que se semble le ris d'un cardinal.

A cardinal would laugh like that

I brood intensely on, and try to analyze,
the laughs men make today. There's one who, as
he twists his neck, laughs with his eyes;
another laughs behind his teeth; another has
such ghastly laughter everyone can see
that laugh and laugher aren't in harmony
and that dementia is underneath his hat:
a cardinal would laugh like that.

Some people laugh out of hypocrisy,
(they have no gift for laughter, only will),
some laughter has no trace of mockery
and comes from pleasure only, not from skill;
some laughter is half-hearted, more a smirk;
some laughter is from malice, tit for tat;
and some men's laughter puts their ears to work:
a cardinal would laugh like that.

Another man will laugh from madness, he
lacks laughter's reasons; someone else will be
joyful, shouting at the top of his voice,
laughing with nothing on his mind but to rejoice;
another laughs in treachery and at
some depth, for his laugh comes from the dark,
and in such cases it is normal to remark:
a cardinal would laugh like that.

Oncques ne vis gens ainsi requinier[35]

fol 218d Tristes, pensis, mas et mornes estoye
Par mesdiser et rappors de faulx dis
fol 219a A une court royal ou je dinoye
Ou pluseurs gens furent a table assis;
Maiz oncques mais tant de moes ne vis
Que ceulx firent que l'en veoit mengier.
D'eulx regarder fu de joye ravis:
Oncques ne vis gens ainsi requinier.

Li uns sembloit truie enmi une voye
Tant mouvoit fort ses baulifres toudiz;
L'autre faisoit de ses dens une soye;
L'autre mouvoit le front et les sourcis;
L'un requignoit, l'autre torcoit son vis,
L'autre faisoit sa barbe baloier;
L'un fait le veel, l'autre fait la brebis:
Oncques ne vis gens ainsi requignier.

D'eulx regarder trop fort me merveilloye
Car en machant sembloient ennemiz.
Faire autel l'un com l'autre ne veoie:
L'un machoit gros, l'autre comme sourez;
Je n'oy oncques tant de joye ne ris
Que de veoir leurs morceaulx ensacher.
Or y gardez, je vous jure et diz:
Oncques ne vis gens ainsi requignier.

L'envoy
Princes, qui est courroussez et pensis
Voist gens veoir qui sont a table mis.
Mieulx ne porra sa trisse laissier.
Des grimaces sera tous esbahis
Que chascun fait; j'en fu la bien servis:
Oncques ne vis gens ainsi requignier.

I never saw such faces as these people made

I was dispirited, saddened, troubled, by
the spiteful gossip, all the malice, I
was hearing at a royal reception where
I banqueted with many people nearby.
I'd never seen such grimaces as played
across the faces of those eating there.
When I saw them, joy came to my aid:
I never saw such faces as these people made.

One looked just like a pig, a roadside sow,
so vigorously did he chomp his lips;
one used his teeth to saw his food in strips,
another moved his forehead and his brow;
one scowled; one twisted up his face somehow,
another managed to get his beard splayed;
one acted like a sheep, another like a cow;
I never saw such faces as these people made.

As I kept looking at them I became
awe-struck, since they seemed demons as they chewed;
I didn't see two people eat the same:
one chew was like a mouse, another lewd.
It gave more laughs than any other game
to watch the ways in which they stuffed down food,
Take a good look! I swear the joy won't fade.
I never saw such faces as these people made.

Envoy
Prince, a man who's sad won't find a thing to beat
watching a group of people as they eat.
He won't find better ways to overcome dull care;
he'll be astonished at the grimaces displayed,
of which I got a generous helping there:
I never saw such faces as these people made.

Je n'en vueil point; varlet soit il au diable![36]

fol 220c "J'ay un varlet qui le vouldroit louer,
Que son pareil ne trouveroit on mie."
"De quoy sert il?" "De boire et de jangler;
Il het chevaulx, ne leva en sa vie
Sanz lui trois foiz appeler;
En cuisine ne scet un oeuf peler,
Non pas servir lui-meismes a la table,
Mais il scet bien viande demander."
fol 220d "Je n'en vueil point: varlet soit il au diable!"

"Ba! Si ferez: il se met a lever
En trestous temps plus de lieue et demie,
N'il n'est homme qui le feist haster
Que sa teste ne fust avant pignie;
Son maistre laisse aprester
Tout a par li sanz venir
Fors au disner; la est il servissable
Pour desservir souvent sanz commander."
"Je n'en vueil point: varlet soit il au diable!

Toutevoie scet il lire ou chanter
Ne escripre chose que l'en lui die?"
"Certes, nenil, mais bien scet murmurer
Et esmouvoir riote a la mesnie.
Trousser ne veult ne maler,
Chambre fournir ne cheval estaler,
Car il se tient pour varlet honourable;
Vous ne povez nul meilleur recouvrer."
"Je n'en vueil point: varlet soit il au diable!"

"No, I don't want him; let him serve in hell."

"I have a servant who is up for hire;
you'll never find his equal." "What can he do?"
"He can drink, and he can gossip, too;
he hates a horse; he's never got up in his entire
life without three yells.
In the kitchen, he can't break an egg too well,
and at the table, he's never any good
at serving, but he can ask for food."
"No, I don't want him; let him serve in hell."

"Come on, you do. To get up in his style
takes more time than to travel a full mile,
and no one in the world can make him hurry
until the combing of his hair is through.
He allows his master to
get ready by himself; he'll never scurry
except to lunch: there you don't have to compel
and he, unasked, can often clear the table well."
"No, I don't want him; let him serve in hell.

But, nonetheless, is he able to read or sing?
Can he write it down, if you tell him what to do?"
"Of course not, but he certainly can bring
some discontent to your house, and complain to you.
No packing, loading, or
preparing rooms, or stabling horses, for
he thinks that, though a servant, he's a swell.
You couldn't find a man who is superior."
"No, I don't want him; let him serve in hell."

Et panduz soit qui ainsi m'assena![37]

fol 220d La fievre quarte et la double tiercaine,
Le mau Saint Leu et le Saint Matelin,
La rage es dens ou chief, goute, migraine,
Les tranchoisons du ventre et de l'avertin,
La goute es flans et le mau Saint Quentin
Puist avoir qui mari me donna,
Et le gros mal au soir et au matin,
Et panduz soit qui ainsi m'assena.

D'ydropisie ait il la pance plaine,
Thisiques soit et ethiques en fin,
La grabelle ait XVIII foiz la sepmaine,
Esquivance soit son corps palasin,
De Saint Fiacre puist estre pelerin,
Et de Saint Mor, qui par goutes fina,
fol 221a Et a tous mauls soit offert et enclin,
Et panduz soit qui ainsi m'assena.

Honteuse mort lui soit briefment prochaine,
Car mon baron m'est trop cruel voisin;
Je n'ose aler en bois, ville ne plaine,
Dancer, chanter, manger, boire de vin,
Que le villain, a guise d'un mastin,
Ne m'abbaie, crians: "Que fais tu la?"
Perdue suis, maudis soit, cy deffin,
Et pandus soit qui ainsi m'assena.

L'envoy
Princes, qui a franchise en son demaine,
Se saiges est ja ne le guerpira;
Or ay mari qui me fait trop de paine,
Et panduz soit qui ainsi m'assena.

And may he hang who sentenced me to this

May four-day fever, double ague, may
all ills Saints Leu and Matelin convey,
may raging aches in teeth or in the head,
may gout, and vertigo, and may migraine,
and grippe, Saint Quentin's dropsy, stomach pain,
strike at whoever made me husbanded,
and may he, night and day, have epileptic fits,
and may he hang who sentenced me to this.

May his belly fill with dropsy, may he be
tubercular, and end consumptive, and may he
eighteen times a week have stones when he goes to piss,
have pains in the throat, suffer paralysis,
have Saint Fiacre's hemorrhoids, and gout,
and die of it like Saint Maur did, and may he
be prone to every ill, and may they find him out,
and may he hang who sentenced me to this.

May he soon meet a shameful death since he,
my baron, is too near and cruel to me.
If I go to the woods, the town, the fields, or dare
to dance or sing or eat or drink some wine,
that low-life, like a dog, barks his one line
and shouts at me, "What are you doing there?"
I'm lost; let him be cursed; that's all there is;
and may he hang who sentenced me to this.

Envoy
Prince, those free to roam in their domain,
if they are wise, will not let go that bliss.
I have a husband now who gives me only pain,
and may he hang who sentenced me to this.

C'est Alixandre le poing clos[38]

fol 224d Je scay un large despensier
Qui conquiert tout par pertuesse;
A sies autrui est le promier;
La scet il monstrer sa largesse,
Tout demande et prant, rien n'y lesse;
La sert chascun de trop beaus mos,
Et se vous demandez qui esse,
C'est Alixandre le poing clos.

Il scet blamer le bouteillier,
Le queux, le maistre et la maistresse
fol 225a S'ilz ne font bien appareillier;
La veult de gent veoir grant presse
Et que la viande ne cesse
Et que toudis ait vin en pos;
. . . .
C'est Alixandre le poing clos.

Chies li ne veult riens espargnier;
Il boit vin de vingne gouesse,
Pain halé, froumaige en quartier,
Lart, vergus, c'est toute richesse,
Trois et trois quart oeufs, trop se blesse,
Donne maintefois, tant est souls,
Aux estrangiers honnour l'adresse,
C'est Alixandre le poing clos.

He's rich as Alexander, but he's tight

I know a man who is a great spendthrift,
who digs successfully in every place he roams.
He's first to arrive at other people's homes
where he displays his generosity, his gift.
He asks for everything, and takes it, and he gives
nothing, except the eloquence by which he lives.
You want to pick him out on sight?
He's rich as Alexander, but he's tight.

He can reproach the cook, and he's not too proud
to go at host and hostess head to head
if they don't lay out an impressive spread.
He's keen to see their houses with a crowd;
unlimited supplies of food are his by right;
an empty pitcher must be filled at once with wine
. . . .
He's rich as Alexander, but he's tight.

At his own house there's nothing he won't spare;
he drinks cheap wine and eats dry bread, and as for cheese
he cuts in quarters whatever he can pare,
and there's all the lard and verjuice that you please,
and he quarters eggs and hands them out in threes.
and so runs wild, and ruins himself with appetite.
He seeks out strangers from a love of honor, he's
rich as Alexander, but he's tight.

Adieu Paris, adieu petiz pastez[39]

fol 225b Adieu m'amour, adieu douces fillettes,
Adieu Grant Pont, Hales, estuves, bains,
Adieu pourpoins, chauces, vestures nettes,
Adieu harnois tant clouez comme plains,
Adieu molz liz, broderie et beaus sens,
Adieu dances, adieu qui les hantez,
Adieu connins, perdriz que je reclaims,
Adieu Paris, adieu petiz pastez.

Adieu chapeaulx faiz de toutes flourettes,
Adieu bons vins, ypocras, doulz compains,
Adieu poisson de mer, d'eaue doucettes,
fol 225c Adieu moustiers ou l'en voit les doulz sains
Dont pluseurs sont maintefoiz chapellains,
Adieu deduit et dames qui chantez:
En Languedoc m'en vois comme contrains,
Adieu Paris, adieu petiz pastez.

Adieu, je suis des or sur espinettes
Car arrebours versera mes estrains.
Je pourray bien perdre mes amourettes
S'amour change pour estre trop loingtains.
Crotez seray, dessirez et dessains
Car le pars est destruit et gastez
Si diray lors pour reconfort au moins,
Adieu Paris, adieu petiz pastez.

Farewell to Paris, farewell my little pies

Farewell my love, farewell girls who are sweet,
farewell to the Great Bridge and Halles, and baths, and heat,
farewell to doublets, breeches, clothes that are clean,
farewell my armor, full of nails and studs,
farewell embroidery, white breasts, soft beds,
farewell to the dance and those who haunt the scene,
farewell to rabbit, partridge, on which I rhapsodize,
farewell to Paris, farewell my little pies!

Farewell to floral hats, and every flower arrayed,
farewell fine wine, spiced drink, good company,
farewell to fish from rivers and the sea,
farewell to churches where sweet saints have prayed
and often worked as chaplains, ministering,
farewell to pleasure, and to women who sing;
I'm sent to be constrained under Languedoc skies:
farewell to Paris, farewell my little pies!

Farewell, I'm pricked by anxiety, as you see,
because the hay has fallen off my cart.
I'll lose the *amourettes* who now love me
if hearts can change when lovers are apart.
I and my clothes will be dirty, torn, unlaced,
because the countryside has been laid waste.
And so I'll say, and you will sympathize,
farewell to Paris, farewell my little pies!

Pour ce vous lo porter quene de martre[40]

fol 226a Vous qui avez vostre teste pelée
Par accident ou de foible nature,
fol 226b Qui cheveulx a soit sa hure avalée;
Au lieu couvrir devez mettre cure;
Un pigne aiez toudis a l'aventure
Et chapelet pour le vent;
Voz crins derrier faictes venir devant
Se mestier est pour bien convoitier l'astre;
C'est grant meschief de deffubler souvent;
Pour ce vous lo porter queue de martre.

Car se martre est dessus le chief posée,
Les cheveulx fait tenir a leur droiture;
Pour ce en yver est la teste eschaufée
Et se puet l'en garder de la froidure
Et si ne puet percevoir creature
Le mehaing legierement;
Qui ainsi fait, il euvre saigement
Car a son chief fait gracieus emplastre;
Mais cilz est foulz qui le fait autrement;
Pour ce vous lo porter queue de martre.

Et se la teste est derrier desnuée
Et vous avez devant cheveleure,
La cosme doit derrier estre menée;
Adonc sera la besongne plus seure;
Aler devez a chevaulx l'embleure
Que voz crins n'aillent balant;
Deffublez vous toudis en avalant
Sanz rebourser qu'en voye l'emplastre
Ou vous serez diffamez laidement;
Pour ce vous lo porter queue de martre.

The best thing is a coon-skin cap, I'd say

You who are bald by accident, or through
foible of nature, here is what to do:
if you've a bald spot, flatten your hair down
and concentrate on covering up the place;
a comb should be kept handy, just in case;
in wind, a hat protects your crown;
bring hair at the back of the head fully into play
if dignity requires it for your family's sake.
To often take your hat off is a grave mistake;
the best thing is a coon-skin cap, I'd say.

For if a coon-skin cap is on the head
it keeps the hair where it should rightly be
and in the winter there is warmth instead
of one poor freezing unprotected head,
and—also—there'll be no one who can see
your affliction easily.
A man is wise indeed who acts this way,
who makes a gracious plaster his resource
but he's a fool who follows another course.
The best thing is a coon-skin cap, I'd say.

Now, if the back is where you have a spot,
and, of the hair in front, you have lost none,
you'll have to train the hair you still have got
backwards, and then the needed will be done.
When you go riding, let the pace be such
it won't blow hair too much;
when you dismount, remove your hat with care
so you don't show the world your plastered hair
or else your name will be in disarray.
The best thing is a coon-skin cap, I'd say.

Par mon conseil, refusez la a tous[41]

fol 233a "Compains, je suis en dolereus parti;
Belle femme ay et si l'aim loyaument;
Pour ce me plust qu'elle fust delez mi
Pour mon soulas et pour mon esbatement.
Or voy seigneurs qui trop communement
La me viennent pour festes empruncter;
Si je l'octroy, je ne fais que muser;
En refusant suis appelez jaloux;
Conseilliez moy comment j'en doy ouvrer."
"Par mon conseil, refusez la a tous."

"Vous dictes bien mais j'aray lors le cri
Que je mescroy ma femme aucunement.
Les emprunteurs diront: 'Vostre mari
Dame, vous fait blamer couvertement;
N'estes vous pas de bon gouvernement?
Oil, par Dieu!' Lors la feront errer,
Disans: 'Je croy qu'il vous veult enserrer;
Il ne deust pas suspeconner de vous.'
Elle plourra; comment puis je ordonner?"
"Par mon conseil, refusez la a tous."

"En bonne foy, chier compains, je languy;
Cure n'ay plus de tel empruntement;
VI ou VIII jours s'en va au virely
Dancer sanz moy ma femme en parement.
Si jaloux suis, venir puet autrement
Car li cucus pourra pour moy chanter;
Par telz empruns ne me puis exempter
Que sur la fin n'aie trop male toux."
"C'est donc le mieulx que de la refuser:
Par mon conseil, refusez la a tous."

L'envoy
fol 233b "Compains, par Dieu, de voz sens vueil user;
Dessus garder vueil ma femme et dessoubz."
"Faictes donc tant qu'om ne s'en puist ruser:
Par mon conseil, refusez la a tous."

"My advice to you is: do not let her go."

"My friend, my situation's bad, you know:
I have an attractive wife, and I love her so!
I'd like her to be more by my side, as it were;
My joy and consolation is to be with her.
But titled persons keep on saying, 'Sir,
may we borrow your wife to grace our party?' If
I agree to it, I lie here worried stiff,
but I get labelled jealous if I say no.
Advise me how to act: I want to know."
"My advice to you is: do not let her go."

"You're right, and wise, but then people will say
that I'm distrustful of her in some way.
The borrowers will say, 'Your husband, lady,
is out to make your reputation shady.
Can't you behave yourself? By God, you do!'
I believe that they will lead my wife astray.
'I think he wants to lock you up' they'll say.
'He shouldn't be suspicious about you.'
How can I set things right? She'll cry, I know."
"My advice to you is: do not let her go."

"In all good faith, dear friend, I'm in distress:
I don't like loaning her at such a rate.
My wife goes off to balls in a fancy dress
and dances for days without me—six or eight.
If I get jealous, things won't turn out the best
since the cuckoo's song won't give me any rest.
With loans like this I know I won't get off:
I, too, will end up catching some bad cough."
"The best thing is to give them a straight 'No!'
My advice to you is: do not let her go."

Envoy
"By God, my friend, you're here to tell me to
keep her both high and dry. I will do so."
"And make sure no one pulls some ruse on you:
my advice to you is: do not let her go."

Com viel roncin, mourir a la Saussoye[42]

fol 233b Plus sui muez en forme merveilleuse
Qu'Yo ne fut, qui en vache mua,
Ne qu'Antheus en la fourest doubteuse
Quant cerfs devint, qui d'angoisse sua
Devant ses chiens dont l'un mort le rua,
Pour la forme bestial qu'il avoit;
Mais j'ay trop pis: cheval suis, qui me voit,
Viel recreant dont nature s'esmaie
Et qui pis est, l'en m'envoie tout droit
Com viel roncin, mourir a La Saussoye.

Qu'est devenu ma force vertueuse?
Ou l'est le temps que mes corps s'esprouva?
Qu'est devenu ma jonesce joyeuse?
Ou est amour qui lors me gouverna?
Ou est un seul de ceuls qui lors m'ama?
Chascuns me fuit; nul d'eulx ne me congnoit
Car viellesce sanz cause me decoipt;
D'omme en cheval pour moy muer s'essaye
Qui me tramet desor comment qu'il soit
Com viel roncin, mourir a La Saussoye.

En ce lieu a mainte religieuse:
Beguinaige est que li roys y fonda;
Les dames ont de droit, et leur prieuse,
Les vieux chevaulx du roy; sont menez la
Quant usez sont, mais on leur coupera
fol 233c L'oreille avant; or ne scay que doit;
Je suis menez auques par cest endroit;
Cheval me sens; doleur n'est que je n'aye;
Aler me fault, se Dieux ne me pourvoie,
Com viel roncin, mourir a La Saussoye.

L'envoy
Hé, jeunes gens! Avisez par deca:
Vieulx devendrez; il n'est chose plus vraie.
Pensez de vous car lors l'en vous menrra
Com viel roncin, mourir a La Saussoye.

To die like some old nag at La Saussaye

I have acquired a shape more strange
than Io after she'd made the change
to cow, or Antaeus in the forest full of dread
when he became a sweating stag and fled
from his own dogs but still could not escape
the one that killed him in his transformed shape.
And I'm worse off: a horse is what's become of me,
a tired old shame of nature, as all can see.
And to compound it I'm being sent away
to die like some old nag at La Saussaye.

What happened to the time when I was fit?
The joy of youth! What has become of it?
And my great strength, where can that be?
Where is the love that ruled my will?
Of those who loved me then, who loves me still?
Not one of them admits to knowing me.
Old age betrays me and, without a cause,
it tries transforming me from man to horse—
and sells me down the river, come what may,
to die like some old nag at La Saussaye.

A large number of nuns live on that site:
the king established their community
and granted them, and their prioress, the right
to care for the king's old horses, which are shipped
there, worn out, after their ears are clipped.
And who knows what will happen to me?
I'm being led, somehow, off to that place.
I've had all kinds of pain; like a horse, I've run my race.
If God does not provide, I must be on my way
to die like some old nag at La Saussaye.

Envoy
Hey, youngsters! Learn from this, and I mean you:
you'll become old; nothing is more true.
Take heed! when your time comes you will be led away
to die like some old nag at La Saussaye.

Car vostre amour trop fort au cuer me touche[43]

fol 236b “Tredoulz amis, parlerez vous a moy,
Qui chascun jour sui pour vo fait tancée?”
“Dame, de qui?” “De mon pere, par foy,
Qui me met sus que je suis fiancée.”
“A qui?” “A vous.” “Onques n’y oy pensée
Fors par honour, du gré de voz amis.”
“Je vous en croy; ma mere m’a amis
Que vous m’avez baisiée enmi la bouche.
Ce scavez vous, ne me chaut de leurs dis,
Car vostre amour trop fort au cuer me touche.

Mais l’en m’a dit de vous je scay bien quoy;
Pour ce est vers vous ma mere forsenée,
Que vous avez autre amie en requoy
Dont vous voulez faire vostre espousée;
Je seroie contre raison moquée,
Et bien scavez que vous m’avez promis.”
“N’en creez riens; ceuls sont mes ennemis
Qui ce dient pour moy faire reprouche;
De voz parlers suis forment esbahis,
fol 236c Car vostre amour trop fort au cuer me touche.”

“Puis qu’ainsis est, a vous du tout m’octroy;
Mais fort sera que vous soye donnée
De mes parens, car a chascun dire oy
Que vostre amour est trop habandonnée;
Je n’en puis mais; je l’ay belle trouvée.
Se vous estes de mon pere escondis,
Maintenez bien que vostre suis toudis;
Ne vous chaille se pere ou mere grouche;
Au fort diray vous estes mes plevis
Car vostre amour trop fort au cuer me touche.”

Because your love is deep within my heart

"Sweetheart, will you come and talk with me?
I'm being chided every day because of you."
"My lady love! By whom?" "It's father. He
accuses me of having got engaged." "To?" "You."
"I swear to you I wouldn't dream of it
unless your family thought that I was fit."
"I trust you. But my mother scolds, calls me a tart;
she says you've kissed my mouth. But, anyway,
you know I don't care what they say
because your love is deep within my heart.

But I've been told of something they say is true—
which would explain why mother's furious with you.
It's said you have another girl, and you intend
for her to be the one you'll marry in the end,
and I'll be mocked, though that's absurd
since, as you know, you've given me your word."
"Don't you believe them; people such as these
just want to cause me trouble; they're my enemies.
I am astounded at the news that you impart
because your love is deep within my heart."

"In that case I can give myself to you.
But it will still be difficult to get
my parents to give their consent as yet
since people say you're free with love. They do.
But I can't help it, since I love you so.
If you're turned down by father, tell him you
will be, for all eternity, my beau.
Don't let my parent's grumbling scare you. Play your part,
and I'll say you're the one I gave my promise to
because your love is deep within my heart."

Balade 911 (cont'd)

"En telz dangiers trop petit me congnois;
Ce qui est mien demander ne m'agrée;
Ce n'est qu'oneur, voire, mais c'est anoy;
Vostre ami suis et vous estes m'amée;
Ja ne vueillez estre femme clamée,
Car en telz cas est chascuns asservis;
Franche vivez en amour, je frans vis;
Des mariez servitute s'aprouche."
"Vous dictes voir, or demourons ainsis,
Car vostre amour trop fort au cuer me touche.

L'envoy
Adieu, Picart." "Adieu, douce Bietrix;
A ce depart fault que je vous atouche;
Baisier vous vueil; soufrez vous; c'est trop amis
Car vostre amour trop fort au cuer me touche."

Balade 911 (cont'd)

"Such trivial dangers are not where I shine;
I never like to ask for what is mine;
it may be what's expected but I will get,
since I am yours and you are mine, upset.
Surely you don't want to be a wife:
In all these cases everyone has strife.
Be free, and live in love, as I am free.
There's servitude in marriage from the start."
"I see what you are saying, so we'll just be,
because your love is deep within my heart.

Envoy
Goodbye, Picart." "Goodbye, sweet Beatrice.
I must come close to you before we part.
I want to kiss you. You are kind. We kiss
because your love is deep within my heart."

J'estoie trop mal imformez[44]

fol 236c "Cergens, prenez moy ce larron;
Trop est de male renommée!"
fol 236d "Voluntiers: venez en prinson
Puis que la chose est commandée."
"Je n'ay meffait a ame née;
Que je parle au prevost a part."
"Adieu! Il est huimais trop tart."
"Je lui diray se vous voulez."
"E que n'a il ou coul la hart?
J'estoie trop mal imformez."

"Veoir vous veult; il y fait bon."
"Alons y, mais pres de l'entrée
Retournez; tesmoin n'y voulon."
"Lierres, par la vierge honourée,
Vo gueule sera estranglée!
Je vous livreray au frappart."
"Prevost, pour Dieu, aiez regart
A cent frans que vez ci; tenez;
Je suis prodoms." "C'est vray, Colart:
J'estoie trop mal imformez.

Je m'en revois en no maison.
Sergens, reslargissiez l'entrée
De ce varlet; c'est un prodom."
"Par la char Dieu, c'est grant fumée!
C'estoit un larron a l'entrée,
Mais en tant d'eure qu'il espart,
Faictes d'un larron papelart;
En po de temps gens reformez."
"Cilz ci n'a pas mangié le lart:
J'estoie trop mal imformez."

I wasn't well-informed, as it turns out

"Officers of the Court! That man there is of bad
repute! So get him for me, will you?" "Glad
to do it. Custody for you, my lad!
Orders are to put you in the hole."
"But I haven't harmed a living soul.
Let me talk in private to the judge."
"By God, it's now too late to budge."
"If you won't do it, I can raise a shout."
"Where's rope for the neck of this layabout?
I wasn't well-informed, as it turns out."

"OK, he wants to see you." "Good; let's go,
but stay back near the entrance so
there won't be any witnesses."
"Hey, thief! By all the Blessed Virgin blesses,
I'll see your dirty face being strangled; I
will hand you to the hangman by and by."
"Hey, Judge! have a look, for heaven's sake,
at the hundred francs I've brought for you to take;
I am an honest man." "Colart, no doubt,
I wasn't well-informed, as it turns out.

I'm on my way; I'm going home; it's late.
Officers of the court! please open up the gate
and let this guy out; he's an honest man."
"By the body of God! what's going on?
He was a crook when he came in,
but quick as a flash the crook is gone,
and he becomes a model citizen.
In such short time, you bring reforms about!"
"The one who got the bacon's not this con.
I wasn't well-informed, as it turns out."

Chanson Royale 912 (cont'd)

"Or me dictes comment fait on
Si tost prodomme a la volée
D'un murdrier, d'un mauves garcon?"
"Quant son innocence est trouvée;
Par cent tesmoings l'a cilz prouvée;
Saichiez, ce n'est pas un coquart;
Dire ne scaroie le quart
fol 237a Des biens qui sont en lui trouvez;
Ne m'en enquerez plus, Lietart;
J'estoie trop mal imformez."

"A tout le moins, qui paiera mon
Salaire de celle journée?"
"Souffrez vous, sergent, j'en respon;
Tenez dix soulz." "Pas ne m'agrée."
"Vous avez tort; c'est grant boursée;
Je les preste, se Dieu me gart."
"Vo bourse est devenue happart
Puisque les larrons y pandez!"
"Souffrez vous, car par Saint Lienart,
J'estoie trop mal imformez.

L'envoy
Sergens!" "Maistre!" "Nous delivron
Ce varlet qui fut arrestez.
Voist a Dieu." "C'est assez raison:
Vous estiez trop mal imformez."

Chanson Royale 912 (cont'd)

"Tell me, how was it you created
this honest man? Is it possible for you
to remake a murderer, and so quickly, too?"
"His innocence was amply demonstrated.
A hundred witnesses say it is so.
He's certainly no fool, you know.
I couldn't begin to tell you a quarter
of the good you can find in him if you search about.
Lietart, no more questioning of this order:
I wasn't well-informed, as it turns out."

"Nonetheless, who's going to pay
the wages of the work I did today?"
"Be quiet, officer. I'll do as I see fit:
here are ten sous." "That's not enough, as you know."
"You're wrong, it's quite a lot of dough.
God save me, but I'm giving it."
"Your purse must be equipped with hooks
to hang from it so many crooks."
"Accept things! By St. Leonard, there's no doubt
I wasn't well-informed, as it turns out.

Envoy
Officers!" "My Lord." "We're setting free
the guy who was detained. And may God be
with him." "That there are reasons, who could doubt?
You were not well-informed, as it turns out."

C'est de dancier au son des chalemiaulx[45]

fol 240a Des merveilles de quoy on puet parler
Et qui cheent en raison de nature
Qu'om puet veoir deca et dela mer
Treuve on bien cause et certaine figure,
Pourquoy se font; mais une est trop obscure
Entre les gens et aux festes royaulx;
La ne voit on sens, raison ne mesure:
C'est de dancier au son des chalemiaux.

Car un soufleur qui commence a soufler
En une piau cornant la turelure
Fait entour lui mainte gent assembler
Qui de joie n'ont a celle heure cure;
Com hors du sens sautent a desmesure,
Balans des piez, des mains et des trumeaulx;
La ne voit on sens, raison ne mesure;
C'est de dancier au son des chalemiaux.

Sotie est grant d'ainsi gens demener
Au son d'un foul; encor plus grant laidure
D'euls tenir coiz quant on laisse a corner;
Vous ne verrez lors mouvoir creature;
Le vent n'est rien nul proufit n'y procure
Fors le soufleur, gent qui fait telz aviaulx;
La ne voit on raison, sens ne mesure;
C'est de dancier au son des chalemiaulx.

L'envoy
Prince, l'en puet en tout cause trouver
Des ars mondains, excepté du dancer
fol 240b Aux instrumens des hommes bestiaulx
Qui par leur son font les gens enchanter
Et hors du sens maintefois ressembler;
C'est de dancier au son des chalemiaux.

I mean the dancing when the bagpipes play

If we consider all those mysteries
to which our reason grants a natural cause,
and which are seen both here and overseas,
and can be well explained by clear-cut laws,
there's one among these wonders gives us pause
when it occurs at royal festivities.
There is no sense or wit or measure here, I say:
I mean the dancing when the bagpipes play.

Whenever any piper starts to puff
into his bag, and the pipes begin to sound,
he brings a great crowd round him soon enough,
but it's not for joy alone they gather round.
They jump as if demented and the place they meet
fills up with hands and legs and flying feet.
There is no sense or wit or measure here, I say:
I mean the dancing when the bagpipes play.

These people must be in some mindless cult
of lunatic musicians. It's even difficult
when they have fallen silent, when all that piping stops
although no creature then so much as hops.
This blowing is just worthless wind except
these revels seem to keep the piper kept.
There is no sense or wit or measure here, I say:
I mean the dancing when the bagpipes play.

Envoy
Prince, there are explanations to be found
for every art, but not this dance around
an instrument of savages which has a sound
that seems to hold the people in its sway
and make them act in this demented way:
I mean the dancing when the bagpipes play.

Ja sur mon corps n'en cherroit une goute[46]

Se tout li cielz estoit de fueilles d'or,
Et li airs fust estellez d'argent fin,
Et tous les vens fussent plains de tresor,
Et les goutes fussent toutes flourin
D'eaue de mer, et pleust soir et matin
Richesces, biens, honeurs, joyauls, argent,
Tant que remplissent en feu toute la gent,
La terre aussi en fust moilliée toute,
Et fusse nuz, de tel pluie et tel vent
Ja sur mon corps n'en cherroit une goute.

Et qui pis est, vous puis bien dire encor
Que qui donrroit trestout l'avoir du Rin,
Et fusse la, vaillant un harenc sor
N'en venrroit pas vers moy vailant un frelin;
Onques ne fuy de nul donneur a fin;
Biens me default, tout mal me vient souvent;
Se j'ay mestier de rien, on le me vent
Plus qu'il ne vault, de ce ne faictes doubte.
Se beneurté plouvoit du firmament
Ja sur mon corps n'en cherroit une goute.

Et se je pers, ja n'en aray restor;
Quant rien requier, on chante de Basin;
Se je faiz bien, neant plus que d'un tor
N'est congneu; tousjours sui je Martin
Qui coste avoit, chaperon et roucin,
Pain et paine, congnoissance ensement,
Son temps usa, mais trop dolentement,
Car plus povre n'ot de lui en sa route.
Je sui cellui que s'il plouvoit pyment
Ja sur mon corps n'en cherroit une goute.

L'envoy
Princes, ii poins font ou riche ou meschant:
Eur et meseur, l'un aime et l'autre doubte;
Car s'il [povoit] plouvoir mondainement,
Ja sur mon corps n'en cherroit une goute.

Not a single drop, not one, would fall on me

If all the sky were made of pure gold leaf,
and the air all starred with silver filigree,
and all the winds brought treasures beyond belief,
and every drop of water in the sea
a florin, and it rained down night and day
more riches, honors and goods than you could say
and the earth soaked too, and everyone quite free
to take and take until they were satiated,
and in that wind and rain I stood stark naked,
not a single drop, not one, would fall on me.

And what is worse, and I'm the one who's telling,
if all the treasure of the Rhine were given away
and I were there, not even a pickled herring,
no, not a single farthing, would come my way.
I've never fled a giving man; goods flee
from my poor self, ill-fortune seeks me out;
if I need anything, it's sold to me
for more than it's worth, that cannot be in doubt.
If luck rained down from heaven above you'd see
not a single drop, not one, would fall on me.

And if something's lost, I never get it back;
when I ask for anything, they sing me an old song;
if I do good, they cut me no more slack
than if it were a crime; I'm always the sad sack
to whom only a gown, and a hood, and a nag belong,
and bread and sweat, and who accepts this grand design,
and uses up his time so cheerlessly,
for no one is so poor in all his company.
So this is who I am: if it rained spiced wine
not a single drop, not one, would fall on me.

Envoy
Princes, two things determine wealth or poverty:
Good luck, and bad; and one I love, and fear the other one
because, if all good things on earth fell down as rain,
not a single drop, not one, would fall on me.

Dieux nous vueille garder et Nostre Dame![47]

Charongne a vers, povre fragilité,
Qui puez estre comparée a la rose
Qui est boutons et naist ou temps d'esté
Enmi le jour s'espanit, lors desclose
Odoure un pou et plaist, mais la nuit close,
Flour et bouton et rose est amatie:
En mains d'un jour est sa beauté perie;
Certes autel est il d'omme et de femme;
En un moment perdons corps, ame et vie:
Dieux nous vueille garder et Nostre Dame!

Ne muert enfans en sa plus grant beauté,
Femme en jouvent, homs aussi? Comment ose
Orgueil avoir, fors que simplicité
Et craindre Dieu? Comme trespo de chose
De fer, de fust ou de fievre l'enosse
Un povres vers, yraingne ou orillie,
Le mors d'un chien ou beste qui le lie
Le fait mourir et mettre soubz la lame
En moins de temps que flour n'est espanie.
Dieux nous vueille garder et Nostre Dame!

Las! que nous vault nostre grant parenté,
Noz grans palais, nostre grant cité close,
Noz grans tresors, li regne conquesté,
Force de corps, nostre sens et la glose:
Tout ce ne puet deffendre nostre fosse.
Sanson est mort, Alixandre et Urie,
Crises, David, Salemon, Jheremie,
Et tuit mourrons en paiant celle drame.
Es biens mondains ne soit nulz qui se fie:
Dieux nous vueille garder et Nostre Dame!

L'envoy
Prince et seigneur, ne vous confiez mie,
Ne homs mortelz, en chose qui varie.
Le corps mourra; or pensons donc de l'ame,
De Dieu servir et la vierge Marie,
Ou autrement nostre gloire est perie:
Dieux nous vueille garder et Nostre Dame!

God save us! May the Virgin intercede!

Carrion for worms, a poor fragility
which may be likened to a rose,
a bud born in the summer which we see
appearing with the dawn, then blooming to disclose
its scent and pleasure; but, as day must close
with night, the bud, the flower, the rose will be
no more: its beauty only lasts a day or so,
and men and women are the same, as we all know.
Then body, soul and life are gone indeed.
God save us! May the Virgin intercede!

At their height of loveliness, haven't children died
and men and women in their youth? Can we have pride
or anything except humility
and fear of God? How small the thing can be
of iron or wood or fever in the bone,
a little worm, an earwig, spider, these alone,
the bite of a dog or beast, are all we need,
these are enough to stretch us in the tomb
in less time than it takes a flower to bloom.
God save us! May the Virgin intercede!

Alas, what use is noble ancestry,
great mansions, city walls, a treasury
that's large, conquered kingdoms, or great
strength of mind or body, the power to discriminate?
None of these things defend us from the grave.
Samson is dead, and Alexander and Uriah,
and Croesus, David, Solomon and Jeremiah;
we pay our penny, and are perishing
Let no one trust in any worldly thing.
God save us! May the Virgin intercede!

Envoy
My Prince and Lord, don't put your trust in mortal men;
don't put your faith in things which cannot last.
The body dies. Let us consider, then,
the good of the soul, or else our glory's past.
Serve God and serve Our Lady in word and deed.
God save us! May the Virgin intercede!

Faictes sur ce vo jugement[48]

fol 270a "A vous, maistre d'ostel, me plain
Du ventre Jehan de Saint Symon,
Car il a fait son sac si plain
Que je n'ay jambes ne talon
Qui puist souffrir tel estalon
Ne moy porter." "Et qui es tu?"
"Certes, je suis son graile cu,
Qui l'ay servi treslonguement;
Or est trop pesant devenu;
Faictes sur ce vo jugement.

"Trop s'emplist le soir et le main
De char de buef et de mouton;
Toudis a le voirre en la main;
Tant boit qu'il en devient breton;
Perdriz n'est, connim ne chapon
Qui ne soit par lui retenu;
Il vole au gros et au menu;
Maint brouet chascun jour respant;
Du servir ne suis plus tenu:
fol 270b Faictes sur ce vo jugement.

"Il semble que je soye un nain
Au regart du ventre felon;
De sa courroie me complain,
De sa tasse et de la facon;
Le martel semble d'un macon;
Son poys me fait estre bossu,
Et je ne suy pas si fessu
Que je fu anciennement;
Plus ne vueil servir tel pensu:
Faictes sur ce vo jugement.

L'envoy
"Maistres d'ostel, je suis perdu
Se par vous ne suis secouru;
Je ne puis durer longuement;
Faictes jeuner ce malostru;
Donnez lui eaue et orge cru:
Faictes sur ce vo jugement."

And this requires a clear decision from you

"Hey! housekeeper! I simply must complain
about Jean de Saint Simon's belly, or, rather, pot.
He's stuffed its bag so full it's got
to the point where my poor legs and heels are numb
from such a weight, and cannot bear the strain."
"And may I ask from whom does this voice come?"
"The honest truth is, I'm his tiny butt
and I've been in his service a long time. But
his weight is now too much; it's something new,
and this requires a clear decision from you.

"All he does, morning and night, is stuff
his beef and mutton in, and he drinks enough—
he always has a glass in hand—to get
as drunk as any Breton. There
is not a partridge or a capon or a hare
which has escaped his clutch as yet.
He steals from the great and from the humble, too.
Every day he pours down soup and stew;
You can't expect me to keep serving as I do,
but this requires a clear decision from you.

"I know I look a dwarf compared to that
unruly belly and its rolls of fat.
And let me bitch about his scrotum—balls to you—
and his breeches, and the doings that they do.
His hammer looks as if it could break stones in two.
Its weight has brought a hump to me,
and I'm not as chubby as I used to be.
And as for his pot-belly, I will not
be in service any longer to that pot.
But this requires a clear decision from you.

Envoy
"Housekeeper, I'll soon be a thing of the past
if I don't get some kind of help from you.
Just how much longer do you think I'll last?
Please put this lout on an extended fast;
raw barley and some water should see him through,
but this requires a clear decision from you."

En tous temps fait bon couchier a par soy[49]

fol 271a On dit qu'il fait bon avoir compaignie,
Mais on mains cas s'en pass'on de legier;
Uns glous la fuit quant il a glotonnie;
Tous seulz vouldroit sa viande mangier;
Homs en grace vouldroit autre estrangier,
Sanz compaignon estre et demourer seulx;
Compaignie vouldroit bien uns tigneux,
Et homs blasmez pour un qu'ilz fussent troy;
Ne scay comment gent dorment deux et deux;
En tous temps fait bon couchier a par soy.

Prouver le puis par maint qui se marie;
Quant il fait chaut et il sent le dangier
De femme avoir qui l'esvente et tarie
Ou s'il fait froit qui le veult approuchier;
Lors le convient coudre, poindre et brochier
Ou cuirien et restouper les treux
Ou il orra maint mot suspeconneux;
Adonc voulsist plus estre seulx que doy;
Lors de certain dit, sans estre doubteux,
En tous temps fait bon couchier a par soy.

Tenez vous donc que ce soit bonne vie
fol 271b De deux et deux communement couchier?
L'un veult couvrir, l'autre ne le veult mie
Si ne se puet ne l'un ne l'autre aisier;
L'un veult dormir, l'autre veult divisier;
Contraires sont, descouvers et fruilleux;
La rongne en vient, la toux, boces et cloux,
Si vault trop mieulx chascun en son recoy
Dormir a part, pour le moins perilleux;
En tous temps fait bon couchier a par soy.

L'envoy
Princes, moult fault scavoir de l'escremie,
A couchier deux, soit ami ou amie,
Car trop de plaiz et de dangiers y voy;
Robe tirer toute nuit anuitie
Sanz reposer; pour ce, quoy que nul die,
En tous temps fait bon couchier a par soy.

It is, at all times, best to sleep alone

Most people claim it's good to have company,
but when we are alone, we're often glad to be.
A glutton, when he's in an eating mood,
prefers to be alone with his heaps of food.
When someone is in favor, he is distant
from friends and others who might be persistant.
Men in disgrace, and those with lousy skin,
like company, so it can hedge them in.
How can you sleep in someone else's zone?
It is, at all times, best to sleep alone.

I give you the case of many a married man.
He senses danger from his wife; it's hot;
she fans him, and requires what he has got.
And when it's cold she cuddles up, tells him he can
stitch her, sew her, put the needle in her hide,
and fill in every hole, or she'll be snide
and he'll be pricked by many a barbed remark.
Single is better than the twosome of this ark
and he won't hesitate to say so, with a groan:
it is, at all times, best to sleep alone.

Now tell me, do you really think the strife
of sleeping with another makes for a happy life?
One wants the blankets off; the other, on;
and so, the ease of both of them is gone.
One wants to talk, the other wants to sleep.
Cold and uncovered, strife is all they reap.
This brings the plague, a cough, and boils, and itch.
It's better to just curl up on your own
and sleep in safety, there in your own niche.
It is, at all times, best to sleep alone.

Envoy
Prince, sleeping with a partner in your bed
is combat, hand to hand, no matter who.
The fact of the matter is, as I have said,
bed-clothes are hauled about the whole night through.
Whatever people claim, rest is unknown.
It is, at all times, best to sleep alone.

"Sire, souviengne vous de moy"[50]

fol 271c Chascuns se prant a amender
Et se confesse chascun jour;
En conseillant vont demander
Pluseurs argent a leur seigneur,
Li grant, ly moien, li menour,
Soit a duc, a prince ou a roy,
Ne font que dire sanz sejour:
"Sire, souviengne vous de moy.

Faictes mes lettres commander;
Parlez au Flament en destour;
Vueillez les generaulx mander
Que paiez soye sanz retour."
Et l'autre dit pour le meillour:
fol 271d "De voz cofres plus brief n'y voy."
Chascun fait ainsi sa clamour:
"Sire, souviengne vous de moy."

Par derrier la table au disner
Et a leur souper vont a leur tour
Les compaignons pour confesser
L'un apres l'autre et font leur plour;
On les rassoult de leur folour;
Response ont souvent troy et troy,
Disans partans, plains de dolour:
"Sire, souviengne vous de moy."

L'envoy
Prince, puis qu'om veult Dieu doubter
Et sa conscience ordonner
Encor sera bonne la loy;
Chascuns va pour soy dolouser
Vers vous en disant ce parler:
"Sire, souviengne vous de moy."

"My lord, remember me"

Everyone aspires to a higher self
and goes to confession seven times a week.
Help is what many seem to seek
as they go ask their patron for some pelf.
The least, the middling and the great
keep saying, early and late,
to duke, prince, king or other pedigree:
"My lord, remember me.

Please have my letters of payment sent;
speak privately to Monsieur Le Flament;
order the treasurers not to delay;
make sure payment goes through."
And the other one, of course, will say:
"I see no payment here from you."
This is the way each man will make his plea:
"My lord, remember me."

And even at lunch and dinner, everyone
sneaks from their table one by one;
to go and say a prayer, and to confess
to all the sorrows they express.
They get an absolution for their mistakes
but the answers may confuse, and then each takes
leave in grief, saying as they flee:
"My lord, remember me."

Envoy
Prince, the fact that the fear of God still gives
people's consciences a tweak
proves that religion lives.
Everyone goes off to make his plea
to you, and these are the words they speak:
"My lord, remember me."

Pour l'amour Dieu, envoiez moy requerre[51]

fol 273b Depuis le jour que des dames parti
Et que je fus boutez en bailliaige,
Joie, deduit n'eus, ne joieux parti,
Bien ne doucour fors que doleur et raige,
Matin lever, contrefaire le saige,
Oir plaider et rendre jugemens,
Seoir toudis et escoutez les gens;
La suis plentez comme ydole de terre.
Aiez pitié dames de mes tourmens:
Pour l'amour Dieu, envoiez moy requerre.

Car il n'est bien que puist avoir bailli,
Mais li convient oir de dur langaige;
De pluseurs est par derriere assailli
Pour faire droit ou garder l'eritaige
De son seigneur et s'omme de paraige
Muert pour ses maulx, hais est des parens;
Se juges faint, lors s'est il parjurens;
Nul tel estat ne doit ja frans cuers querre,
Car c'est de vie uns grans abregemens:
Pour l'amour Dieu, envoiez moy requerre.

Hostel de roy et de royne autressi
En voz deux cours a plus joieux usaige,
Plus franchement y vit l'en, Dieu merci,
Las! Dolereus et pour quoy vous lessai ge?
De cest escript faiz vers vous mon messaige,
Soiez de moy, mes dames, souvenans;
fol 273c Damoiselles, a vous me recommans;
Pour mon depart de vous li cuers me serre;
Se par vous n'est, je mourray languissans:
Pour l'amour Dieu, envoiez moy requerre.

L'envoy
Noble princesse, humblement vous suppli
Que je vous serve; autrefoiz vous servi;
De la doleur m'ostez qui trop m'enserre,
Car je suis ja presque tout amorty,
Se n'y pourveez briefment, je languy:
Pour l'amour Dieu, envoiez moy requerre.

For the love of God, have me recalled to court

Ever since the day I took my leave
of the ladies, kicked to this distant bailiwick,
I've lost all joy and pleasure; I've been sick
with grief and pain; they give me no reprieve;
from early morning I am in assize,
hear cases, render judgment, imitate the wise,
always in session, hearing what people say;
I'm planted there like some idol made of clay.
Have pity, ladies, I am so distraught:
for the love of God, have me recalled to court.

A bailiff has no pleasure, he is just
obliged to hear harsh words. A bailiff must,
if he protects an owner or tries to act
with justice, expect to be attacked
from behind; if he puts some important man
to death for crimes, he's hated by that clan,
but if he hides the truth he breaks the law:
it's a post no decent person should aim for;
it takes the years away, it cuts life short:
for the love of God, have me recalled to court.

The king's court, and the queen's court, too, is where
a happy normal life is to be found;
people live in greater freedom there,
thank God. Alas! Why did I leave you, bound
for the dumps? This note delivers my message: do
keep me, my ladies, in your every thought;
young women, I commend myself to you;
I left, and now my heart is broken; I am blue;
I languish, dying; you're my last resort:
for the love of God, have me recalled to court.

Envoy
My noble princess, I am begging you
to put me in your service as before.
I'm in despair at what I'm going through;
my courage fades away; I have no more.
I'll perish. You must quickly give support:
for the love of God, have me recalled to court.

A gens qui sont en maladie[52]

fol 325b Qui veult paix et repos avoir
En maladie et en destour,
Ce puet bien cilz appercevoir
Qui a Fymes gist en la tour,
Car la se logent tout autour
Choes, cahuans, estourneaulx,
Grans corbes, suettes, moyneaulx,
Qui sanz cesser y font grant bruit,
Aucuns de jour, autres de nuit.
C'est une estrange melodie
fol 325c Qui ne semble pas grant deduit
A gens qui sont en maladie.

Premiers les corbes font scavoir
Pour certain si tost qu'il est jour;
De fort crier font leur povoir
Le gros, le gresle sanz sejour;
Mieulx vauldroit le son d'un tabour
Que telz cris de divers oyseaulx.
Puis vient la proie, vaches, veaulx,
Crians, muyans, et tout ce nuit,
Quant on a le cervel trop vuit;
Joint de moustier la sonnerie
Qui tout l'entendement destruit
A gens qui sont en maladie.

A souleil couchant sur le soir
Deslogent de leur carrefour
Cahuans, suettes, pour voir,
Qui chantent chans plains de tristour;
Toute la nuit font grant freour
Aux veillans: de mort sont appeaulx;
Lors doubtent malades leurs peaulx.
Sages est qui tel logis fuit;
De dormir n'y a sauf conduit;
Puces font la dure escramie
Et tous les vens, c'est lieu mal duit
A gens qui sont en maladie.

By those who are gripped by malady

Those wanting peace and quiet
in sickness and in solitude
will find them with great ease
by sleeping in Fismes castle,
for all around that place
live jackdaws, brown owls, starlings,
great crows, screech owls, sparrows,
making an endless din,
some by day, others by night.
It's a strange melody
not appreciated much
by those who are gripped by malady.

First, the crows are sure
to speak as day dawns;
they shriek, hard as they can,
large and small, with no break;
the beat of drums is better
than all these bird-calls.
Then cattle come, cows, calves,
crying, lowing, all night,
when one's mind is void;
then church bells join in
destroying all sanity
of those who are gripped by malady.

At sunset, as evening falls,
they emerge from meeting-places:
brown owls, and screech owls too,
singing plaintive songs,
bringing dread all night,
hints of death, to the sleepless,
the sick who fear for their skin.
The wise avoid such lodging
where sleep is uncertain
and fleas fight vigorously,
as do all winds, a place unfit
for those who are gripped by malady.

Balade 1202 (cont'd)

L'envoy
Princes, saichent toutes et tuit
Qu'Eustace imformé et instruit
Sui de tout ce que je publie
Par III moys dont le cuers me cuit.
C'est froit hostel et mal reduit
fol 325d A gens qui sont en maladie.

Balade 1202 (cont'd)

Envoy
Prince, make clear to each and all:
Eustache has been told and taught
all that is here recorded publicly
by three months of buffetings.
It's a frosty lodge, an evil inn, for
those who are gripped by malady.

Atten encor jusqu'a demain[53]

fol 333d "Pour Dieu, donnez maille ou denier
A ce povre qui ne voit goute."
"Va t'en sanz chandoille couchier;
D'ardoir ton lit es hors de doubte."
"Ha! Sire, je ne menjus goute;
Aler ne puis par maladie."
"Tu ne doiz donc point de chaucie;
Saint Mor ne te fera fremir."
"Sire, je ne puis gesir;
Donnez moy pour avoir du pain."
"Tu as d'estre droit bon loisir:
Atten encor jusqu'a demain."

"A! Doulz Sires, ne puis durer;
Mon chief pers, le bras et le coutte."
"Du coustel ne pourras fraper;
D'amende paier n'aiez doubte."
"A! Sire, j'ay la jambe route."
"Or fay qu'elle soit reboulie;
Pran aucun drapel si la lie."
"Sire, je ne faiz que languir;
Donnez moy: pense de mourir."
"Tout seroit perdu en ta main."
"Helas! Vueillez moy secourir."
"Atten encor jusqu'a demain."

"Saint Anthoine me vent trop chier
fol 334a Son mal; le feu ou corps me boute."
"D'achater buche n'as mestier;
Fay ton lit en Seine et ta couste
Pour refroider." "Sire, j'ay goute
De saint Mor." "Ne la retien mie."
"Sire, je suy en frenaisie."
"Donques te doit chascuns fuir."
"Doulz Sires, j'ay tant a souffrir
Que je ne dor ne soir ne main;
Vueillez moy quelque chose offrir."
"Atten encor jusqu'a demain."

Keep waiting for tomorrow

"For God's sake give a farthing or if you can,
a penny to a completely blind poor man."
"To bed without a candle, I've heard said,
preserves from fear of burning up your bed."
"Ah, Lord! I've eaten nothing; please!
I cannot move because of this disease."
"So there's no tolls you'll have to pay,
and St. Maur's gout won't hold you in its sway."
"My Lord, I can't lie down to rest my head;
give me a little something to buy bread."
"You've plenty of time to stretch out in your sorrow:
keep waiting for tomorrow."

"Ah, sweet my Lord! I can't endure another day;
My head and arm and elbow waste away."
"So you'll be saved, since you can't jab a knife,
from paying fines for getting into strife."
"My Lord! This leg of mine, I've broken it."
"You've got to see that it heals up a bit
so bind it, go and find a rag and cord."
"I feel my life just wastes away, my Lord;
make me a gift: think of death's sting."
"So it's a waste to give you anything."
"Alas! Please help me in my sorrow!"
"Keep waiting for tomorrow."

"Saint Anthony has charged too much to hire
his illness out; it covers me with fire."
"So you've no need for wood, and don't complain
since there's a bed and pillow in the Seine
to cool you off." "My Lord, I have the gout
of good St. Maur," "Then give it back, you lout."
"My lord, I believe I'm going mad."
"Then we should try avoiding you, my lad."
"Sweet Lord, I've suffered more than I can say;
I cannot sleep at night, or in the day;
please give a little something for my sorrow."
"Keep waiting for tomorrow."

Balade 1230 (cont'd)

L'envoy
"Princes, je ne me puis aidier."
"Nulz te doit donc avoir chier,
Car l'en te feroit bien en vain."
"Sire, j'ay le mal saint Riquier;
Donnez moy, pour Dieu, le requier."
"Atten encor jusqu'a demain."

Balade 1230 (cont'd)

Envoy
"Prince! I'm a completely helpless man."
"So no one should concern themselves with you
since helping is a useless thing to do."
"My Lord, Saint Riquier has sent a fever; can
you make me a gift: for the sake of God, and sorrow."
"Keep waiting for tomorrow."

Si j'en puis nullement finer[54]

fol 334b J'ay mon mari qui se rigole
De moy et s'en va jardinant
Avecques mainte femme fole
Chascun jour ou le plus souvent
Et ne me tient pas bien couvent
Mais me sert d'estrange langaige
fol 334c Et puis qu'il me fait tel oultraige
Je lui feray sanz jardiner
Avoir cucu en son mesnaige
Si j'en puis nullement finer.

Car j'ay assez qui m'en escole
Et qui ses faiz m'est rapportant
Et comment il baise et acole
Les fillettes et va donnant
Nostre avoir; tel vie est menant
Dont il ne fait mie que saige;
Mais je pourverray a ma caige
D'un oisel pour moy conforter
Qui appaisera mon couraige
Si j'en puis nullement finer.

Ouil, par Dieu! Maint m'en parole
Qui me va cuer et corps offrant.
Je ne suy ne laide ne mole
Dont il me dust estre laissant;
J'en trouveray bien pour un cent.
Puis qu'il brise son mariage
Par Saint Arnoul, aussi feray je.
D'autel pain vueil souppes tremper
Et prandre de ce doulz ouvraige
Si j'en puis nullement finer.

L'envoy
Prince amoureux, qui fait tel raige
En amours s'on lui rent tel gaige,
Vous n'en devez nullui blamer
Et pour ce par mon pucellaige
Prendray ce bien qui assouaige
Si j'en puis nullement finer.

If it's the final thing I do

I have a husband who is mocking me
by getting laid, by going off
with many women who do that type of thing,
each day, or very often anyhow,
and so he doesn't keep his pledge to me,
but since he treats me in this dreadful way
I'll raise for him, without his getting to plough,
a cuckoo to have in his nest
if it's the final thing I do.

I've heard about it all from many people
who tell me stories of what he's been doing,
and how he kisses and embraces
the girls, and how he goes off spending
what's ours; that is the life he leads,
which isn't doing something wise;
but I'll be able to provide my cage
with a small bird to comfort me,
and this will make my spirits calm
if it's the final thing I do.

Oh yes, by God! Men speak to me
and offer me their bodies and their hearts.
I am not ugly, and haven't spread too much,
so he had no reason to let go of me;
I'll find, for sure, a hundred in exchange.
Since he is breaking up our marriage,
then by Saint Arnoul I will do it, too.
I'll dip the same bread in the soup
and take a taste of that sweet work
if it's the final thing I do.

Envoy
Prince Cupid, those who commit such crimes
of love must then be made to pay;
there should be no reproach for this by you
and so I swear by my own maidenhead
I'll take the pleasure that assuages me
if it's the final thing I do.

Seule en tes faiz au royaume de France[55]

fol 337c Muse eloquent entre les ix, Christine,
Nompareille que je saiche au jour d'ui:
En sens acquis et en toute dotrine,
Tu as de Dieu science et non d'autruy;
Tes epistres et livres, que je luy
En pluseurs lieux, de grant philosophie,
Et ce que tu m'as escript une fie,
Me font certain de la grant habondance
De ton scavoir qui tousjours monteplie,
Seule en tes faiz au royaume de France.

Dieu t'a donné de Salemon le signe,
Cuer enseignant qu'il demanda de lui;
A l'estude es, ou tu ensuis la ligne
Du bon maistre Thomas, que je conguy,
De Boulongne, Pizain, recors en suy:
Ton pere fut docteur d'astronomie;
Charles le Quint, roy, ne l'oublia mie,
Mais le manda pour sa grant souffisance,
Et tu l'ensuis es vii ars de clergie,
Seule en tes faiz au royaume de France.

Ha! quelle honeur entre les femmes digne
Et les hommes! Pour aprandre a toy fuy
Qui trop te plains de la fausse nature
Dont le fruit fait a tout le monde ennuy;
Par t'espitre le voy, que je recuy
Benignement, dont cent foiz te mercie;
Mais plus a plain scaras de ma partie,
fol 337d Qui en tous cas te faix obeissance,
Le remede de ta grief maladie,
Seule en tes faiz au royaume de France.

L'envoy
O douce suer, je, Eustace, te prie,
Comme ton serf, d'estre en ta compaignie
Pour bien avoir d'estude cognoissance;
Mieulx en vaudray tous les temps de ma vie,
Car je te voy, com Boece a Pavie,
Seule en tes faiz au royaume de France.

You are alone in France in what you've done

Of the nine muses you're most eloquent, Christine.
I know of none to match you in our days:
accomplished both in wisdom and in doctrine,
you got your science from God and no one else;
your letters and your books, all filled with thought,
which I have read in many places,
and also what you'd written to me once,
make me quite certain of the great abundance
and ever-building knowledge that is yours:
you are alone in France in what you've done.

God granted you what He gave to Solomon
at his request, which is, a knowing heart.
And in your study you are in the line
of the good master Thomas, whom I knew,
from Pizan and Bologna, as I recall:
Your father was a doctor of astronomy,
whom Charles V, the king, did not forget
but rather praised for his capacity;
you follow him in learning's seven arts.
You are alone in France in what you've done.

So! You have honor now among the worthy women
and among the men! I want to learn from you;
for you've my sympathy for the false doctrine,
the fruit of which is troubling all the world.
Your letter was received without a problem
for which I give you thanks a hundred times,
but you will soon receive more news from me,
and I, in any case, bow down to you,
the remedy for your great malady:
you are alone in France in what you've done.

Envoy
Sweet sister, I, Eustache, now pray to you
to let me, like your servant, keep you company
so that I can acquire some knowledge of your learning
and be better off for it all the days of my life,
since I see that, like Boethius in Pavia,
you are alone in France in what you've done.

Toute chose est part tout mal ordenée[56]

fol 338d En mon cuer n'a ce jour de may verdure,
Joye, deduit n'amoureus sentement.
Pourquoi? Pour ce que mainte creature
Voy au jour d'ui en paine et en tourment
Ne je ne voy nul bon gouvernement
Au bien commun ne en fait de justice;
De la loy Dieu, de la foy est esclipce,
Division et convoitise est née
Entre pluseurs, orgueil et avarice:
Toute chose est par tout mal ordonnée.

L'un a l'autre fait mal, tort et injure;
Pour extorquer or, joyaulx et argent,
On bat, on ment, on rapine, on parjure;
En mains pais va tout desloyaument,
Et le plus fort en fait a son talent;
Pité n'a lieu, nulle amour n'est propice,
Et verité ne fait pas son office;
L'eglise Dieu est par tout divisée;
Vertu ne voy regner fors que tout vice;
Toute chose est par tout mal ordonnée.

Des prodommes anciens n'a nulz cure;
Reboutez sont; l'en fait eslectement
Des non sachans; se telz temps longues dure,
Et se scet Dieu, l'en verra bien comment
La fin sera et le pugnissement
Des malfaicteurs et de leur grant malice,
Car en brief temps fault que mauves perice
Et que bonté soit aux bons guerredonnée;
C'est loy de Dieu; gart soy qui en mal glice;
Toute chose est par tout mal ordonnée.

L'envoy
Prince, avisez que tout voist autrement;
Nobles et clers et peuples ensement
fol 339a Crions mercy; soit no vie muée
En bonnes meurs et an amendement,
Ou tout se pert a nostre dampnement;
Toute chose est par tout mal ordonnée.

Everything is totally corrupt

There's no life in my heart on this May Day
or joy, or love, or even happiness.
Why so? The reason is that all I see today
is the trouble of so many, the distress,
and though I sought, I saw good government
in neither state nor law, whichever way I went.
God's word and true religion are held in scorn,
and faction and self-seeking have been born
among the people; pride and avarice erupt:
everything is totally corrupt.

Each heaps on the other harm and injury
in order to extort jewels, silver, gold;
they fight, they lie, they plunder, use perjury.
In many countries treachery's extolled,
and the strong do what they like. As for compassion,
it has no place, and love is out of fashion,
and truth doesn't have the influence it is due.
God's church is now divided through and through.
I find vice only, virtue is bankrupt:
everything is totally corrupt.

No one has time for men of integrity;
they're pushed aside, and the preferred is he
who is ignorant. If the world continues as it's been,
God knows it will undoubtedly be seen
that in the end some punishment will come along
for sinners and their wickedness: you'll see,
the sinful man cut down before too long
and the good man rewarded. This is God's decree:
beware of evil, for the fall's abrupt:
everything is totally corrupt.

Envoy
Prince! the needed change is up to you;
nobles, clerics, and the common people, too,
cry out for mercy. Our lives must have new norms;
we must start now to institute reforms
or else we'll lose the lives you must disrupt:
everything is totally corrupt.

Ce sont les signes de la mort[57]

fol 344c Je deviens courbes et bossus,
J'oy tresdur, ma vie decline,
Je pers mes cheveulx par dessus,
Je flue en chascune narine,
J'ay grant doleur en la poitrine,
Mes membres sens ja tous trembler,
Je suis treshastis a parler,
Impaciens, desdaing me mort,
Sanz conduit ne scay mes aler:
Ce sont les signes de la mort.

Convoiteus suis, blans et chanus,
Eschars, courroceux; j'adevine
Ce qui n'est pas et loe plus
Le temps passé que la dotrine
Du temps present; mon corps se mine;
Je voy envix rire et jouer,
J'ay grant plaisir a grumeler,
Car le temps passé me remort;
Tousjours vueil jeunesce blamer:
Ce sont les signes de la mort.

Mes dens sont longs, foibles, agus,
Jaunes, flairans comme santine;
Tous mes corps est frois devenus,
Maigres et secs; par medicine
Vivre me fault; char ne cuisine
Ne puis qu'a grant paine avaler;
Des jeusnes me fault baler,
Mes corps toudis sommeille ou dort
Et ne vueil que boire et humer:
Ce sont les signes de la mort.

L'envoy
fol 344d Princes, encor vueil cy adjouster
Soixante ans, pour mieulx confermer
Ma viellesce qui me nuit fort,
Quant ceuls qui me doivent amer
Me souhaide ja oultre la mer:
Ce sont les signes de la mort.

These are the signs of death

I'm hunched; my life's begun to creak;
my hearing isn't what it was;
my hair is thinning out; my nose—
both nostrils—must have sprung a leak;
I have a bad pain in my chest;
my limbs now tremble and protest;
I'm impatient, hasty when I speak;
I'm scorned; that lot's now mine.
I can't walk alone, I've grown too weak.
These are the signs of death.

I'm greedy now, and bald and white;
suspicious without cause; I'm tight,
I'm irritated; full of praise
for old opinions, not today's;
my body seems to shrink away;
I envy those who laugh and play;
and grumble with a great delight
because I mourn the past with all my might;
I think the young are asinine:
these are the signs of death.

My teeth are weak, long, pointed, always smell
of bilge; they're broken, yellowing;
my body's always got a chill;
I'm thin and dry; and as for living,
there's medicine; and if a food needs chewing,
like meat, it's a great effort; I make
a feast out of a fast for feasting's sake;
my body is asleep or trying to take
a nap; if I can't slurp it, then I must decline:
these are the signs of death.

Envoy
Prince, to all of this I still desire
to add another sixty years of dire
old age, that bears so heavily on me,
and those who ought to love me pine
for when I have already crossed the sea:
these are the signs of death.

Onques amour ne fut sanz Jalousie[58]

Qui aime bien, il a pou de repos,
De son amour toudis perdre se doubte;
Il tremble, il frit, il n'a ne cuir ne os,
Cuer ne penser ou paour ne se boute;
Il craint, il plaint, il ne repose goute.
Tele est amour entre ami et amie:
Tousdis enquiert, cerche, oreille et escoute:
Onques amour ne fut sanz Jalousie.

Si n'en doit on pas dire villains mos,
Ne l'appeller fausse, vielle ne glote,
Si comme on fait; qui la blasme il est folz,
Car s'elle fust desloial ne estoute,
Amour l'eust pieca destruite toute;
Mais pour son bien l'a en sa compaignie,
C'est son escu, sa servant, son escoute:
Onques amour ne fut sanz Jalousie.

Qui n'aime a droit, il est d'elle forclos,
De ce qu'il het en tel cas ne fait doubte,
Donc est amour en Jalousie enclos;
Dame et ami l'un de l'autre fordoubte,
Et bon signe est de sivre droicte route,
De vray amour: jaloux ne seroit mie
Cilz qui harroit, pour ce ne la reboute:
Onques amour ne fut sanz Jalousie.

No love without Dame Jealousy

The man who really loves has little peace;
his fear of losing love will never cease;
he trembles, he quivers; dread, he'll find,
invades his skin, his bones, his heart, his mind;
he is afraid, complains, he has no rest.
Such is the love all lovers have possessed:
they spy, they probe, they listen, ears ever free:
no love without Dame Jealousy.

And yet we mustn't say harsh things of her,
or call her greedy, false, or old, though slur
is common; whoever blames her has gone mad,
for if she really were so proud and bad,
love would have long ago got rid of her;
it's for love's good he keeps her company.
His servant, guard and watch is she;
no love without Dame Jealousy.

Only the man without true love is free of her,
what he dislikes gives no anxiety;
so love must be enclosed in Jealousy;
in mistress and in lover doubts recur,
and that's the sign they're on the highway of
true love, for those who do not love
don't feel her pangs. Do not reject her; let her be:
no love without Dame Jealousy.

Le pais est un enfer en ce monde[59]

fol 355c De paradis ne scaroie parler
Ne je n'y fu onques jour de ma vie
Mais en enfer vous feray bien aler
Se vous voulez passer en Lombardie
Ou cheminer le pais de Hongrie
Entre les mons; la sont glaces et nois
Grans froidures par tous les XII moys
Et habismes jusqu'en terre parfonde
Et la ne croist fors que sapins et rapois:
Le pais est un enfer en ce monde.

Charrettes ou chars n'y pourroient passer
Et le souleil qui est hault n'y luist mie;
N'y n'est oisel qui y puist demourer
Pour la froideur volent autre partie.
Mais le chemin n'a pas piet et demie:
Qui mespasse, s'il chiet, mors est tout frois;
fol 355d Et se chevaulx s'encontrent a la foys
La convient que l'un l'autre confonde.
Pour les griefs pas et les chemins estrois
Le pais est un enfer en ce monde.

Verdeur n'y a, cerf, biche ne cengler,
Vignes ne blez, ne nulle melodie.
Ours et chameulx voit on les mons ramper
Mais leurs vuires que nul d'eulx ne mendie
Leur quierent ailleurs; du main jusqu'a complie
Sont tenebres, vens et horribles vois
Et Lucifer, qui est des diables roys,
Ou hault des mons o ses freres habonde
Qui en tous lieux depart gelée et frois:
Le pais est un enfer en ce monde.

L'envoy
Prince, qui veult corps et ame dampner
D'un grant pecheur, face loy condempner
Entre ces mons et la lui mettre bonde
Du remanoir sanz povoir retourner:
Le pais est un enfer en ce monde.

That country really is a hell on earth

Of paradise, I don't know what to say
since I have never been there in my life
but I can certainly point out the way to hell
if you are willing to go to Lombardy
or travel between the mountains to
the land of Hungary, where there is ice and snow
and bitter cold for twelve months of the year
and many an abyss that goes down to the depths,
where nothing grows except some scrub and pine:
that country really is a hell on earth.

No cart or wagon gets through all the way,
and the sun, when high, does not illuminate,
there is no bird which can survive up there
but due to cold, they fly to other lands.
The road is only one or two feet wide:
make one false step and you'll fall to cold death;
if horses there come face to face,
then one of them destroys the other one.
Because of its hard passes and narrow paths
that country really is a hell on earth.

No verdure, no stag, no hind, no wild boar,
no vines or wheat, or any melody.
You'll see the bears and chamois climb the peaks
but neither of them scavenge so they must
go seek their food elsewhere; from morn to night
there's darkness, winds and ghastly howls
and Lucifer, who is the devils' king,
roams freely with his brothers on those heights
and all about him casts forth ice and snow:
that country really is a hell on earth.

Envoy
Prince, those who want to damn both flesh and soul
of some great sinner should have him condemned
to live between the mountains, forcing him to stay
under a bond without right of return:
that country really is a hell on earth.

Que sont partout les maronniers[60]

fol 355d Je croy qu'entre joueurs de dez,
Coquins, courratiers de chevaulx,
Sarrasins, Juifs, larrons prouvez,
Mourdreurs, rufiens et ribaux,
Charretiers, cabuseurs et traitres faulx,
Pillars, coureurs sur les chemins,
Sorciers, sorcieres et devins,
Depuis qu'Adam fut faiz premiers,
fol 356a Ne fut plus faulx ne plus malings
Que sont partout les maronniers.

Trop a eulx ne vous attendez:
Aux pelerins font trop de maulx
En la mer, ce mot entendez,
En eaue douce sont ilz maulx
Soiez toudis encontr'eux caux.
Ceuls qu'ilz treuvent sont mieulx que prins.
Aux gens font pis que Sarrazins.
En nave, en galée, en craiers
N'est au jour d'ui pires venins
Que sont partout les maronniers.

Pluseurs sont par eulx desrobez
En la mer les gectent tous chaux
Se riches sont et defoulez
Sont les povres par leurs travaulx.
A paine en treuve on nulz loyaulx.
Eulx donner viande ne vins
Fors leur loyer c'est bien estins:
Gré n'en scevent, tant sont loudiers.
Gens ne sont pires a toutes fins
Que sont partout les maronniers.

L'envoy
Prince, depuis qu'Adam fut nez
Ne fut gens plus desordonnez
Ne plus desloyaulx patarins
Plus mauvais ne plus faulx trovez
Entre toutes gens esprouvez
Que sont partout les maronniers.

Than sailors, everywhere that they exist

I think, among the gamblers with dice,
those who steal horses, rogues, and Jews,
and Saracens, convicted criminals,
and ruffians, and louts and murderers,
and wagoners, deceivers, traitors, thieves,
and those who roam the roads to rob,
all warlocks, witches, soothsayers,
who've lived since Adam first was born,
not one has been more cunning or more false
than sailors, everywhere that they exist.

Don't get your expectations up for them:
they play a lot of tricks while they're at sea
with pilgrims—listen carefully to this—
and on fresh water they are just as bad
so always be on guard when you're with them.
Those in their keep are worse than prisoners.
They have less pity than the Saracens.
In boats, in galleys, in the greatest ships,
there is, today, no venom that is worse
than sailors, everywhere that they exist.

Many people get stripped down by them
and then thrown in the ocean while still warm
if they are rich, and if they're poor
they're trampled the exact same way.
You almost never find an honest one.
Don't ever give them any food or drink
since anything but wage is pure loss:
they are such boors they won't give thanks.
No other group is of more perfect evil
than sailors, everywhere that they exist.

Envoy
Prince, since the time of Adam's birth
there's never been a group that's so disorderly;
a group of more disloyal souls,
more wicked or more false, you'll never find
than sailors, everywhere that they exist.

Il ne scet rien qui ne va hors[61]

fol 356b Ceuls qui ne partent de l'ostel
Sanz aler en divers pais
Ne scevent la dolour mortel
Dont gens qui vont sont envahis,
Les maulx, les doubtes, les perilz
Des mers, des fleuves et des pas,
Les langaiges qu'om n'entent pas,
La paine et le traveil des corps.
Mais combien qu'om soit de ce las:
Il ne scet rien qui ne va hors.

Car par le monde universel
Qui est des nobles poursuis,
Sont choses a chascun costel
Dont maint seroient esbahis:
De la creance, des habis,
Des vivres, des divers estas
Des bestes, des merveilleux cas,
Des poissons, oiseaulx, serpens fors,
Des roches, des plains et des lieux bas
Il ne scet rien qui ne va hors.

De vir les montaingnes de sel,
Les baings chaux dont maint sont garis
Dont le cours desquelz est naturel
Par vaines de soufre tramis,
Les divers fruis, ermines, gris
Minieres d'or, d'argent a tas,
De fer, d'acier, d'estain verras,
De plomb, cuivre, arain et alors
A toutes gens dire pourras:
Il ne scet rien qui ne va hors.

L'envoy
fol 356c Princes, nulz ne sera sutils
Saiges, courtois ne bien apris,
Tant soit riches, puissans ou fors,
S'en divers voyages n'est mis
En jeunesce, pour avoir pris:
Il ne scet rien qui ne va hors.

A man knows nothing who hasn't been overseas

Those folk who've never left their home,
who've never been in countries not their own,
don't know the misery, the pain,
the suffering, of those who go,
the hardships, perils, fear and strain,
from rivers, mountain passes, seas,
the languages you do not know,
the body's torment and disease.
But, weary though one gets of these,
a man knows nothing who hasn't been overseas.

For in this world that is so wide,
so travelled by nobility,
there are so many things on every side
you'd be amazed at what is there to see:
I mean the creeds, the clothing, food,
the sheer diversity of what's found good,
of animals, the strangest congeries,
and fish, and birds, huge serpents, and
rocks, and plains, the low lands:
a man knows nothing who hasn't been overseas.

To see salt mountains, white and pure,
hot baths in which so many get their cure,
the origin of which, it has been found,
are natural sulphur channels underground,
the diversity of fruits, and furs like ermine,
gold mines, and piles of silver, tin,
and iron, and steel, you'll come to know,
and copper, bronze and lead, and so
you can say to all as often as you please:
a man knows nothing who hasn't been overseas.

Envoy
Prince, no one will be clever or well-taught,
or wise, or good to have at court,
though rich or powerful or strong, if he's
never travelled widely in his youth
on journeys which will make him less uncouth:
a man knows nothing who hasn't been overseas.

Poulz, puces, puour et pourceaulx[62]

Poulz, puces, puour et pourceaulx
Est de Behaingne la nature,
Pain, poisson sallé et froidure,
Poivre noir, choulz pourriz, poreaulx,
Char enfumée, noire et dure;
Poulz, puces, puour et pourceaulx.
Est de Behaingne la nature,
Vint gens mangier en deux plateaux,
Boire servoise amere et sure,
Mal couchier, noir, paille et ordure,
Poulz, puces, puour et pourceaulx
Est de Behaingne la nature,
Pain, poisson sallé et froidure.

Lice, fleas, pigs, mold

Lice, fleas, pigs, mold,
the gist of the Bohemian soul,
bread and salted fish and cold.
Black pepper, leeks, a rotten cabbage roll,
smoked meat as hard and black as coal;
lice, fleas, pigs, mold:
the gist of the Bohemian soul.
Ten people eating from one bowl,
a bitter drink—it's beer, I'm told—
bad beds, and dark, straw, filth, a hole,
lice, fleas, pigs, mold,
the gist of the Bohemian soul,
bread and salted fish and cold.

Tousjours arez d'uy a demain[63]

fol 364c Vous, ambasseur et messagier,
Qui alez par le monde es cours
Des grans princes, pour besongnier,
Vostre voyage n'est pas cours
Car on quiert tant de divers tours
Depuis que vous serez ois
De journées, de mos polis.
De venir au soir et au main,
Mais ne soiez pour ce esbahis:
Tousjours arez d'uy a demain.

Qui vous durra un mois entier,
Voire bien trois, et tous les jours
Vous fault poursuir a dangier
Vostre response. On n'est pas sours
De vous respondre par amours:
fol 364d "Ne soiez mie si hastis!
Il fault que vostre fait soit mis
Au conseil, pour respondre a plain.
Attendez encor mes amis:
Tousjours arez d'uy a demain.

Il fault parler au chancelier
De vostre fait et a plusours.
Vous vous pourrez bien empeschier
De tenir trop pres noz seignours!"
Temps passe et tout vient arrebours;
Argent fault hors de son pais,
La desplaisance qui fait pis.
De teles poursuites me plain
Et des moz dont on est servis:
Tousjours arez d'uy a demain.

L'envoy
Princes, il sont maint estrangier
Qui seulent les cours estrangier
Quant ilz n'y voient mot certain
Et n'en veulent plus approuchier;
Pour ce mot que nulz homs n'a chier:
Tousjours arez d'uy a demain.

Tomorrow is another day

Ambassadors and envoys! you
who go around the world to do
your work at some great prince's court:
your voyages will not be short
because of all the problems people raise;
you won't be heard until you've worked for days
and listened to the polished words which you
will come to hear the whole day through,
but please don't get downhearted; as we say,
tomorrow is another day.

This will go on; a whole month will be lost
or even three, and every day
you'll have to hunt, at your own cost,
the response you want. And they're not deaf since they
reply with great affection: "Give us a break!
Don't be in such a hurry, for heaven's sake!
Your business has to be put before
the council, which of course must weigh
its answer. Friends, please wait a little more:
tomorrow is another day.

We'll need to speak to the chancellor who
must think about your business, and to others, too.
it's likely you will harm your case if you
insist on pressing our principals too long!"
Time passes; everything goes wrong.
You're in a foreign country and your purse
is empty, and the stress of it all is worse.
I know these hassles, and here record dismay
at every serving of the following cliche:
tomorrow is another day.

Envoy
Prince, there are many strangers who
become estranged from courts that never do
give the straight answers that they sought,
and who no longer wish to approach the court
because of that phrase no man should say:
tomorrow is another day.

Jamais a table ne serrai[64]

fol 388c Jamais a table ne serray
Si je ne voy le vin tout prest
Pour boire et verser sanz arrest.
Au premier morsel tel soif ay
Que mort suy se boire n'y est;
Jamais a table ne serray
Si je ne voy le vin tout prest.
Comment il m'en va, bien le scay;
Rolant en mourut; si me plest
Boire tost puisque vin me pest;
Jamais a table ne serray
Si je ne voy le vin tout prest
Pour boire et verser sanz arrest.

I don't sit down to eat unless I see

I don't sit down to eat unless I see
some wine has been poured out for me
or, if not poured, about to be.
At the first morsel, I become so dry
that if there isn't any drink I'd die.
I don't sit down to eat unless I see
some wine has been poured out for me.
That's how it goes, I know, with me.
It's said that Roland died of thirst, and I
do like to drink, since wine does nurture me:
I don't sit down to eat unless I see
some wine has been poured out for me
or, if not poured, about to be.

Un chien doit presque tout scavoir[65]

fol 434c Je ne me puis trop merveillier
De ce qu'om dit communement
Quant on veult aulcun desprisier:
"Ne q'un chien n'a d'entendement;
Il ne scet riens." Mais vraiement
Chiens par droit doit bien estre saige
Car en tous lieux va par usaige,
Au palais, au conseil, c'est tout voir,
En la taverne, au labouraige:
Un chien doit presque tout scavoir.

Il va chascun jour au moustier
Sur l'abit du prestre pissant,
Aux noces, au corps, au bouchier,
Au sermon, en chambre souvent,
En cloistre, en dortoir, en couvent,
En cuisine, en chascun mesnaige;
S'on fait armes ou vassellaige,
La puet on chiens souvent veoir:
J'en tray heraux a tesmoinaige,
Un chien doit presque tout scavoir.

Les chiens vont en sale au mangier,
Soubz les tables se vont mucent;
Ilz vont les tripes barguignant,
Couchier en lit de parement;
Ilz vont les tapiz dessirent
Et au marchié querir frommaige,
fol 434d Au four, moulin ou jardinaige,
En cellier des coups recevoir,
Es vaisseaulx sur l'eaue au passaige:
Un chien doit presque tout scavoir.

L'envoi
Prince, se chien eust beau langaige,
De guerre, de sens et de gaige,
De tout, ce vous fais assavoir,
Deust parler et de mariaige;
Et puisqu'ilz ont tel avantaige,
Un chien doit presque tout scavoir.

Most of what we know a dog must know

I marvel more and more each day
at a phrase so common it's become cliche:
when people want a put-down now they say,
"He's got the brain of a dog; he's about
as ignorant as can be." But I'd point out
a dog is very well informed since he
wanders where he wants habitually:
to palace, council—isn't it the truth?—they go
to taverns, and to fields, and to, and fro:
most of what we know a dog must know.

Dogs go to churches every single day
and piss on the vestments of the priests,
and go to funerals and wedding feasts,
to butchers, and orations, bedrooms; they
go to the cloister and the dorm, and go
to convents and kitchens, every household. Where
there are feats of arms, bold deeds or fair,
many dogs are often gathered there.
The heralds will confirm that this is so:
most of what we know a dog must know.

Dogs go to eat in dining rooms, and they
can hide and quarrel while they are below
the table, bickering over offal; they can go
into the houses of the great and find a way
to sleep in those grand beds, and tear
the carpets up, and go to markets where
there's cheese, and to the mill, the baker's, go
to gardens, cellars, where they're beaten, and dogs lie
on all the river barges passing by:
most of what we know a dog must know.

Envoy
Prince, if a dog had language, he
would use his speech to talk, and to talk well,
of war, and wisdom, and of salary
and marriage, and of all that I can tell.
Since dogs can go more places than we go,
most of what we know a dog must know.

Toute maladie me nuit[66]

fol 442a J'ay perdu doulz apvril et may,
Printemps, esté, toute verdure;
Yver, janvier de tous poins ay
Garniz d'annoy et de froidure.
Dieux scet que ma vieillesce endure
De froit et reume jour et nuit,
De fleume, de toux et d'ordure:
Toute maladie me nuit.

Pour mon costé crie: "Hahay!"
Maintefois et a l'aventure
Une migrayne ou chief aray.
Autrefoiz ou ventre estorture
Ou en l'estomac grief pointure.
Aucunefois le cuer me cuit;
Autreheure tousse a desmesure:
Toute maladie me nuit.

Tant qu'en lit me degecteray
Si qu'il ny remaint couverture.
La crampe d'autre part aray
Ou le mal des dens me court sure
Ou les goutes me font morsure.
Quelque part ou ventre me bruit;
Toudis ay medecin ou cure:
Toute maladie me nuit.

L'envoi
Prince, de santé je vous jure
Que moult s'afoiblist ma nature
Pour maint grief mal qui me destruit.
Vieillesce m'est perverse et dure,
Ne je ne scay comment je dure:
Toute maladie me nuit.

I am attacked by every malady

I've lost sweet April and May,
spring, summer, all green signs of life.
Winter, January, is where I stay,
my life is filled with freezing and with strife.
I suffer in old age, as God can see,
from frost, and colds, all night, all day,
and phlegm and cough and filth inhabit me:
I am attacked by every malady.

I cry out "Oy" from pains I get
in my side, or when I feel a migraine set
to strike, and know my head will shortly split.
At another time the colic does its bit
or stomach pains become an agony
or heart-burn suddenly will hit;
or I get shaken by a coughing fit:
I am attacked by every malady.

It's gotten so when I'm in bed, I writhe about
until the covers all depart.
Cramp seizes me in another part
or a toothache will have found me out,
or I'll be bitten by the gout;
or else my belly's rumbles start.
I'm always needing medicine, some remedy:
I am attacked by every malady.

Envoy
Prince, my health's a theme I must expound;
I can assure you it's become unsound;
because of pains and ills, I'm barely alive.
Old age is harsh, it is my enemy;
I don't know how I've managed to survive:
I am attacked by every malady.

Mais je n'ay peu demourer en ce point[67]

fol 442b Bien m'a li temps et nature, tous deux,
Mué mes meurs et mon gouvernement,
Car a vint ans fus gais et amoureus,
Plain de chaleur et de foul hardement,
Jolis, joieux, sains et entreprenent,
Ne me chaloit de sens ne de folie.
Jusqu'a XXX ans force et cuider me lie,
Crespes et blons, vestus d'un seul pouepoint,
Dancant, chantant, sanz craindre mort ne vie,
Mais je n'ay peu demourer en ce point.

A XL ans devins malicieus
Et m'avisay que j'eu fait folement.
Lors me retray de mes faiz perilleus.
A acquerir me mis terre et argent
A grant doleur, a paine et a tourment.
Tiray X ans pour avoir seignourie
Mais assez tost chey en maladie:
Estomac froit trouvay qui me point
Mon jeune temps perdu lamente et crie,
Mais je n'ay peu demourer en ce point.

Devenus suis maigres, pelez, frilleux,
Po voyant, sourt, sec, annuieux, chargent,
Tousseux, roingneux, graveleux et gouteux,
Courbes du corps, po mangant, trop buvent.
Chascun jour ay un nouvel accident:
Bout en costé ou autre maladie.
L'an LX pour mourir me deffie
Qui a la fin de mon eage se joint.
Du jeune temps ay regret et envie,
Mais je n'ay peu demourer en ce point.

L'envoy
O foul cuidier, j'ay de ta cuiderie
Long temps m'as fait paier la muserie
En un espoir qui de moy se desjoint
D'estre jeunes et d'avoir chiere lie
fol 442c Sanz envieillir et sanz merancolie,
Mais je n'ay peu demourer en ce point.

But I could not continue at this stage

Time and nature have—how can I put it?—
together changed compulsive habit.
At twenty, I was merry and amorous,
filled with warmth and a foolhardiness,
joyful, healthy, enterprising, jolly,
as uninterested in wisdom as in folly.
Up to thirty I was gripped by power and arrogance,
had primped blond hair, and owned one pair of pants,
and danced and sang, not fearing death or age,
but I could not continue at this stage.

At forty I became a cunning man
and came to think I'd been a fool before.
I gave up risky actions, and began
acquiring land and money, but got my store
with difficulty and distress and pain.
Status took ten years for me to gain.
But I soon fell sick: my stomach went,
seized up with cramps that I could not assuage.
My lost youth's what I grieve for and lament
but I could not continue at this stage.

Now I've got thin, and bald, and my sight is spent,
I'm chilly, deaf, a withered burden, full of moans,
and suffer coughs, scabs, gout, and bladder stones;
don't eat or drink too much; and my body's bent.
And every day there's a new accident:
a bump on the side or some other malady.
I'm due to die at sixty years of age
which is the time that's been allotted me.
I long for the young years regretfully,
but I could not continue at this stage.

Envoy
Foolish presumption! I let you have your way
for quite a while, and I'm being made to pay
through loss of the hope, which now is cold,
of being young and never in a rage,
not melancholy, and not growing old,
but there was no remaining at this stage.

Souflez, nostre vie n'est rien[68]

Ou est Nembroth le grant jayant,
Qui premiers obtint seigneurie
Sur Babiloine? Ou est Priant,
Hector et toute sa lignie:
Achilles et sa compaingnie,
Troye, Cartaige et Romulus,
Athenes, Alixandre, Remus,
Jullius Cesar et li sien?
Ilz sont tous cendre devenus:
Souflez, nostre vie n'est rien.

Ou est David le combatant,
Judas Machabée et Urie:
Ou est Charlemaine et Rolant,
Godefroy qui fut en Surie,
Baudouin, leur chevalerie,
Josué, Daires et Artus
Et ceuls qui conquirent le plus
Sarrazin, Juif et Crestien?
Ilz sont mis en pouldre et corrups:
Souflez, nostre vie n'est rien.

Ou est Atille le tyrant,
Caton plain de phillosophie,
Hercules, Jason conquerant,
Socrates et son estudie,
Augustin en theologie,
Le pouete Virgilius,
Es estoilles Tholomeus,
Ypocras le phisicien?
De mort n'est d'eulx eschapez nulz:
Souflez, nostre vie n'est rien.

L'envoy
Prince, il n'y a que les vertus,
Bien faire et esjouir ca jus
Et departir pour Dieu du sien
Aux povres, pour regner la sus;
No eages est tantost conclus:
Souflez, nostre vie n'est rien.

This life of ours is nothing, a puff

Where is that giant named Nimrod,
the first to be the overlord
of Babylon? Where are Priam,
and Hector, and all their line?
Achilles and all his company,
Carthage, Romulus, and Troy,
and Remus, Athens, Alexander,
and those who followed Julius Caesar?
All have gone to dust's rebuff:
this life of ours is nothing, a puff.

Where can the hero David be,
Uriah, Judas Maccabee?
Where is Roland, Charlemagne,
Godfrey of the Syrian campaign,
and Baldwin, and all the chivalrous,
Joshua, Arthur, Darius,
and those who conquered the most of men,
Jew and Christian and Saracen?
Gone to powder, corrupted to snuff:
this life of ours is nothing, a puff.

Where can Attila the Hun now be,
Cato, full of philosophy,
Jason the conqueror, Hercules,
the understanding of Socrates,
and Augustine of theology,
Virgil of epic poetry,
and the star-gazing Ptolemy,
and the physician, Hippocrates?
Death's pursuit not one could slough:
this life of ours is nothing, a puff.

Envoy
Prince, it's only virtues we should not forgo:
do good, and enjoy life here below,
and, for the sake of Heaven, give
to the poor, so that on high we'll live.
Our years will end up soon enough:
this life of ours is nothing, a puff.

Escoutez, Monseigneur dit voir![69]

fol 444a Je vi, encor n'a pas longtemps,
Un homme merveilles compter,
Qu'il avoit veu cent asnes blans,
Une truie un cerf pourceler,
Et qu'il avoit veu avaler
Le matin en guise du soir.
Lors dist un varlet hault et cler:
"Escoutez, Monseigneur dit voir!"

Le seigneur dist: "J'ay dyamens
Si gros com teste de sanglier;
J'ay veu mille moulins moulens
Moudre sanz eaue et sanz venter;
J'ay veu un heran en la mer
Qui povoit mille frans valoir;
Prins fut, tant en voulsisse donner."
"Escoutez, Monseigneur dit voir!"

"Je vis dix mille combatans
Par six hommes prandre et tuer,
Et XIIII mille oliphans
De IIII brebis estrangler;
Je vy un toreau ressembler
A la fourme d'un chien tout noir,
Et vy les montaignes voler."
fol 444b "Escoutez, Monseigneur dit voir!"

L'envoy
Prince doit amer ses sergens
Quant ilz font ainsi leur devoir,
Disens de tout devant les gens:
"Escoutez, Monseigneur dit voir!"

"Believe me, all my lord has said is true."

I saw, and I'm not talking of times now dead,
a man who spoke of miracles: he said
he'd seen white donkeys, at least a hundred head,
observed a stag born to a sow right in her pen,
and after that he'd seen the sun set when
it was the morning not the evening. Then
a lackey said, and spoke up loudly, too:
"Believe me, all my lord has said is true."

"I own some diamonds," I heard the noble say,
"as large as any wild boar's head;
I've seen a thousand mills grinding away
without water or wind." And then he said,
"I've seen a herring in the sea, I swear to you,
for which I'd pay, if it were caught,
a thousand francs—indeed, that's what I thought."
"Believe me, all my lord has said is true."

"I saw ten thousand soldiers who had been
captured and killed by six men; I have seen
fourteen thousand elephants and the four
sheep which strangled them, and then I saw
a bull whose shape transformed and grew
into a jet black dog, and then I saw
mountains that lifted up and flew."
"Believe me, all my lord has said is true."

Envoy
A prince can only be delighted when
he's served with such devotion by his men,
who say, in public, and without ado,
"Believe me, all my lord has said is true."

Dame, aiez pité de tettine![70]

fol 447d Puis que tettine se monstra
En tous lieux si generalment
Convoitise en pluseurs entra
Pour le ravir couvertement
Pour ce qu'il fait soudainement
Par veoir maint cuer dolereux
A des gens trouvé si creulx
Que prins l'ont et mis a gehine.
A Paris, c'est un cas piteux:
Dame, aiez pité de tettine!

Car ce qui en ce point mis l'a
Est par juenesse seulement,
Rons, petiz, durs: lors se cela
Sanz monstrer si publiquement
Puis s'abandonna folement,
Molz devint, lours, maugracieux
Et pour ce a esté mis en deux
fol 448a Sacs cousus parmy la poitrine
Estrains de cordes et de neux:
Dame, aiez pité de tettine!

Ou certes en ce ploy mourra;
Tenus est trop estroictement
Du delivrer grant bien sera
Et de lui faire aligement
Car il seufre trop grief tourment
Pour avoir esté gracieux.
Amoureuses et amoureux
Qui d'amours scavez le couvine
Faictes secours au langoreux:
Dame, aiez pité de tettine!

L'envoi
Princes, qui ne le secourra
En adventure se mettra
De saillir hors: prinson le mine,
Ou tous ses liens rompera
Lors en fosse avalez cherra:
Dame, aiez pitié de tettine!

Lady, take pity on the breast!

Ever since the breast displayed itself
in every place quite generally,
the desire has entered many minds
to come covertly and ravish it
because it gives so suddenly
heart pangs to many just by seeing it,
and it has found people were so cruel,
they took it prisoner and tortured it.
In Paris, it is in a piteous state:
Lady, take pity on the breast!

What got it into this predicament
is only the result of youth.
Round, small and firm: it didn't then
display itself so openly,
but then it foolishly let go,
turned flabby, heavy, unattractive,
and so it was divided into two,
sewn into bags across the bosom
and bound up with all sorts of cords and knots:
Lady, take pity on the breast!

Surely, it will die if in this plight:
it's trussed up far too tightly now.
It would be good indeed to deliver it
and give it at least some relief
because it suffers such tormenting pain
for having been of such a gracious shape.
Those women who are lovers, and those men
who understand the ways of love,
bring succor to this victim who is languishing:
Lady, take pity on the breast!

Envoy
Princes! if someone doesn't help,
it's possible it will leap out;
since prison is sapping all its strength,
or else it will break all its bonds
and then fall straight into a ditch:
Lady, take pity on the breast!

Femme est plus fort lien qui soit[71]

fol 452c On parle de larrons lier
Et d'estraindre de fors liens,
De gresillons, corde acoler,
Laisses de poil pour tenir chiens,
Nerfs, grans chables pour nefs, merriens
Entailliez a queue d'aronde,
D'estre en fers en une tour ronde;
Mais c'est tout rien qui bien y voit,
Et tien que des choses du monde
Femme est plus fort lien qui soit.

Car on a veu maint prinsonnier,
Sarrazins, Juifs et Crestiens,
Rompre fers, leurs cordes mangier,
Miner, yssir hors de lyens
De leurs prinsons a Orliens,
En Chastellet et de parfonde
Fosse ou ilz furent foiz seconde;
Mais femme prandre estraint si roit
Que nulz homs prins n'ist de sa fonde;
Femme est plus fort lien qui soit.

Si fort neue homme au marier;
Et sache que ly mariens
fol 452d Ne puet ce lien deslier,
Mais fault qu'il demeure prins ens
Jusqu'a la mort; voy se n'est sens
Et sur quel tourment homs se fonde
Qui en mariage s'affonde
Et qui en telz las se decoit;
S'on l'en blame, die et responde:
Femme est plus fort lien qui soit.

L'envoy
Prince, toute contrainte est riens
Au regart de femme; si tiens
Que cilz qui bien s'adviseroit
N'aroit cure d'avoir telz biens,
Car saichent juenes et anciens:
Femme est plus fort lien qui soit.

The bondage of a wife is the strongest bond

Some talk of how a thief is bound,
constrained by ties that bind him round,
the manacles and neck ropes used together,
of dogs held down by leashes made of leather,
great hawsers anchoring ships before they sail,
wood pillories shaped like a swallow's tail,
of being clapped in irons in a tower, but we
know these are nothing; anyone can see,
as I maintain, in all this world, if not beyond,
the bondage of a wife is the strongest bond.

For we've seen many prisoners, no matter whose—
Christians or Saracens or Jews—
break iron, bite through all cords that cause their pain,
dig their way out, escape from every chain,
even from prison at Orleans, the keep
in the Châtelet, and from the deep
of a pit where they were sent in double jeopardy;
but taking a wife binds so inflexibly
no man imprisoned in her bag can abscond:
the bondage of a wife is the strongest bond.

So tightly knotted up is man to wife,
you know whoever's in the married life
can never manage to untie the knot
but must remain a captive, like it or not,
until his death—does this make sense?—
and what torment it is that will commence
for one who sinks himself in marriage, and who
laces himself in self-deception, too.
But if anyone would blame him, I'd respond:
the bondage of a wife is the strongest bond.

Envoy
Prince, other constraints amount to nothing much
compared to any wife: and so I hold
that anyone who thinks at all of such
would not desire it, and could not be conned,
for, all should understand, both young and old:
the bondage of a wife is the strongest bond.

Miroir de mariage[72]

"Vous avez nostre chamberiere
Requis d'amour ii foiz ou trois;
Vous estes alez pluseurs fois
Veoir Helot et Eudeline,
Ysabel, Margot, Kateline
Et couché aux femmes communes.
De la me viennent les rancunes,
Car lerres le larron mescroit,
Ne ly mauves le bon ne croit,
Ains cuide que chascuns soit lerres:
On ne verroit en nulles terres
Plus mescreant de vous sanz failles;
Tousjours avons plaiz et batailles
J'ay long temps souffert vo pechié:
Comment m'avez vous reprouchié
Que j'estoie trop villotiere?
Meilleur vous sui et plus entiere
Que vous ne m'estes, par ma foy!
Lasse! vous doubtez vous de moy?
Je ne suy pas du lieu venue
Que pour fole soye tenue;
En mon linaige n'a putain:
Prenez les vostres par la main
Et celles de vostre linaige."
Et lors fait semblant qu'elle enrraige,
Et crie si horriblement,
Et ploure si parfondement
Qu'il samble qu'elle soit dervée:
"Helas!" fait elle, "il me vée
Neis que je voise au moustier!
Si n'ay je Robin ou Gautier
Ne homme, dont je soie acointe!"
Ainsis ly ment, ainsis l'apointe,
Ainsis le decoit et confont,
Ainsis pluseurs femmes le font.

The Mirror of Marriage

"You've asked our chambermaid,
twice or more, to make love;
you've been many times to see
Helot and Eudaline,
Isabel, Margot, Kate,
and slept with prostitutes.
That's why I'm riled up;
one thief distrusts another,
the bad disbelieve the good
and think all men are rogues.
There isn't, anywhere on earth,
for sure, a man as faithless as you.
Always, there's quarrels, fights.
I've suffered your sins a good long time.
How can you have reproached me
for being so debauched?
I'm better to you, more faithful,
I swear, than you to me.
Alas, you have suspicions!
My family's not the sort
that gives bad reputations,
I'm not from a line of whores!
Take charge of your own women
and those of all your family."
And then she pretends to get upset
and cries so terribly
and sobs so deeply
it seems she's lost her mind.
"Alas," she says, "I'm miserable.
He blocks me even from church!
I don't have a Robin or Walter,
no man with whom to connect."
This is the way she lies, twists,
this is the way she deceives, defeats,
this is what many women do.

Notes to the Poems

For the convenience of the reader, for each poem two identifying numbers are provided: the number of the poem as it appears in BNF Fonds français 840 and the volume and page number of the Société des Anciens Texts Français (SATF) edition. Also, a metrical analysis of each poem's first strophe is provided.

1. **Balade 24**, 1:103. Decasyllabic: *ab*ab*b*ccd*cD**, envoy *b*d*b*D**. **Line 3**: *failliz et passez*, a legal doublet. **Line 6**: SATF misread this line as *li hystorier* and then emended it to simply *ystorier*. **Lines 10 and 20**: MS reads *presteray*, which produces a line of 11 syllables. **Line 15**: MS has *donnas*, which may be a mistake for *donner*. **Lines 18 and 31**: these are unusual because the caesura would appear to occur after the fifth and not the fourth syllable. Note the reinforcement of two of the strong points in the line, the first word and the word forming the caesura in *p* in the refrain.
2. **Balade 37**, 1:121. Decasyllabic: *ab*ab*b*cb*C*. **Line 7**: This line would make better sense with the emendation suggested by the SATF, substituting *homme* for *honneur*, but this emendation produces a line of 11 syllables. **Line 21**: SATF suppresses the *en* to return the line to 10 syllables; perhaps the *ei* in *obeissant* is counted as one syllable only.
3. **Balade 58**, 1:151. Octosyllabic: *ababbcbC*, envoy *bcbC*, only masculine rhymes. **Lines 11 and 18**: The mouse is a lady by grammatical gender and for the convenience of the translators, who needed to keep the pronouns straight. The poem may have been written at Sluys in 1385–86, when an invasion of England was planned there. This plan was never carried out. Balade 1085 was clearly written on the theme of the French hesitation to invade at this time, and refers to the fabled difficulty of belling the cat: "Mais il convient, comme dist la souris, / Vir qui pandra la cloquette au mynon" ("As the mouse says, it is wise to know who will bell the cat") (lines 13–15). The SATF notes that this fable is not ancient (1:348) but points to *Isopet I* number 62 as a source (11:202).

4. **Balade 84**, 1:187. Decasyllabic: *ab*ab*b*ccd*cD**, envoy *ad*aD**. Note that the *-er* infinitives in the poem rhyme with words such as *mer* and *cler*. This poem is also present in MS BNF Nouvelles acquisitions françaises 6221. We have not ourselves transcribed the variants from this version but taken them from SATF 1:187–88. See also SATF 2:li. **Line 11**: 6221 has a better spelling at the rhyme: *tumber*. **Line 23**: 6221 has *Et pour ce fait les undes trescouper*. **Line 15**: Has only nine syllables; 6221 has a better version: *Pour la pueur vomir mainte guelée*. SATF corrects the line by adding a *la* before *vomir*. **Line 25**: Appears to be missing. **Line 26**: Has only nine syllables; 6221 has the better text: *poulz et puces et raz*. **Line 31**: 6221 has a better text: *Enfans, vueillez tost a terre aborder*. SATF corrects the line by adding *ici* after *vueillez*. **Line 22**: The nautical terms *pouge* and *ourse* present a critical crux. Even Deschamps's editors disagreed about it: Sainte-Hilaire annotated them as leeward and windward; Raynaud, as starboard and port. Old French dictionaries are also split. The line might, therefore, be equally well translated "To windward, to leeward, as their song is sung."
5. **Balade 169**, 1:301. This is a heterometric poem: all lines are decasyllabic except for lines 6, 16, and 26, which are heptasyllabic: *a*b*a*b*b*ccdcD*. **Line 14**: MS has *fois* but the emendation is necessary for sense. **Line 20**: MS has *Bien*; we emend to *Riens* to preserve the sense. Boudet and Millet include an annotated edition of this poem (153–54).
6. **Balade 208**, 2:30. Decasyllabic: *ababbcC*, only masculine rhymes. Note that this poem also exists in Lydgate, R.3.20, Trinity College, Cambridge. There are no significant variants in this later manuscript, but it is at least of interest in so far as it indicates interest in Deschamps's verse in England in the fifteenth century. The manuscript adds: *Autre balade de la maniere d'estre a la court*.
7. **Balade 225**, 2:52. A heterometric poem: all lines are decasyllabic except lines 5, 14, and 23, which are heptasyllabic: *a*b*a*b*ccd*cD**. It is difficult to know how much autobiographical significance to attach to this poem. In real life, Deschamps was a salaried royal officer and kept his post as bailiff of Senlis until shortly before his death. He also owned several properties and had some independent means. One may be confident that he was never reduced to rags or poverty. That said, the poem does fit some of his career, first as a student at Orléans and then as a *bailli*. **Line 4**: The word *practiqué* is just an alternative spelling for the preterit rather than the past participle. **Line 8**: Has 11 syllables, but if the mute *e* in *diminue* is not counted, a liberty known as the epic caesura, admittedly rare in Deschamps's work, the line would be regular. **Line 6**: In medieval times, it was thought that there were two kinds of stars, the erratic and principal. The erratic or wandering stars are the planets. The principal are those that did not move. **Line 24**: The French *indigens* means poverty-stricken, but "left out in the cold" suited the translation better if less exactly.
8. **Balade 235**, 2:65. Decasyllabic: *ab*ab*b*c*b*C**, envoy *aac*aaC**. Note that lines 27 and 28 have only nine syllables. Again note how the *-er* infinitive rhymes with *amer* and *mer*. Deschamps's poem makes a contrast with Balade 1309, on the advantages of travel (see p. 186). **Line 27**: MS could just as easily be read as *conars*, but *couars* makes more sense.

9. **Balade 285**, 2:138. Decasyllabic: *a*b*a*b*b*ccdcD*, envoy *a*a*da*a*D*. *Anglux* is a dense reference. Raynaud identifies him as Angelus or Giles of Rome, an obscure "good practitioner" (11:204). Others, including Jenkins, Young, and Lampe, have taken him to be Aulus Gellius, author of *Noctes Atticae* (*The Nights*), an extremely popular man of letters, and a judge. Mieszkowski and Kooijman concur. Brutus, the descendent of Aeneas, is the eponymous founder of Britain—not to be confused with the murderer of Julius Caesar. The word *pandras* presents a critical crux. It has been read as Pandarus of Chaucer's *Troilus and Cressida*, eponymous source for Modern English *pander*, but if Deschamps refers to Chaucer himself in that way, the meaning is simply the contemporary one that he is a go-between. (See Lerch, who posits that Deschamps could read the English poet's work, and Mieskowski, who contends that Deschamps was familiar with the Italian and French versions of the Troilus story.) Raynaud takes the reader in a different direction and suggests that *pandras* is Pandrasus, a Greek king, whose daughter Ignogne married Brutus, Aeneas's great-grandson, the mythical founder of Britain (although Raynaud is off by one generation, calling Brutus Aeneas's grandson). This reading grants Chaucer a royal ancestor in the founding line of Britain. More modestly one might read *pandras* as part of the verb *pander*, which perhaps means to open. This reading would reinforce Deschamps's profile of Chaucer as a great translator since it would present him as the one who opened up a foreign language, French, to those speakers of English who were ignorant of it. The translation skirts the issue. (For further discussion of *pandras*, see also Toynbee, Jenkins, Spurgeon, and most recently, Pearcy.) Similarly, Angela the Saxon princess could be read in the MS as "angel of the Saxons," but such a reading confounds the sense of the poem. The princess is the better reading, based on Deschamps's being very likely intimately familiar with the *Roman de Brut* (see Pearcy). Raynaud also identifies such a princess, again in the *Roman de Brut*. That this story was current in Deschamps's time is also borne out by its citation by Christine de Pizan (*City of Ladies*, 2.61.3). **Line 30**: MS has only *Gieffroy*. **Line 30**: SATF corrects *destruye* to *deservie*. It could be that Chaucer is a knight or even standard-bearer in the service of the allegorical figure of praise or even honor. **Line 11**: Albion is England. **Line 14**: *Angleterre*, that is, England, in three French syllables. **Line 16**: Chaucer did translate *Le Roman de la Rose* by Jean de Meun and Guillaume de Lorris. **Line 21**: Helicon is the fountain of the Muses, associated with poetic inspiration. **Line 29**: Deschamps sent Chaucer a laudatory balade delivered by Sir Lewis Clifford, possibly in 1386. The extent of the relationship between Deschamps and Chaucer is the topic of considerable critical debate.
10. **Balade 341**, 3:56. Octosyllabic: *a*b*a*b*b*cb*C*, envoy *a*ca*C*. There is no title *balade* in the MS. SATF supplies it silently. **Lines 1 and 8**: These lines have *ca* instead of *sa*. **Line 22**: SATF corrects to *et va* to supply the missing syllable. **Line 27**: MS reads not *denree* but *derree*. **Line 38**: SATF corrects to *ces bestes*, which makes better grammar but spoils the image of servile beasts. The translation opts for the better grammar.
11. **Balade 348**, 3:71. Decasyllabic: *ababbcbC*, envoy *bbcbbC*, only masculine rhymes. **Line 46**: In the refrain, *preudoms* has been emended to *prodoms*.

12. **Balade 404**, 3:194. Octosyllabic: *ababbccdcD*, envoy *bbdbbD*, only masculine rhymes. Line 3 has only six or seven syllables, according to whether *fiction* is pronounced with two or three syllables. Title *balade* is on fol. 138c. *Aucuns dient* . . . on fol. 115b, gives us Deschamps's self-image as a moralist-poet. **Line 3**: SATF prints *en parla* as a correction. Ovid was the Latin poet who wrote the *Metamorphoses*, *Ars Amatoria*, and the *Amores*. *L'Ovide moralisé*, a tremendously popular work written in the early fourteenth century, presented the text of the *Metamorphoses* accompanied by exegetical and moral commentary. **Line 17**: The pig is actually full grown, but he couldn't fit into the rhyme whole hog. **Line 25**: *denz de baleine* may be a narwhal horn, mistaken in the Middle Ages for that of the unicorn. It can here refer perhaps to shoes that were as long and pointy, and maybe the mechanics that let them stand up straight: there was a mode for shoes with extra-long toes, sort of an inversion of the platforms of the 1970s and 2000s. Such sartorial excesses were the subject of scorn and derision by the Church and the practical such as Deschamps. The French name for those long-toed shoes is *souliers à la poulaine*, or Polish shoes.
13. **Balade 447**, 3:259. Decasyllabic: *ababbcC*, only masculine rhymes. **Line 18**: Has only nine syllables. Also, this is one of Deschamps's earliest balades that can be dated: it was written shortly after Machaut's death. Did Deschamps's other early balades also lack an envoy? The fact that it has only masculine rhymes may suggest a certain lack of metrical sophistication, but the matching Balade 493, which follows, is more elaborate—and also deals with the interesting topic of Deschamps's apparent lack of success with Peronne. The only metrical elegance is in the "grammatical rhyme" in lines 8–9, the *rime équivoque* in lines 13–14, and the leonine rhyme in lines 16 and 18. *Emmuys*, misread as *emmutys* by SATF, is a "fancy" word. **Line 21**: *amy*. **Line 4**: Ovid's *Remedia amoris* is a kind of answer to his *Ars amatoria*. The Peronne to whom the poem is addressed has to be the Peronne of Machaut's *Voir Dit*, a work in prose and verse in which Machaut corresponds with an admirer, Peronne d'Armentières. The work has been recently reedited by Daniel Leech-Wilkinson and translated by R. Barton Palmer. Machaut died in 1377, and Deschamps's poem is likely to have been written shortly thereafter.
14. **Balade 493**, 3:318. Decasyllabic: *ab*ab*b*c*C**. Leonine rhymes in lines 2 and 4, 9 and 11, 13 and 14. **Line 6**: Has 11 syllables unless, as in Balade 225, line 8 above. The mute *e* at the end of the word forming the caesura, here *supplie*, is not reckoned in the syllabic count and is described as an epic caesura. The poem appears to be a companion piece to Balade 447. It may suggest that neither poem was to be taken too seriously. Also an early datable balade without envoy. Is the poem an elaborate joke? Gauteronne is a suspiciously good rhyme for Peronne. **Line 15**: Looks like a joke at the expense of the whole of the French courtly tradition; certainly Deschamps, most of whose work lay outside that tradition, did not require the allegiance of a courtly lady to relieve him of authorial sterility. **Line 7**: MS, *personne*. The characters mentioned are all troubling as examples of fickle classical lovers. Helen, later of Troy, left her husband Menelaus to run away with Paris; her departure occasioned the Trojan War, hers being the "face that launched a thousand ships," and Paris came to a sad end after the defeat of the Trojans. Jason did indeed win the Golden Fleece but later abandoned Medea, who

had helped him steal the Fleece, to marry the princess of Corinth; Medea killed the two children she had had with Jason, the princess and Jason's future father-in-law, and fled to safety in Athens in a dragon-drawn chariot. Jason later died a miserable death. Dido was the queen of Carthage, whom Aeneas loved and left at his mother's command; she committed suicide after he left her. Line 11's syntax is somewhat compressed; the addition of another word, perhaps "o" ("or"), might make the syntax more clear but would spoil the scansion. The only other possible explanation for this crux is Deschamps or the scribe confusing Dido's name with that of Jason's fiancée. Narcissus was a human beloved of the nymphs, whom he scorned to pine away for his own reflection.

15. **Virelai 548**, 4:1. Heptasyllabic: *AAB*B*A b*b*a b*b*a aab*b*a AAB*B*A*. Only the first line of the complete refrain appears in the MS, followed by *etc*, and it is repeated after each strophe. **Line 13**: SATF emends silently to *Wacarme*, a Flemish battle cry. **Line 22**: Has only six syllables. SATF corrects to *Quant il pleut la*. **Line 29**: One line is missing in this strophe. It could occur at this point or between lines 27 and 28. SATF places the lacuna after line 30. **Line 31**: Has only eight syllables. SATF suppresses the *y*. Also, *ventance* means literally "a boast" rather than a confession. **Line 40**: Has only six syllables; SATF corrects to *J'i ay esté entrepris*. **Line 45**: SATF emends to *Voist i*. The Lys is a river that formed a border between France and Flanders. The poem is perhaps the most original and unusual of all Deschamps's virelais, given its novel theme in a genre normally devoted to conventional love poems.
16. **Rondeau 554**, 4:8. This heptasyllabic poem, described by BNF Fonds français 840 first as a *rondel double*, which is crossed out by the copyist, and then as a *virelay*, does not in fact belong to either of these genres, at least as far as the conventional fixed forms of the fourteenth century are concerned. It has more in common with the looser refrain poems of the thirteenth century. For a fuller discussion of the piece, see I. S. Laurie, "Verbal Polyphony in Deschamps" (in Sinnreich-Levi 1998, 97–107). The poem is also unusual insofar as it is constructed on two assonances in *e* and *i*: *A*bba*Bbba*A**. The present editors have maintained the traditional presentation of this poem in thirteen short strophes. They do, however, suggest an alternative view of the poem in six eight-lined strophes with this structure (only the first preceded by a refrain) and a view of the last four-lined strophe as a variety of envoy with the structure *bb?A**. Viewed this way, the second form of the refrain then is more easily construed as a midstrophic pause as compared to the finality of the final refrain. **Line 51**: So identified by a question mark, it is imperfect since it has only six syllables and it does not match the assonance in *e* expected. It may be that Deschamps wrote *chansonnette* rather than the dubious "chansonnelle" preferred by SATF. **Line 5**: The girl's eyes are not green but literally lively (*vers* < Lat. *varius*). **Line 8**: BNF Fonds français 840 adds an *etc* here and also after the refrain in strophes 2 and 6 but not in the others. The editors prefer to think that no further repetition is intended. **Line 10**: Literally, "long slender arms and fingers, too." Boudet and Millet have included an annotated edition of this poem in their anthology (224–26).
17. **Rondel 579**, 4:38. Octosyllabic: *ABBabABabbABB*, only masculine rhymes. Note the *rimes équivoques* in lines 1, 46, 8, and 11. **Line 6 and line 11**: MS reads

Je n'ose etc. Raynaud identifies Charles de Savoisy as one of Deschamps's persecutors. Savoisy served several royal masters, including the duke of Orléans, and died in 1405. Philippe de Poitiers also served the house of Orléans and the duke of Touraine. Both Savoisy and Poitiers traveled widely for their royal masters. Deschamps mentions them both again in Balade 803 (cf. Boudet and Millet, 201–2); they are among a list of nobles Deschamps reviles for mocking him. Balade 1199 recounts the same grievance. **Line 9**: The plovers had to roost in this note because there was no room for them in the translation.

18. **Rondeau 596**, 4:55. Decasyllabic: *ABBabABabbABB*, only masculine rhymes. This poem was written perhaps about the same time as Deschamps sent his poems to Chaucer. **Line 1**: *veul* and *dane*. **Line 3**: *c'on*. **Line 4**: *veul*; SATF misreads *mattas*. **Line 5**: *n'espoir a vous*. **Line 6** and again in **line 10**: MS reads simply *Est cilz aise etc.* **Line 7**: *veul*; SATF misreads *oir* but the reading is fairly clearly *oit*, which in any event makes better sense if a new sentence is begun with this line. Oton de Grandson was a poet and friend of Deschamps's. Indeed, Grandson played a trick on Deschamps, making him think himself a prisoner of the English at Calais in Balade 893. **Line 4**: Medieval mattresses rested on ropes strung on a frame, an early predecessor of the modern box spring.
19. **Rondeau 631**, 4:90. Decasyllabic: *ABaAabAB*, only masculine rhymes. **Line 1**: *veul* and *dane*. **Line 3**: *c'on*. **Line 4**: *veul*. **Line 5**: *n'espoir a vous*. **Line 7**: *veul*. The rhymes in the refrain are examples of "grammatical rhyme." This poem also appears as an example of the genre in *L'Art de dictier* (p. 90). It also appears, without variants, in the other manuscript that contains *L'Art*, BNF Nouvelles acquisitions françaises 6221. **Line 5**: the *n* before *espoir* may be an unusual contraction of *en*. Such a contraction is common in Occitan but not in French. There are similar Latin abbreviations for words beginning with *n* such as *nec*. **Line 1**: The verb *muser* can mean to think about, to waste one's time, to trick, to play the musette, to write poetry, to write music, or even to hum. It is not, therefore, exactly cognate with modern English "muse." **Line 2**: *musart*, a lazy person, a fool or someone who wastes time wooing women. Like a molting bird, such a person is not active. **Line 3**: The verb *amuser* is a translator's false friend. It means to walk around like a lovesick cow with one's muzzle in the air, i.e., waste time.
20. **Rondeau 635**, 4:94. Decasyllabic: *ABaAabAB*, only masculine rhymes. Note the *rimes équivoques* in lines 1, 3, 4, and 7. This rondeau is no more than a slightly modified version of the opem with which Machaut opens the *Voir Dit*: "Cil qui encores ne vous vit" (ll. 203ff.). BNF Fonds français 840, line 4: *Cil etc* and lines 7–8 *Cil etc*. Note that this poem is used as an example of the genre in *L'Art de dictier*. There are two copies of *L'Art*, one in BNF fr 840 (fols. 394a–400c), the other in BNF Nouvelles acquisitions françaises 6221 (fols. 28d–32d). There are no significant variants in the two other versions of this poem, but it is worth noting that the version in the BNF Fonds français 840 copy of *L'Art de dictier* is closer to Machaut's poem in that it omits the word *oncques* in the initial and in the medial refrain, reducing this refrain to the original eight syllables of Machaut in the process. 6221 uses the spelling *cilz*.
21. **Rondel 657**, 4:116. Heptasyllabic: *AB*aAab*AB**. **Line 7**: MS has simply *jubilé etc.*

22. **Rondeau 706**, 4:167; *L'Art de dictier*, p. 90. Decasyllabic: *ABBabABabbABB*, only masculine rhymes. **Line 4**: *cilz*. **Line 6**: *Au monde n'a etc*. **Line 9**: *chascuns* and also *puis*. **Line 10**: *au jour d'ui* and also *ces deux etc*. The poem also appears in 6221, fols. 32a and b. Variants in that MS are line 1, *d'ui*; line 4, *puet*; line 5, *lui puet ne nuire*; line 7, *Mais bien se gart toudis*; line 8, *Car il ne puet*; line 9, *Chascun li nuit si puet*. The last two lines are not in the BNF Fonds français 840 but were added by the editors to complete the refrain. The full refrains in the MS are replaced by *au monde n'a etc* in the medial refrain, and then *au monde n'a au jour d'ui que ces deux etc* in the end refrain.
23. **Virelai 752**, 4:235. Hexasyllabic. The poem is a very irregular virelai, not only because it is based on assonance not rhyme but also because of the lack of full parallelism between the tierce and the refrain: both these features had been characteristic of earlier virelai-type forms in the thirteenth and early fourteenth centuries but were archaic by the time Deschamps wrote; perhaps they match the archaic theme since the genre of the song of the unhappy nun was much more common in this earlier period. All three strophes are analyzed: *A*BA* a*b c*b a*a*ba* A*BA* a*b a*b a*a*ba* A*BA* d*e d*e a*a*ba* A*BA**. **Line 8**: If the word *escolle* is viewed as a manuscript mistake for an assonance in *e*, at least one small irregularity can be removed. **Line 12**: MS "Oez etc"; **Line 23**: MS follows this line with *etc*. **Line 26**: Has only five syllables. SATF reads *moniage*: probably a MS mistake. **Line 34**: MS follows this line with *etc*.
24. **Balade 774**, 4:273. Heterometric: line 6 of every strophe is heptasyllabic and all the remaining lines are decasyllabic, except for the defective lines 25 and 27, which have nine syllables, and line 23, which has eleven: *a*ba*bbccdcD*, envoy *a*da*D*. **Line 12**: Could be *More* and mean "Moor"; the mottled surface of a mulberry makes better sense. Deschamps is also playing on his own name, Morel. The mulberry was sometimes used in medieval slang to indicate a Moor or Muslim; some have taken this line to mean that Deschamps was dark-skinned. **Line 13**: The word *pintelez* is described as unknown by the Raynaud, but Godefroy, giving only this example from Deschamps, lists it as meaning *peindre* or *barioler*. **Line 23**: Has eleven syllables; MS reads *sappre nature*. **Line 25**: Has nine syllables. **Line 27**: The text is corrupt and perhaps the *fait* is a mistake for *faut*, but this reading still leaves the line with only nine syllables. **Line 31**: MS repeats word *envoy*. **Line 18**: Dwarves and people with physical anomalies provided entertainment at many medieval courts; Deschamps may be claiming that his appearance outdistances such characters'.
25. **Balade 776**, 4:276. Octosyllabic: *ababbcbC*, envoy *acaC*, only masculine rhymes. **Line 6**: *mon*. Also, literally, he has many ways. **Line 21**: Missing. **Line 23**: Literally, "He has no concern for people with no money." The word Deschamps uses, *croix*, was slang for the reverse of a coin. The translators here have opted for a different fiscal pun.
26. **Balade 780**, 4:282. Octosyllabic: *ababbc*bC**, envoy *bc*bC**. **Line 20**: MS reads *geste*; we accept SATF's correction. **Line 26**: *graine* can indicate malaguetta pepper, otherwise styled grains of paradise or guinea grains. For a discussion of Deschamps's attitudes toward food, see Scully, "Manger pour vivre: The Gourmet Deschamps" (in Sinnreich-Levi, 1998, 247–52). For a general

discussion of food in the Middle Ages, see Barbara Santich, *The First Mediterranean Cuisine*. During the Middle Ages, there were three main meals in the day: *dejeuner, disner, souper*.

27. **Balade 813**, 4:331. Decasyllabic: *ababbc*c*dD*. The caesura in line 2 divides the word *office*. Again in line 14, the caesura divides the word *nature*. Line 14 has eleven syllables: if the mute *e* at the end of *nature* is not included in the syllabic count (a poetic license called the "epic caesura"), the line and the caesura become regular. **Line 23**: The literal sense of this line is, "There's no point in arguing about it," which is what one might expect a *bailli* used to hearing endless arguments in court to say.
28. **Balade 833**, 5:2. Heterometric: *ab; abccdcD*, only masculine rhymes. The fifth line of every strophe is heptasyllabic, the others are decasyllabic except for line 11, which has only nine syllables; the correction from *dont* to *doit* suggested by SATF seems reasonable. **Line 7**: SATF misread the MS, taking *plourira,* as *plouvra*, and then further emending by adding *il* in *il scet*. **Line 17**: SATF misread *airer* as *curer* and corrects the line to *de li cure ne tien*. **Line 26**: MS reads *la trippe*; SATF corrects to *l'agrippe* and *saint Mor*. Saint Julien was the patron saint of hospitality and even general well-being and good cheer; Saint Maur was the patron saint of gout.
29. **Balade 834**, 5:4. Decasyllabic: *ababbcC*, only masculine rhymes. Note the alliteration in *d* on the words forming the caesura and rhyme in the refrain. **Line 1**: SATF misreads *veiller*. In lines 7 and 14, the refrain reads *que fors le*. **Line 21**: *fors le*. SATF corrects to *fors que* in all the refrains. **Line 11**: Has only nine syllables, possibly even only eight if the *e* in *que* is elided. SATF corrects to *que l'on en ait*.
30. **Balade 837**, 5:7. Heterometric. The fifth line of every strophe is heptasyllabic; the others are decasyllabic: *ababccd*cD**. Irregular lines include the refrain, which has eleven syllables, line 4, which has nine, and line 20, which has eleven and also divides the word *destruire* at the caesura. However, if the mute *e* in this word is not included in the syllabic count (the epic caesura), the line becomes regular.
31. **Balade 838**, 5:8. Decasyllabic, *a*b*a*b*b*c*C**, only feminine rhymes. **Lines 4 and 20**: These lines have only nine syllables. There appears to be a change of scribe on fol. 217d after line 2, on the same side. It may be that this change of hands can account for the curious form *aureuse* in line 6. SATF prints *amoureuse* instead, which would involve repetition of the same rhyme as in line 20. *Aureuse* meaning "happy" does, however, exist. See also Tobler under *euros* where *aureus* is listed; also Godefroy, Complement, under *euros* lists *aurouzes*. *Aur-* for *eur-* is Picard; perhaps the new scribe was Picard? **Line 12**: Could as easily be *Crotin*. Raynaud identifies Saint "Trotin" as a variant spelling of *Trotteins*, but gives no further information. The current editors have not been able to further identify this saint. **Line 19**: SATF reads *feroit, which* is also possibly correct.
32. **Balade 839**, 5:9. Decasyllabic, *ab*ab*b*c*C**. **Line 2**: Mary Magdalene, a woman who followed Jesus after he cured her of demonic possession, witnessed his crucifixion and was among the first to bear witness to his empty tomb. The medieval idiom *faire la madelaine* means to pretend to repent, pretend to humility. **Line 13**: *effeit* here probably means as a result, conclusion, or effect. That is,

the line perhaps means that they hide color beneath their wings. They go around in somber, deathly colors and rags, but in reality, they have color concealed beneath their drab wings (rather like some mainland Chinese in the 1980s, who stitched bright colors into the sleeves of their obligatory, dark Mao jackets). **Line 17**: SATF corrects to *faisant*. The wafer of the refrain is the Eucharist, the bread used in the Catholic liturgy, offered on a paten.

33. **Balade 840**, 5:10. Decasyllabic: *a*ba*bbcbC*. Lines 5, 7, 15, and 17 have eleven syllables. **Line 5**: SATF suggests *Et il se par* . . . **line 7** *Mais j'en reprends*. Both suggestions are reasonable and the second avoids splitting a word at the caesura. SATF regularizes **line 11** by deleting the *re* in *reconfort* and line 17 by removing *ce*, but the latter correction, while not unreasonable, is based on a faulty reading of *n'est traye*. The rhyme in **line 18** is defective; SATF corrects it to *suppli*. **Line 12**: Cf. Morawski proverb 1701: *Por un perdu, deus retrovez*; and Hassell (110). **Line 20**: MS reads *assez amens*, but this phrase is obviously a copyist's mistake for *a ces amens*. Preserving *assez amens* renders the line incomprehensible.
34. **Balade 843**, 5:14. Decasyllabic: *a*ba*bbcbC*. **Line 21**: Has only nine syllables unless the *eu* in *traiteusement* is reckoned as two syllables. **Line 7**: Missing. The translators have supplied one in the English verse. **Line 9**: Has only nine syllables; SATF corrects to *Aucuns si font* . . ., which also produces a better caesura. **Line 12**: Has only nine syllables; SATF corrects to *Du bon du cuer*, which we have not found as in idiom in either Tobler-Lommatsch or Godefroy. The difficulty is removed if *cuer* is pronounced as two syllables.
35. **Balade 844**, 5:15. Decasyllabic: *a*ba*bbcbC*, envoy *bbcbbC*. **Line 2**: SATF misreads: *mesdisance*. **Line 5**: SATF misreads *nices*. **Line 20**: SATF misreads *souriz*. **Line 23**: has only nine syllables; SATF corrects to *je vous le jure*. **Line 27**: Has only nine syllables; SATF corrects *trisse* to *tristesse*. **Line 30**: MS, *onques*. **Line 15**: The calf grew up to fit the rhyme.
36. **Balade 852**, 5:26. Heterometric: the fifth line of every strophe is heptasyllabic. All the others except line 15 are decasyllabic: *ab*ab*aac*aC**. **Line 14**: MS reads for *maistre* simply *m* with an *e* above it. SATF misreads as *s'on ne le laisse*, adding the *le* for meter. **Line 15**: Corrupt: it has only seven syllables like the line before it and ends in *-lir*, not with the expected rhyme in *-er*. It may be that the copyist failed to complete the line after *venir* and that it should have continued *li aider*.
37. **Balade 853**, 5:27. Decasyllabic: *a*ba*bbcbC*, envoy *a*ca*C*. The poem is decasyllabic but line 6 has only nine syllables, unless *puist* is reckoned as two syllables. **Line 4** has eleven syllables. **Line 27**: SATF misreads as *Vray mari* and then adds an *ai* for meter. Saint Leu was patron saint of epilepsy; Saint Matelin, madness; Saint Fiacre, hemorrhoids; and Saint Quentin, dropsy. The poem renews the twelfth- and thirteenth-century genre of the song of the unhappy wife, *la chanson de mal mariée*.
38. **Balade 869**, 5:49. Octosyllabic: *ab*ab*b*cb*C*. In the Middle Ages, Alexander the Great had a reputation for great generosity, but it had waned by the fourteenth century. Raynaud points out that Deschamps preserved the tradition in numerous poems (SATF 11:204). **Line 2**: *Pertuesse* is cited by Godefroy and interpreted as "action de faire des pertuis a la lune." **Line 7**: Could read *esse*; SATF prints

demandes: "*Qui esse*?" The refrain appears only once, in line 8, as *le poing clos*; in lines 16 and 24 it appears as *au poing clos*. The reading *au* reduces the line to seven syllables. **Line 15** appears to be missing in the MS. *Gouesse* is listed as a term of abuse in Godefroy and is probably a variant of *gouaulx*, *gol*, *goet*, which mean cheap wines made from inferior grapes. **Line 21**: The abbreviation for *quarts* could as easily be interpreted as *quatre* or even as *quatre mille*, which would make no sense. It could read 4,000 almost as easily as 3/4, 3/4 making more sense in context. This line, therefore, presents textual and interpretive difficulties. The translation is a compromise. Our cheapskate is so mean that he won't even serve four whole eggs if he can get away with 3 3/4, just as he serves foods of no value: lard and verjuice. **Line 24**: To make an English rhyme, the refrain gave up one word to the previous line.

39. **Balade 871**, 5:51. Decasyllabic: *a*ba*bbcbC*. The alliteration in *p* in the refrain is worth noting. **Line 5**: SATF *seins* may make better sense and avoids duplicating the rhyme in line 14. **Line 6**: MS has *chantez*, but we accept SATF emendation to *hantez*, which makes better sense. **Line 17**: MS has *espurettes* and SATF corrects to *espinettes*. This correction would have Deschamps outside, not up on his spurs, but poised on thorns—perhaps metaphorical thorns of anxiety about the behavior of his lady friends in his absence. The word *espinette* is also linked to love in such courtly works as Froissart's *L'Espinette amoureuse*. **Line 22**: The line has only nine syllables. SATF correction to *pays* makes better sense and restores the syllabic count. **Line 24**: *petis*. There were luxury shops on the Grand Pont (today the Pont au Change). It was one of the most popular among the upper classes (SATF 1:349, notes for Balade 62). Les Halles, today a shopping mall, was a great market place. Medieval people bathed considerably more often than the modern popular imagination believes. In Deschamps's time, bathing and taking steam baths were widespread at all levels of society. For a discussion of bathing and other details of personal life, readers should consult Georges Duby's *A History of Personal Life*, especially pp. 600–10. **Line 18**: That is, the speaker is now down on his luck, or has botched matters beyond repair. **Line 22**: The countryside has been laid waste by warring parties such as are deplored in "Out with your money, out!" Boudet and Millet have included an annotated edition of this poem in their anthology (154–56).
40. **Balade 874**, 5:55. Heterometric: line 6 of every strophe is heptasyllabic; the others are decasyllabic, *a*b*a*b*b*ccd*cD**. **Line 4**: Has only nine syllables; SATF corrects to *devez bien mettre*. **Line 10**: MS omits *vous*. **Line 28** has only nine syllables; SATF corrects to *que l'en*. **Line 10**: Actually, Deschamps advocates marten fur, but he didn't know about Davy Crockett. Both animals have bushy tails, so the translators, who all lived in the United States at the beginning of their collaboration, opted for this more regionally understandable rendering.
41. **Balade 900**, 5:90. Decasyllabic: *ababbccdcD*, envoy *cdcD*, only masculine rhymes. **Line 3**: *delez*. The word *envoy* is missing. **Line 4**: Has eleven syllables; SATF corrects by suppressing the second *pour*. **Line 6**: SATF misreads *emprunter*. **Line 26**: Since the cuckoo sings for the cuckolded husband, his serenade is to be avoided.

42. **Balade 901**, 5:91. Decasyllabic: *a*ba*bbccd*cD**, envoy *bd*bD**. **Line 12**: SATF corrects to *Ou est*. **Line 26**: Has only nine syllables. Perhaps the copyist omitted *ce* in *que ce doit*. SATF corrects to *or je ne sçay que doit*. **Line 29**: SATF corrects to *pourvoit*. **Line 34**: The refrain in the MS reads *La Saussaye*. The translation retains this spelling because it makes for better rhymes. **Line 33**: SATF misreads *l'on*. Royal horses were put out to pasture at the abbey at La Saussaye. Io was seduced by Jove and then turned into a cow to avoid the jealous anger of Juno (Ovid, *Metamorphoses* 1:583ff). Antheus (Antaeus) is a mistake for Actaeon, who was turned into a stag and killed by his own hunting dogs for having seen the goddess Diana naked (Ovid, *Metamorphoses* 3:137ff). Raynaud noted this mistake (11:161).
43. **Balade 911**, 5:107. Decasyllabic: *ab*ab*b*ccd*cD**, envoy *cd*cD**. Note the *rimes équivoques* in lines 6, 7, and 43. This poem, with four strophes and an envoy, may be considered an irregular short chanson royale or an irregular long balade. There is no break in the sense to suggest that a strophe is missing. **Line 1**: SATF misreads *tresdoulz*. **Line 12**: MS reads *fiforsenee*, which could be a mistake for *si forsenée*, but this reading would produce a line of eleven syllables. **Line 26**: MS has *este*. **Line 32**: MS has *demandez*. **Line 43**: Has eleven syllables; SATF corrects to *c'est amis*.
44. **Chanson Royale 912**, 5:109. Octosyllabic: *ab*ab*b*ccdcD*, envoy *adaD*. This is a character lyric; *à personnaiges* is the description commonly given such poems. A minidrama, it tends to strain within its five strophes and envoy, and does not always ensure end-stopping (e.g., line 41). The meaning of the refrain changes from the first strophe where it probably implies: "If I'd known about him earlier, he'd have been punished already" to the remaining strophes, where it implies, "We were wrong to have arrested him in the first place." The refrain changes meaning because the speaker of it changes. **Line 1**: SATF misreads *Sergens*. **Line 9**: SATF misreads *Et*. Lienart is identified by Raynaud as Saint Leonard, the patron saint of thieves. **Line 33**: The murderer is also styled a *mauves garcon*, or criminal. **Line 36**: Literally, subjunctive "Let it be known!"
45. **Balade 923**, 5:127. Decasyllabic: *ab*ab*b*cB*C*, envoy *aacaaC*. There is a change in the word order of the refrain in line 23, that we have not corrected: *La ne voit on raison, sens ne mesure*. MS reading for this final refrain in line 30 is *chalumiaux*. A balade with a two-line refrain is unusual in Deschamps. It reduces to one line in the envoy, but given the symmetry of the rhyme scheme—*aacaaC*—the reduction seems deliberate. The bagpipe is an instrument whose origins are ancient, attested by Aristophanes, Suetonius, and Martial. Some early medieval bagpipes such as the French *estive* were "soft" instruments, classed with the harp and the fiddle. Bagpipes were played in France for many centuries before and after the fourteenth, but they developed similarly to the much louder instruments known today. Deschamps was not the only medieval person who found the volume of such bagpipe music unpleasant, and during the later Middle Ages, bagpipes were played less indoors. For a thorough discussion of the history of the bagpipe, see Sadie, "Bagpipe."
46. **Balade 928**, 5:136. Decasyllabic: *ababbccd*cD*, envoy *cd*cD**. Line 7, which has eleven syllables, is corrupt. SATF makes sense of it by suggesting *Tant que*

remplie en feust toute la gent. **Line 14** also has eleven syllables. **Line 28**: *povre* could also be read as *painé*, troubled or distressed. **Line 34**: We accept the SATF's emendation, adding *povoit* to make sense of the line and restore the scansion. Raynaud identifies Basin as a king of Thuringia, celebrated in a work that does not survive. From the same source, Martin is either the patron saint of sore throats or the generic name for a cleric, or, in this case, a name given to personify a *vilain* or poor man.

47. **Balade 969**, 5:204. Decasyllabic: *ab*ab*b*c*c*d*c*D**, envoy *c*c*d*c*c*D**. MS rubric has *autre balade*. This balade is a Christian *ubi sunt* poem. The biblical hero Samson, noted for unsurpassed physical strength, was defeated after being betrayed by Delilah. Alexander the Great, king of Macedonia, was later one of the medieval Nine Worthies. King David had his loyal retainer Uriah sent into battle so that David might have Bathsheba, Uriah's wife. David died and was succeeded by his son, Solomon. Jeremiah was a biblical prophet, and Croesus a famously rich Greek king. Deschamps's point in this poem has been made over and over by poets: neither wealth nor riches nor connections can save any person from eventual death. **Line 28**: Since a *drame* is a drachma or small coin, "We all pay our mortal dues" is the sense of this line.
48. **Balade 1024**, 5:294. Octosyllabic: *ababbccdcD*, envoy *ccdccD*, only masculine rhymes. **Line 15**: *connim* is probably the copyist's mistake for *connin*. Raynaud identifies Jean de Saint-Simon as belonging to the house of Louis of Orleáns, *ecuyer de la cuisine de la reine* in 1391 (BNF Pièce originale 2776).
49. **Balade 1028**, 5:300. Decasyllabic: *a*ba*bbccdcD*, envoy *a*a*da*a*D*. This poem appears twice more in the MS and in the SATF edition: 5:332 (fol. 276c), and 5:300 (fol. 277a). There are no significant variants: line 4 *seuls*; line 8 *blamez*; line 15 *queudre*; line 16: *En cuirien* . . . ; line 25 SATF corrects to *devisier*; line 27 *tous*, SATF corrects to *cleux*; line 31 *Prince*; line 33 *plais*. **Line 12**: Besides the cognate "danger," *dangier* can also mean power, domination, enjoyment, will, caprice, the right to use, marital authority, mastery, captivity, resistance. **Line 31**: Although friends of both sexes, *ami* and *amie*, are mentioned, Deschamps is making no sexual comment. Travelers at inns often slept even ten to a bed, at least, so Deschamps claims in Chanson Royale 1325. Cf. Balade 1317, in which he praises Paris, among other reasons, as a place one needn't share a bed. Other poems about staying at inns include Balades 1305 and 1318; Rondeaux 1303, 1323, and 1326 (see p. 96).
50. **Balade 1030**, 5:303. Octosyllabic: *ababbcbC*, envoy *aacaaC*, only masculine rhymes. The poem could be viewed partly as a satire on his own behavior when seeking payment of sums of money promised him by Charles VI but delayed by the royal treasurers (e.g., in Balades 788, 902, and 1168). Jean le Flament was one such treasurer. The image of the confessional, which is well developed throughout the poem, does not, however, appear elsewhere in association with late payment of debts. **Line 4**: SATF corrects to *seignour*. **Line 18**: Has nine syllables; SATF corrects to *Et a souper*. . . .
51. **Balade 1036**, 5:313. Decasyllabic: *ab*ab*b*ccd*cd**, envoy *aad*aaD**. Note the *rime équivoque* in lines 1 and 3. **Line 7**: Probably a MS mistake for *escouter*; SATF misreads *escouter*. **Line 35**: A word is split at the caesura.

52. **Balade 1202**, 6:188. Octosyllabic: *ababbccdde*dE**, envoy *dde*ddE**. The word *publie* in the envoy is of interest insofar as it may suggest that Deschamps viewed this poem as an open letter to the court as a whole, not to any one person in it. MS adds: *Balade du deduit et estrange melodie des oyseaulx demourans en la Tour de Fymes ou Eustace des Champs demoura malades par III moys, qui nuit et jour en fut servis.* **Line 22**: MS reads *lassonnerie.* The castle at Fismes was given to Deschamps by Charles VI in the first half of 1381 (see Laurie, 34 n11; SATF 11:33–34).
53. **Balade 1230**, 6:232. Octosyllabic: *ab*ab*b*c*c*ddedE*, envoy *aaeaaE.* Line 9 has only seven syllables. As in Deschamps's character lyrics, the loosening of the conventions with respect to end-stopping is noteworthy in lines 25, 28, and 29. No titles *balade* and *envoy.* **Line 2**: SATF has *goutte.* **Line 13**: SATF misreads *endurer* and amends by suppressing *doulz.* MS crosses out the *en* before *durer.* **Line 15**: SATF misreads *frapper.* Saint Anthony was patron saint of erysipelas, a skin disease; Saint Riquer, fevers; Saint Maur, the gout.
54. **Balade 1232**, 6:235. Octosyllabic: *a*ba*bbc*c*dc*D*, envoy *c*c*dc*c*D.* The refrain in lines 10 and 36 reads *j'em puis.* It has been regularized to *en* in both cases. The poem is an updated version of the traditional *chanson de mal mariée.* Again end-stopping does not always occur in this character lyric: lines 1, 13, 14, and 31. Nearest proverb in Morawski to correspond a little with the *souppes* above is *il estuet avoir du pain a qui veult faire souppes. L'envoy* is missing from the MS. **Line 7**: This agricultural metaphor for sexual intercourse is, of course, an ancient as well as medieval motif. **Line 27**: Saint Arnoul was patron saint of cuckolded husbands. **Line 34**: A droll oath, "by her virginity," long since lost. The translated refrain is very free. Literally, it is, "If there is anything I can do about it."
55. **Balade 1242**, 6:251. Decasyllabic: *a*ba*bbc*c*d*c*D**. **Line 14**: *conguy* must be a scribal error for *congnuy.* **Line 23**: SATF offers *racine* instead of nature. This balade is in response to a verse epistle sent to Deschamps by Christine de Pizan on February 10, 1403, Old Style. Christine de Pizan (c.1365–c.1442) had, around the time of this correspondence with Deschamps (1401–3), been engaged in the exchange of letters about the *Roman de la Rose (Epistres du débat sur le Roman de la Rose* or *Querelle de la Rose*). Christine responded to a treatise by Jean de Montreuil which praised Jean de Meun's section of the *Roman de la Rose.* A vehement epistolary exchange involving several writers developed, to which Christine contributed two more letters. (See, for example, Baird and Kane.) Christine had come to France after her father, Tommaso di Benvenuto da Pizzano, had been invited to become Charles V's court astrologer. When left a widow with three small children, she supported herself and her family with her writing. It is of interest that Deschamps does specifically claim to have known her father (line 14). Also he says that he'll be writing to her separately from this poem (line 27), presumably in prose. This reference, coupled with Deschamps's mention of a remedy or solace for Christine may possibly be construed as a reference to Deschamps's intention to support her in the *Querelle de la Rose,* in which she defended women from traditional misogynist attacks. It is not possible to tell whether Deschamps intended his poem as purely private reassurance to Christine or whether he hoped that it might serve as public support of her. More simply, it may indicate his sympathy for her long illnesses in the late 1390s and

early 1400s. The alliteration in *f* on the words forming the caesura and the rhyme should be noted. *L'envoy* is missing in the MS. Christine's father was from Pizzano, near Bologna. This city was often erroneously identified with Pisa. Elena Nicolini correctly identified the source of Christine's name. We retain the spellings of *Pizain* and *Pizan* to preserve the spelling of the manuscript in the former case, and to preserve the scansion in the latter. **Line 12**: Cf. 1 Kings 10:5–9. **Line 23**: The *fausse nature/racine* (false doctrine) in question stems from the *Querrelle de la Rose*. **Line 35**: Boethius was the author of the *Consolation of Philosophy*, a tremendously popular philosophical work of the Middle Ages. Boethius (c. 480 to 526) wrote the *Consolatio philosophiae* in 523–24. The minister of Theodoric, the Ostrogothic king, in 526, Boethius was charged with treason. His property was confiscated and he himself was condemned to death. He was imprisoned at Ticinum (Pavia), tortured, and put to death at Calvenzano. In 722, Liutprand, king of the Lombards, had a tomb built for him in the church of San Pietro Ciel d'Oro at Pavia. Deschamps may well have seen this tomb during one of his visits to Pavia. Christine cites the *Consolatio philosophiae* in her verse epistle to Deschamps (ll. 70–77 in Kosta-Théfaine, 87). See also Earl Jeffrey Richards, "The Lady Wants to Talk: Christine de Pizan's 'Epistre a Eustace Morel' " in Sinnreich-Levi (1998, 109–22). Deschamps's comparing Christine to one of the best-known authors of the Middle Ages, and a fellow Italian, is quite a compliment.

56. **Balade 1246**, 6:258. Decasyllabic: *a*ba*bbc*c*d*c*D**, envoy *bbd*bbD**. Alliteration on the words forming the caesura and rhyme is to be noted in lines 18, 19, 26, and 33. MS adds *Autre balade comment l'acteur s'excuse de faire aucuns diz amoureux pour ce que tout est mal ordonné ou royaume* (fol. 388c). **Line 10**: Reads *ordenée* in BNF Fonds français 840, and SATF corrects to this reading for all the refrains, although the MS has *ordonnée* in lines 20, 30, and 36. **Line 27**: SATF misreads *mauvais*. **Line 28**: Has eleven syllables; SATF corrects to *guerdonnée*. **Line 31**: SATF misreads *par tout*. **Line 7**: Literally: eclipsed.
57. **Balade 1266**, 7:3. Octosyllabic: *ab*ab*b*ccdcD*, envoy *ccdccD*. Lines 31 and 35 have nine syllables. "Rimes équivoques" in lines 8 and 10. **Line 31**: *L'envoy* is missing from the MS. **Line 32**: This line could also be translated "to talk of those 60 years of dire. . . ." **Line 35**: SATF corrects to *Me souhaident ja oultre mer*. For more on Deschamps and senescence, see Magnan, *Aspects of Senescence in the Work of Eustache Deschamps*, and Magnan, "Eustache Deschamps and the Course of Life" (in Sinnreich-Levi 1998, 229–44).
58. **Balade 1279**, 7:20. Decasyllabic: *ab*ab*b*c*b*C**. The Bibliothèque Nationale de France, on whose microfilm of Fonds français 840 the editors have had to rely for those few poems which Ian Laurie did not transcribe directly from the MS, did not correctly microfilm the folio in which the last two strophes of this poem appear. Exceptionally, therefore, the editors have been obliged to rely on the assistance of a Parisian colleague for these two strophes. Jean-François Kosta-Théfaine was allowed to consult the MS itself for long enough to transcribe the remaining two strophes, and it is his version that we print above. **Line 21**: MS *suire* is a mistake for *sivre*. We accept the SATF's silent correction of the MS's *doute* to *route*. Deschamps, who records how his poetry got lost when his manu-

scripts were borrowed by friends (cf. Balade 24, the first in this collection), might have concluded that six centuries have done nothing to improve the situation. Personifications of Love or Jealousy may not have been Deschamps's intention, but this translation has opted to personify Dame Jealousy.

59. **Balade 1309**, 7:66. Decasyllabic: *ab*ab*b*ccd*cD**, envoy *aad*aD**. The envoy is unusual in that it does not divide into two symmetrical parts. Lines 9 and 25 have eleven syllables; line 18, only nine. As line 25 stands, it is probably corrupt since the caesura splits the word *ailleurs*. SATF correction suppresses *Leur*, which regularizes the caesura and the syllabic count. **Line 1**: MS reads *Oe*. Beside it is a lower-case *d* as a guide to the scribe to make a capital *D*. The capital maker misread the note. **Line 6**: Setting aside Petrarch, it is worth remembering that the view that mountains are beautiful was not medieval. **Line 24**: *vuires*. We accept the SATF emendation to *vivres*. **Line 28**: Lucifer and his companion devils roam or crowd literally in great numbers rather than freely.

60. **Balade 1310**, 7:67. Octosyllabic: *ababbccdcD*, envoy, *aadaaD*, only masculine rhymes. *Rimes équivoques* in lines 12 and 14. Line 5 has ten syllables and line 29 eleven. **Line 33**: *patarins*—Deschamps uses the term for the Patarines, an eleventh-century northern Italian heretical group, to designate all heretical types.

61. **Balade 1311**, 7:69. Octosyllabic: *ababbccdcD*, envoy *bbdbbD*, only masculine rhymes. *Rimes équivoques* in lines 6 and 7. Lines 19 and 23 have nine syllables. **Line 23**: SATF suppresses *Dont* for meter and sense. **Line 25**: MS misplaces this line after the refrain. **Line 36**: MS has *riens*, but we regularized the refrain.

62. **Rondeau 1326**, 7:90. Octosyllabic: *AB*B*ab*AB*ab*b*AB*B**. **Line 1**: The "stink" in the French is given off by the "mold" of the translation. **Line 4**: Poor Deschamps, a man used to the cuisine of the French court, is probably referring to sauerkraut, which is not normally served in a roll. The word "roll," however, gave the harried translators a rhyme in English. In its defense, the translators wish to point out that the cabbage roll is a central culinary concept of Eastern European cuisine, and so not out of place here, and worthy, along with sauerkraut, of all the disdain Deschamps could muster. **Line 8**: Literally, there are twenty people eating from two platters. **Line 11**: MS has *poureaulx*, probably a scribal error.

63. **Balade 1341**, 7:116. Octosyllabic: *ababbccdcD*, envoy *aadaaD*, only masculine rhymes. There is no proverb to match the above refrain in Morawski, but there is the opposite proverb in number 1477: *l'en n'a nul demain*. **Line 24**: "Principals" is diplomatic and business jargon today for "superiors," "those with the power to make decisions."

64. **Rondeau 1385**, 7:236. Octosyllabic: *ABBabABabbABB*. All masculine rhymes. **Lines 1 and 10**: SATF misreads *serrai*. Roland's proverbial thirst is traceable to Laisse 165 of *La Chanson de Roland*. Archbishop Turpin, himself mortally wounded, tries to fetch Roland water from a stream to revive him from a faint, and dies in the attempt. Elsewhere, Deschamps bemoans being sent on campaign far from the amenities of the court (Balade 854, line 14): "Comme Rolant languiroie de soy" ("Like Roland, I'll be racked by thirst").

65. **Balade 1432**, 8:94. Octosyllabic: *ababbc*c*dc*D*, envoy *c*c*dc*c*D*. **Line 8**: Has nine syllables. MS adds: *Balade de desprisier l'un l'autre et de l'acomparagier a un chien*. **Line 4**: SATF misreads *qu'un*. **Line 6**: MS reads *Dhiens*. **Line 8**:

Has nine syllables; SATF corrects to . . . *c'est voir*. **Line 22**: SATF misreads *souz*. **Line 23**: SATF corrects to *barguignier* to restore the rhyme. **Line 5**: Literally: he knows nothing. Dogs were kept as pets in the Middle Ages but also were working animals for hunting, ratting, and herding. Dogs would have accompanied their owners to many of the locations cited in this poem. The translation of the refrain is very free. Literally, "A dog must know almost everything"—and perhaps even more than we do!

66. **Balade 1449**, 8:134. Octosyllabic, *ab*ab*b*cb*C*, envoy *b*b*cb*b*C*. *Rimes équivoques* in lines 28 and 29. MS adds *Balade de doloir pour jeunesse qui s'en va ailleurs*. This poem also exists in BNF Nouvelles acquisitions françaises 6221, fols. 34c–34d. 6221 also has a preamble: *Balade faite de douleurs pour jeunesse qui va ailleurs*. **Line 11**: 6221 has *ay*. **Line 12**: SATF misreads *foyz*. **Line 13**: SATF corrects to *En l'estomac grieve pointure*. **Line 23**: 6221 has *en cure*. Karin Becker has written about Deschamps and illness: "Eustache Deschamps' Medical Poetry" (in Sinnreich-Levi 1998, 209–23).

67. **Balade 1450**, 8:135. Decasyllabic: *ababbc*c*dc*D*, envoy *c*c*dc*c*D*. Note the alliteration in *p* reinforcing the words that form the caesura and rhyme in the refrain. MS adds *Autre balade du regret de jeunesse*. There is also a version of the poem in BNF Nouvelles acquisitions françaises 6221, fol. 34d. It contains one line (line 17) missing in BNF Fonds français 840, adopted here as an emendation on which the translation depends. **Line 8**: SATF misreads *pouepoint*, a scribal error; the abbreviation in 6221 suggests *pourpoint*. **Line 14**: SATF prints *acquerrir*; *acquerir* in 6221. **Line 17**: SATF also adds this line from 6221; 6221 has three versions: *tost apres chey* and *tost tournay*, the two last crossed out; 6221 also reads *froit ay trouvé*, adopted by SATF for meter. **Line 31**: 6221 also has *j'ay de*, but above the *de* is a better reading, *cru*. **Line 23**: *graveleux* means suffering from bladder stones, also sometimes called gravel in English. **Line 27**: Medieval theorists divided life expectancy into six or, more usually, seven decades. For Deschamps's attitudes toward senescence, see Magnan.

68. **Balade 1452**, 8:149. Octosyllabic: *ab*ab*b*ccdcD*, envoy *ccdccD*. MS adds *balade de comment ce monde n'est riens quant a la vie*. Cf. SATF 5:189, 6:22, 7:149. **Line 1**: Nimrod, a mighty hunter, is identified as the founder of Babylon (Genesis 10:8–10). **Lines 3–8**: Priam was the king of Troy, destroyed during the Trojan War. Hector, Priam's beloved son, led the Trojan army and was killed by the Greek hero Achilles, who died soon thereafter. Carthage, once a great city, was the first major stopping point for Aeneas after fleeing Troy. Romulus and Remus were the mythical founders of Rome. Alexander the Great was king of Macedonia (336–23 B.C.E.). Julius Caesar, Roman emperor, was murdered in 44 C.E. **Lines 11–12**: David was a prophet, a king of Israel, and one of the medieval Nine Worthies. David sent his loyal retainer Uriah into battle without support so that David might have Bathsheba, Uriah's wife (2 Samuel 11–12). **Line 12**: Judah Maccabee, another of the Nine Worthies, was a Jewish patriot who led the Jewish people during the revolt c. 164 B.C.E. commemorated by Chanukah. **Line 13**: The betrayal and battles of Emperor Charlemagne's nephew Roland are recorded in *La Chanson de Roland*. **Lines 14–15**: Godfrey of Bologne, who was part of the First Crusade, accepted the crown of Jerusalem but not the title of king. Baldwin

was his younger brother, and became king of Jerusalem in 1100. His rule formed the basis for French domination of Syria and Palestine for the next 200 years. **Line 16**: Joshua was the biblical character most famed for the battle of Jericho (Joshua 6), and for God's stopping the sun in its path during another battle (Joshua 10:12–13). Darius I, son of Hystaspes, attempted to conquer Greece, and was finally defeated at Marathon in 490 B.C.E. Arthur fills a place in British mytho-history analogous to that of the historical Charlemagne in French history. There were three biblical worthies: David, Judah, and Joshua; three classical worthies: Hector, Julius Caesar, and Alexander; and three medieval worthies: Godfrey of Bologne, Arthur, and Charlemagne. (For a full discussion of this topos, see Schröder and McMillan.) **Line 21**: Attila, king of the Huns (434–53 C.E.), led a barbarian invasion of the Roman Empire. **Line 22**: Cato was an important early Roman writer, censor, and model of austerity (d. 149 B.C.E.). **Line 23**: Hercules, a classical demigod whose twelve labors were widely chronicled, died when his jealous wife was tricked into poisoning his garment. Jason led the Argonauts through adventures including the theft of the Golden Fleece; Medea murdered their children (cf. notes to Balade 493 p. 220). **Line 24**: Socrates was the Greek philosopher whose suicide was commanded by the assembly of Athens because of his alleged corruption of the youth of the city. **Line 25**: Augustine was a Church Father. **Line 26**: Virgil was the author of the *Aeneid* and other classical poems. **Line 27**: Ptolomy, whose seminal work *The Almagest* served as the basis for astronomical studies through the seventeenth century, lived in Alexandria in the second century C.E. **Line 28**: Hippocrates, called the father of medicine, lived from 460 B.C.E. to c. 377.

69. **Sote balade 1455**, 8:146. Octosyllabic: *ababbcbC*, envoy *acaC*, only masculine rhymes. The alliteration in *m* is worth noting in strophe 2. **Line 10**: The line would have nine syllables if the *-ier* ending of *sanglier* is reckoned as two syllables; SATF corrects to *sangler*. **Line 15**: The line has nine syllables; SATF corrects to *Prins fust, tant voulsisse donner*. The line then offers an unreal condition: "If the herring had been caught, I would have been willing to pay that sum for it." This reading suits the following *voulsisse* better, but if the MS reading, *fut*, is allowed to stand, the lie is stretched even more than the syntax. Then the fish did actually get caught, and Monseigneur would have been willing to pay that sum for it had it been for sale.
70. **Balade 1469**, 8:169. Octosyllabic: *ababbccd*cD**, envoy *aad*aaD**. MS adds *Balade sur les femmes qui troussent leurs tetins* (*Balade on women who bundle up their breasts*). Brassieres had not yet been invented at this date, but fourteenth-century women did their best to hoist their breasts as near to the neck as possible with something similar. **Line 1**: SATF's *moustra* is just as possible. **Line 21**: As easily *estroittement*. **Envoy**: For this translation, the question of whether *princes* is singular or plural is perhaps not so pressing because the address had become formulaic in the thirteenth century.
71. **Balade 1486**, 8:196. Octosyllabic: *ababbc*c*dc*D*, envoy *aadaaD*. Lines 21 and 22 are in the category of "grammatical" rhyme. MS adds *Balade que femme prandre est le plus fort lien qui soit*. **Line 15**: SATF corrects by adding *Et*. This addition is unnecessary since the termination *-ien* in the poem is sometimes

reckoned as one and sometimes two syllables. **Line 25**: SATF misreads *se c'est sens*. **Line 5**: There are also thongs, but they didn't fit in the line in English. **Line 15**: A castle in Orléans, Amboise, was often used as a prison. **Line 16**: Châtelet was the seat of common-law jurisdiction from the Middle Ages to the French Revolution.

72. ***Le Miroir de mariage***, 9:130–31, ll. 3920–54. *Le Miroir de mariage* is written in octosyllabic couplets rhyming *aa*, *bb*, etc. and a mixture, not regular alternation, of masculine and feminine rhymes. *Le Miroir* focuses on whether the main character, Franc Vouloir (Free Will), should marry. The influence of *Le Roman de la Rose* resonates in *Le Miroir*, as Franc Vouloir's false friends—Desir (Desire), Folie (Foolishness), Servitude (Servility), and Faintise (Deceit)—urge marriage and procreation. Franc Vouloir's true friend, *Répetoire de Science* (Repository of Wisdom), enlists the aid of the entire array of medieval and classical antifeminist tracts and topoi in stating his opposition to the marriage plan. The selection in this volume is one cited by Bryan and Dempster (222) and is therefore, perhaps, familiar to some readers. Bryan and Dempster find parallels to the *Wife of Bath's Prologue* ll. 198–398 *passim*. In an anecdote used to illustrate the caprices of married life, husband and wife are depicted in an argument. The husband has been reproaching his wife. This is her reply.

Bibliography

Baird, Joseph L. and John R. Kane. *La Querelle de la Rose: Letters and Documents*. North Carolina Studies in the Romance Languages and Literatures 199. Chapel Hill: U.N.C. Dept. of Romance Languages, 1978.

Becker, Karin. *Eustache Deschamps: L'état actuel de la recherche*. Orleans: Paradigme, 1996.

Besant, Walter. *The French Humorists from the Twelfth to the Nineteenth Century*. London: Bentley, 1873. Reprint, Freeport, NY: Books for Libraries Press, 1972.

Boüard, Michel de. *La France et l'Italie au temps du grand schisme d'occident*. Paris: Boccard, 1936.

Boudet, Jean-Patrice, Helene Millet, and Karin Becker, eds. *Eustache Dechamps en son temps*. Histoire ancienne et médiévale 44. Paris: Sorbonne, 1997.

Bradley, John W. *A Dictionary of Miniaturists, Illuminators, Calligraphers and Copyists*. 3 vols. London: Quaritch, 1889.

Brewer, Derek, ed. *Chaucer, Geoffrey*. London: Bell, 1974.

Bryan, W. F. and Germaine Dempster. *Sources and Analogues of Chaucer's "Canterbury Tales*." New York: Humanities Press, 1941.

Calin, William. "Deschamps's 'Ballade to Chaucer' Again, or the Dangers of Intertextual Medieval Comparatism." In *Eustache Deschamps, French Courtier-Poet: His Work and His World*, edited by Deborah M. Sinnreich-Levi, pp. 73–83. New York: AMS Press, 1998.

———. *The French Tradition and the Literature of Medieval England*. Toronto: University of Toronto Press, 1994.

Cantor, Norman. *In the Wake of the Plague: The Black Death and the World It Made*. New York: Free Press, 2001.

Cerquiglini-Toulet, Jacqueline. *The Color of Melancholy: The Uses of Books in the Fourteenth Century*. Translated by Lydia G. Cochrane. Baltimore: Johns Hopkins University Press, 1997.

———. *"Un engin si soutil": Guillaume de Machaut et l'écriture au XIVᵉ siècle*. Bibliothèque du XVᵉ siècle 47. Geneva: Slatkine, 1985.

Christine de Pisan. *The Book of the City of Ladies*. Translated by Earl Jeffrey Richards. New York: Persea Books, 1983.

Coleman, Joyce. "The Text Recontextualized in Performance: Deschamps' Prelection of Machaut's "Voir Dit" to the Count of Flanders." *Viator* 31 (2000): 234–48.

Collette, Carolyn P. "Chaucer and the French Tradition Revisited: Philippe de Mezières and the Good Wife." In *Medieval Women: Texts and Contexts in Late Medieval Britain—Essays for Felicity Riddy*, edited by Jocelyn Wogan-Browne et al., pp. 151–68. Turnhout, Belgium: Brepols, 2000.

Coville, Alfred. "Jacques de Nouvion, secrétaire de duc d'Orléans et du roi." *Bibliothèque de l'Ecole des Chartes* 96: 71–90.

Crépin, André. "Chaucer et Deschamps." In *Autour d'Eustache Deschamps, Actes du Colloque du Centre d'Etudes Médiévales de l'Université de Picardie–Jules Verne, Amiens, 5–8 Novembre 1998*, edited by Danielle Buschinger, pp. 37–43. Amiens: Centre d'Etudes Médiévales de l'Université de Picardie–Jules Verne, 1999.

Delachenal, Roland. *Les Grands chroniques de France: Chronique des règnes de Jean II et de Charles V*. 4 vols. Société de l'Histoire de France. Paris: Nogent, 1910–20.

Deschamps, Eustache. *L'Art de dictier*, edited and translated by Deborah M. Sinnreich-Levi. East Lansing, Mich.: Colleagues Press, 1994.

———. "*Le Miroir de mariage* d'Eustache Deschamps: Edition critique accompagnée d'une étude littéraire et linguistique." Monique Dufournaud Engel. *DAI* 36 (1975): 6734A; Ph.D. diss., McGill University, 1975.

———. *Oeuvres complètes de Eustache Deschamps*. Edited by Gaston Raynaud and Henri Auguste Edouard, le marquis de Queux de Sainte-Hilaire. 11 vols. Paris: Firmin-Didot, 1878–1903. Reprint, New York: Johnson Reprint, 1966.

Devaux, Jean. "Images des guerres de Flandre chez Eustache Deschamps et Jean Froissart." In *Autour d'Eustache Deschamps, Actes du Colloque du Centre d'Etudes Médiévales de l'Université de Picardie–Jules Verne, Amiens, 5–8 Novembre 1998*, edited by Danielle Buschinger, pp. 57–72. Amiens: Centre d'Etudes Médiévales de l'Université de Picardie-Jules Verne, 1999.

Duby, Georges, ed. *A History of Private Life*. Vol. 2. *Revelations of the Medieval World*. Translated by Arthur Goldhammer. Cambridge, Mass., and London: Bellknap Press of Harvard University Press, 1988.

Dupont-Ferrier, Gustave. *Gallia Regia: ou état des officiers royaux des bailliages et des sénéchaussées de 1328 à 1515*. 7 vols. Paris: Imprimerie Nationale, 1942–65.

———. "Le Personnel de la cour du Trésor 1390–1520." *Annuaire Bulletin de la Société de l'Histoire de France* (1935): 185–298.

Elsabe, Einhorn. *Old French: A Concise Handbook*. London: Cambridge University Press, 1975.

Flammermont, Jules. "Histoires des institutions municipals de Senlis." *Bibliothèque de l'Ecole des Hautes Etudes* 45. Paris: Viewig, 1881.

Fournier, Nathalie. *Grammaire du français classique*. Paris: Belin, 1998.

Fox, John. *The Lyric Poetry of Charles d'Orléans*. Oxford: Clarendon Press, 1969.

Gardner, Rosalyn, and Marion A. Greene. *A Brief Description of Middle French Syntax*. Studies in the Romance Languages and Literatures 29. Chapel Hill: University of North Carolina Press, 1958.

Godefroy, Frédéric. *Dictionnaire de l'ancienne langue française, et de tous ses dialectes du IXe au XVe siècle composé d'après le dépouillement de tous les plus importants documents, manuscrits ou imprimés, qui se trouvent dans les grands bibliothèques de la France et de l'Europe, et dans les principales archives départementales, municipales, hospitalières ou privées.* 10 vols. Paris: Vieweg, 1880–1902.

Grand Larousse universel. 15 vols. Paris: Larousse, 1994.

Hassell, James Woodrow. *Middle French Proverbs, Sentences, and Proverbial Phrases.* Subsidia mediaevalia 12. Toronto: Pontifical Institute of Mediaeval Studies, 1982.

Hoepffner, Ernst. "Eustache Deschamps: Leben und Werke." Ph.D. diss., Strassburg, 1904. Reprint Strassburg: Karl J. Trübner, 1904. Reprint, Geneva: Slatkine, 1974.

Huizinga, Johan. *The Autumn of the Middle Ages.* Translated by Rodney J. Payton and Ulrich Mammitzsch. Chicago: University of Chicago Press, 1996.

Jenkins, T. A. "Deschamps' Ballade to Chaucer." *Modern Language Notes* 33 (1918): 268–78.

Kendrick, Laura. "Transgression, Contamination, and Woman in Eustache Deschamps's 'Miroir de mariage.' " *Stanford French Review* 14:1–2 (Spring–Fall 1990): 211–30.

Kibler, William. *An Introduction to Old French.* 4th ed. New York: MLA, 1989.

Kooijman, Jacques. "Envoi des fleurs: à propos des échanges littéraires entre la France et l'Angleterre sous la Guerre de cent ans." In *Etudes de langue et de littérature françaises offerts à André Langly*, edited by C. Brucker et al., pp. 173–83. Nancy: Publications Nancy II, 1980.

Kosta-Théfaine, Jean-François. "'L'Epistre a Eustace Morel' de Christine de Pizan." *Le moyen français* 38 (1996): 79–91.

Lampe, David. "The Courtly Rhetoric of Chaucer's Advisory Poetry." *Reading Medieval Studies* 9 (1983): 70–83.

Laurie, I. S. "Biography." In *Eustache Deschamps, French Courtier-Poet: His Work and His World*, edited by Deborah M. Sinnreich-Levi, 1–72. New York: AMS Press, 1998.

Lerch, Eugen. "Zu einer Stelle bei Eustache Deschamps." *Romanische Forschungen* 62 (1950): 67–68.

Longnon, Auguste. *Documents relatifs au comté de Champagne et de Brie 1172–1361.* 3 vols. Paris: Imprimerie Nationale, 1901–14.

Lote, Georges. *Histoire du vers français.* 2 vols. Paris: Boivin, 1949.

Lowes, John Livingston. "Chaucer and the 'Miroir de mariage.' " *Modern Philology* 8.2–3 (1910–11): 165–86, 305–34. Reprint, Chicago: Chicago University Press, 1911.

———. "Illustrations of Chaucer. Drawn Chiefly from Deschamps." *Romanic Review* 2 (1911): 113–28.

———. "The Chaucerian 'Merciless Beaute' and Three Poems of Deschamps." *Modern Language Review* 5 (1910): 33–39.

———. "The Prologue to the "Legend of Good Women" as Related to the French *Marguerite* Poems and the 'Filostrato.' " *PMLA* 19 (1904): 593–683; 20 (1905): 749–864.

Luce, Siméon. *La France pendant la guerre de cent ans: episodes historiques et vie privée aux XIVe et XVe siècles*, 2nd ed. Paris: Hachette 1890: 245–59.

Machaut, Guillaume de. *Le livre dou voir dit*, edited by Daniel Leech-Wilkinson and translated by R. Barton Palmer. New York: Garland, 1998.

Magnan, Robert. "Aspects of Senescence in the Work of Eustache Deschamps." Ph.D. diss., Indiana University, 1985.

———. "Eustache Deschamps and the Course of Life." In *Eustache Deschamps, French Courtier-Poet: His Work and His World*, edited by Deborah M. Sinnreich-Levi, pp. 229–44. NY: AMS Press, 1998.

Marchello-Nizia, Christiane. *Histoire de la langue française aux XIVe et XVe siècles*. Paris: Nathan, 1997.

McMillan, Ann. "Men's Weapons, Women's War: The Nine Female Worthies, 1400–1600." *Medievalia* 5 (1979): 113–39.

Mieszkowski, Gretchen. " 'Pandras' in Deschamps' 'Ballade for Chaucer.' " *The Chaucer Review* 9 (1975): 327–36.

Molinier, Auguste. *Les Sources de l'histoire de France des origines aux guerres d'Italie*. 6 vols. Paris: Picard, 1902–06.

Monfrin, J. "Les traducteurs et leur public en France au moyen âge." *L'Humanisme médiéval dans les littératures romanes du XIIe au XIVe siècle: colloque organisé par le Centre de Philologie et de Littératures romanes de l'Université de Strasbourg du 29 Janvier au 2 Février 1962*, edited by Anthime Fourrier. Paris: Klincksieck, 1964.

Morawski, Joseph. *Proverbes français antérieurs au XVe siècle*. Paris: Champion, 1925.

Neal, Young Abernathy. *Le Chevalier poète Jehan de Garencières, 1372–1415: Sa vie et ses poésies complètes*. Paris: Nizet, 1953.

Nicolini, Elena. "Cristina da Pizzano, l'origine e il nome." *Cultura neolatina* 1 (1941): 143–50.

Olson, Glending. "Deschamps' 'Art de dictier' and Chaucer's Literary Environment." *Speculum* 48 (1973): 714–23.

———. *Literature as Recreation in the Later Middle Ages*. Ithaca: Cornell University Press, 1982.

———. "The Marital Dilemma in the 'Wife of Bath's Tale': An Unnoticed Analogue and Its Chaucerian Court Context." *Speculum* 33:1 (September 1995): 1–7.

Palmer, R. Barton, ed. *Chaucer's French Contemporaries: The Poetry/Poetics of Self and Tradition*. New York: AMS Press, 1999.

Pearcy, Roy J. "Chaucer, Deschamps, and 'Le Roman de Brut.' " *Journal of the Sidney University Arts Association* 12 (1984): 35–39.

Picoche, Jacqueline, and Christiane Marchello-Nizia. *Histoire de la langue française*. 5th ed. Série Linguistique Nathan Université, Faculté Linguistique. Paris: Nathan, 1998.

Poirion, Daniel. *Le Poète et le prince: l'évolution du lyrisme courtois de Guillaume de Machaut à Charles d'Orléans*. Paris: Presses Universitaires de France, 1965. Reprint, Geneva: Slatkine, 1978.

Prieur, Charles. "Eustache Deschamps, Maître de la léproserie de Fismes." *Revue des études historiques* 70 (1904): 505–16.

———. "La Patrie d'Eustache Deschamps." *Revue des études historiques* 67 (1901): 515–41.

Recueil des ordonnances des roys de France de la 3e race recueillies par order chronologique par M. de Laurière. 22 vols. Paris: Imprimerie Nationale, 1723–1869.

Sadie, Stanley, ed. *The New Grove Dictionary of Music and Musicians*. 2nd ed. London: Macmillan, 2001.

Sainte-Palaye, Jean Baptiste La Curne de, ed. *Dictionnaire historique de l'ancien langage français*. 10 vols. Paris: Champion, 1875–82.

Sarradin, Amadée. *Etude sur Eustache des Champs*. Thesis, Faculté des lettres de Paris. Versailles: Cerf, 1878.

Schröder, Horst. *Der Topos der Nine Worthies in Literatür und bildender Kunst*. Göttingen: Vandenhoeck & Ruprecht, 1971.

Shoaf, R.A. "Notes Towards Chaucer's Poetics of Translation." *Studies in the Age of Chaucer* 1 (1979): 105–18.

Sinnreich-Levi, Deborah M., ed. *Eustache Deschamps, French Courtier-Poet: His Work and His World*. New York: AMS Press, 1998.

———. "Eustache Deschamps' *L'Art de dictier*: Just What Kind of Poetics Is It? Or: How Robert O. Payne Launched My Career in Deschamps Studies." In *The Rhetorical Poetics of the Middle Ages: Reconstructive Polyphony—Essays in Honor of Robert O. Payne*, edited by John M. Hill and Deborah M. Sinnreich-Levi, pp. 29–44. Madison and Teaneck, N.J.: Fairleigh Dickinson University Press, 2000.

Spurgeon, Caroline F. E. *Five Hundred Years of Chaucer Criticism and Allusion: 1357–1900*. 3 vols. Chaucer Society, 2nd ser. Cambridge: Cambridge University Press, 1923. Reprint, New York: Russell & Russell, 1960.

Stoneburner, Michelle. "Medieval Misogyny in Deschamps' 'Le Miroir de mariage': Can This Really Be Funny?" *Romance Languages Annual* 8 (1996): 143–47.

Tesnière, Marie-Hélène. "Les manuscrits copiés par Raoul Tainguy: un aspect de la culture des grands officiers royaux au début du XVe siècle." *Romania* 107 (1986): 282–368.

Thibault, G., and E. Droz. *Poètes et musiciens du 15e siècle*. Paris: G. Jeanbin, 1924. Reprint, Geneva: Slatkine, 1976.

Thibault, Marcel. *Isabeau de Bavière*. Paris: Ferrin, 1903.

Thundy, Zacharias P. "Matheolus, Chaucer and the Wife of Bath." In *Chaucerian Problems and Perspectives Presented to Paul Beichner*, edited by Edward Vasta and Zacharias Thundy, pp. 24–58. Notre Dame, Ind.: University of Indiana Presss, 1979.

Tobler, Adolf, and Erhard Lommatzsch, eds. *Altfranzösisches Wörterbuch*. 10 vols. Wiesbaden: Steiner, 1955.

Toynbee, Paget. "The Ballade Addressed by Eustache Deschamps to Geoffrey Chaucer." *The Academy* 40 (1891): 432–33. Reprint, *Specimens of Old French*, edited by Paget Toynbee. Oxford: Clarendon Press, 1892, 314–15; 482–84.

Tuchman, Barbara. *A Distant Mirror: The Calamitous Fourteenth Century*. New York: Ballantine, 1978.

Twigg, Graham. *The Black Death: A Biological Reappraisal*. New York: Schocken Books, 1985.

Verdon, Jean. *Isabeau de Bavière*. Paris: Tallander, 1981.

Wartburg, Walther von. *Evolution et structure de la langue française*. 12th ed. Tübingen and Basel: A. Francke, 1993.

Whiting, Bartlett Jere. *Chaucer's Use of Proverbs*. Harvard Studies in Comparative Literature 11. Cambridge: Harvard University Press, 1934.

Willard, Charity Cannon. "Women and Marriage Around 1400: Three Views." *Fifteenth Century Studies* 17 (1990): 475–84.

Wimsatt, James. *Chaucer and His French Contemporaries: Natural Music in the Fourteenth Century*. Toronto: University of Toronto Press, 1991.

Young, Karl. "Chaucer and Aulus Gellius." *Modern Language Notes* 52 (1937): 347–51.

About the Collaborators

Ian S. Laurie began his career at the Victoria University of Wellington, New Zealand, then spent ten years at the University of Cambridge, five of them as a lecturer in French and Fellow of Clare College. He finally became Foundation Professor of French at the Flinders University of South Australia, retiring as Emeritus Professor of French in 1995. He has been honored by the French government with the rank of Commandeur dans l'Ordre des Palmes Académiques. His numerous articles and book chapters have been principally in the fields of medieval French literature and applied linguistics. He also coedited *Dictionary of Literary Biography* on the *Literature of the French and Occitan Middle Ages: Eleventh to Fifteenth Centuries* (coedited by Deborah Sinnreich-Levi, 1999); *Voices for the Future: A Languages Policy for South Australian Schools* (coedited by Anne L. Martin et al., 1983); *Languages at the Primary Level* (with Alex Gardini, 1980); and *French Profile*, *Nine Languages Project*, NLLIA (National Languages and Literacy Institute of Australia, Melbourne) (with Peter M. Cryle et al., 1993). He also has made contributions to film criticism, been the director of the Adelaide International Film Festival, and spent several years as columnist for the principal daily newspaper in South Australia, *The Advertiser*. Ian Laurie currently resides in Melbourne.

Deborah M. Sinnreich-Levi is Associate Professor of English and Comparative Literature at Stevens Institute of Technology, where she cochairs the biennial Literary Translation Conference, directs the Humanities Resource Center, and teaches medieval literature to engineers. She was awarded distinguished teaching awards in 1997 and 1998, and has twice received funding from Stevens's Technogenesis® Summer Scholars' Program for research assistance building a database of Deschamps's poems. Her publications include *The Rhetorical Poetics of the Middle Ages: Reconstructive Polyphony: Essays in Honor of Robert O. Payne* (coedited by John Hill, 2000), *The French and Occitan Middle Ages: Dictionary of Literary Biography* (coedited by Ian S. Laurie, 1999), *Eustache Deschamps, French Courtier-Poet: His Work and His World* (AMS Press, 1998), *Eustache Deschamps' "L'Art de dictier"* (1994), and *Voices in Translation: The Authority of "Olde Bookes" in Medieval Literature: Essays in Honor of Helaine Newstead* (coedited by Gale Sigal, 1992).

David Curzon has published five books: *Midrashim* (1991); *Modern Poems on the Bible: An Anthology* (1994); *The Gospels in Our Image: An Anthology of Twentieth-Century Poetry Based on Biblical Texts* (1995); *Dovchik* (1995), and *The View From Jacob's Ladder* (1996), and, with Katharine Washburn, a translation of "The Madness of Heracles" (in *Euripides, 4*, edited by David R. Slavitt and Palmer Bovie, 1999). His poems are represented in two Oxford anthologies and in the twentieth-century section of *World Poetry* (1998). Individual poems, translations, essays, and reviews have been published in numerous journals in the United States, the United Kingdom, Israel, and Australia. A translated monologue, Goethe's "Persephone," was produced off Broadway in 1998 at the Harold Clurman Theatre. David Curzon was born in Melbourne, Australia, and holds a Ph.D. in economics and a B.Sc. in physics. He is currently a contributing editor of *The Forward*. He recently retired from the United Nations after twenty-six years, the last twelve as chief of the Central Evaluation Unit.

Jeffrey Fiskin writes. He lives with his family in Hollywood.

General Index

Index of Works

Pages in boldface indicate text of the poem.

www.ingramcontent.com/pod-product-compliance
Lightning Source LLC
Chambersburg PA
CBHW071509110726
47908CB00003B/782

* 9 7 8 1 1 3 8 9 9 3 6 2 4 *

www.ingramcontent.com/pod-product-compliance
Lightning Source LLC
Chambersburg PA
CBHW071528110726
47908CB00003B/983

* 9 7 8 1 8 0 0 7 9 4 1 3 9 *